AF334618

ADVANCED TOPICS
IN SCIENCE AND TECHNOLOGY IN CHINA

ADVANCED TOPICS
IN SCIENCE AND TECHNOLOGY IN CHINA

Zhejiang University is one of the leading universities in China. In Advanced Topics in Science and Technology in China, Zhejiang University Press and Springer jointly publish monographs by Chinese scholars and professors, as well as invited authors and editors from abroad who are outstanding experts and scholars in their fields. This series will be of interest to researchers, lecturers, and graduate students alike.

Advanced Topics in Science and Technology in China aims to present the latest and most cutting-edge theories, techniques, and methodologies in various research areas in China. It covers all disciplines in the fields of natural science and technology, including but not limited to, computer science, materials science, life sciences, engineering, environmental sciences, mathematics, and physics.

Kaizhu Huang
Haiqin Yang
Irwin King
Michael Lyu

Machine Learning
Modeling Data Locally and Globally

With 53 figures

AUTHORS:

Dr. Kaizhu Huang,
Dept. of CSE,
Chinese Univ. of Hong Kong,
Shatin. N.T. HK,
China
Email: kzhuang@cse.cuhk.edu.hk

Dr. Haiqin Yang,
Dept. of CSE,
Chinese Univ. of Hong Kong,
Shatin. N.T. HK,
China
Email:hqyang@cse.cuhk.edu.hk

Prof. Irwin King,
Dept. of CSE,
Chinese Univ. of Hong Kong,
Shatin. N.T. HK,
China
Email: king@cse.cuhk.edu.hk

Dr. Michael Lyu,
Dept. of CSE,
Chinese Univ. of Hong Kong,
Shatin. N.T. HK,
China
Email:lyu@cse.cuhk.edu.hk

ISBN 978-7-308-05831-5 **Zhejiang University Press, Hangzhou**
ISBN 978-3-540-79451-6 **Springer Berlin Heidelberg New York**
e-ISBN 978-3-540-79452-3 **Springer Berlin Heidelberg New York**

Series ISSN 1995-6819 Advanced topics in science and technology in China
Series e-ISSN 1995-6827 Advanced topics in science and technology in China

Library of Congress Control Number : 2008925536

Co-published by Zhejiang University Press, Hangzhou and Springer-Verlag GmbH Berlin Heidelberg

Springer is a part of Springer Science+Business Media
springer.com

Cover design: Joe Piliero, Springer Science + Business Media LLC, New York
Printed on acid-free paper

Preface

Machine Learning: Modeling Data Locally and Globally delivers the main contemporary themes and tools in machine learning including probabilistic generative models and Support Vector Machines. These themes are discussed or reformulated from either a local view or a global view. Different from previous books that only investigate machine learning algorithms locally or globally, this book presents a unified and new picture for machine learning both locally and globally. Within the new picture, various seemly different machine learning models and theories are bridged in an elegant and systematic manner. For precise and thorough understanding, this book also presents applications of the new hybrid theory.

This book not only provides researchers with the latest research results lively and timely, but also presents an excellent overview on machine learning. Importantly, the new line of learning both locally and globally goes through the whole book and makes various learning models understandable to a large proportion of audience including researchers in machine learning, practitioners in pattern recognition, and graduate students.

The Chinese Univ. of Hong Kong,
Jan. 2008

Kaizhu Huang
Haiqin Yang
Irwin King
Michael R. Lyu

Contents

1

Introduction

The objective of this book is to establish a framework which combines two different paradigms in machine learning: global learning and local learning. The combined model demonstrates that a hybrid learning of these two different schools of approaches can outperform each isolated approach both theoretically and empirically. Global learning focuses on describing a phenomenon or modeling data in a global way. For example, a distribution over the variables is usually estimated for summarizing the data. Its output can usually reconstruct the data. This school of approaches, including Bayesian Networks [8, 13, 30], Gaussian Mixture Models [3, 21], and Hidden Markov Models [2, 25], has a long and distinguished history, which has been extensively applied in artificial intelligence [26], pattern recognition [9], and computer vision [7]. On the other hand, local learning does not intend to summarize a phenomenon, but builds learning systems by concentrating on some local parts of data. It lacks the flexibility yet surprisingly demonstrates superior performance to global learning according to recent researches [4, 16, 15]. In this book, a bridge has been established between these two different paradigms. Moreover, the resulting principled framework subsumes several important models, which respectively locate themselves into the global learning paradigm and the local learning paradigm.

In this chapter, we address the motivations of the two different learning frameworks. As a summary, we present the objectives of this book and outline the main models or the contributions. Finally, we provide an overview of the rest of this book.

1.1 Learning and Global Modeling

When studying real world phenomena, scientists are always wondering whether some underlying laws or nice mathematical formulae exist for governing these complex phenomena. Moreover, in practice, due to incomplete information, the phenomena are usually nondeterministic. This motivates to base probabilistic or statistical models to perform a global investigation on sampled data from the phenomena. A common way for achieving this goal is to fit a density on the observations of data. With the learned density, people can then incorporate prior knowledge, conduct predictions, and perform inferences and marginalizations. One main category in the framework of global learning is the so-called generative learning. By assuming a specific mathematical model on the observations of data, e.g. a Gaussian distribution, the phenomena can therefore be described or re-generated. Fig. 1.1 illustrates such an example. In this figure, two classes of data are plotted as $*$'s for the first class and $\circ$'s for the other class. The data can thus be modeled as two different mixtures of Gaussian distributions as illustrated in Fig. 1.2. By knowing only the parameters of these distributions, one can then summarize the phenomena. Furthermore, one can clearly employ this information to distinguish one class of data from the other class or simply know how to separate two classes. This is also well-known as Bayes optimal decision problems [12, 6].

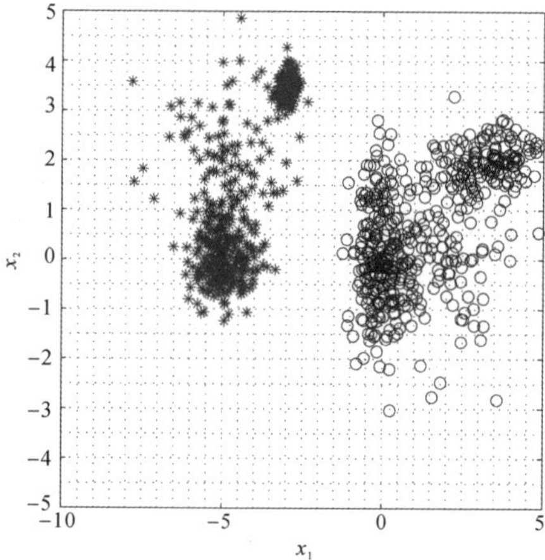

Fig. 1.1. Two classes of two-dimensional data

In the development of learning approaches within the community of machine learning, there has been a migration from the early rule-based methods [11, 32] wanting more involvement of domain experts, to widely-used probabilistic global models mainly driven by data itself [5, 9, 14, 17, 22, 33]. However, one question for most probabilistic global models is what kind of global models, or more specifically, which type of densities should be specified beforehand for summarizing the phenomena. For some tasks, this can be prescribed by a slight introduction of domain knowledge from experts. Unfortunately, due to both the increasing sophistication of the real world learning tasks and active interactions among different subjects of research, it is more

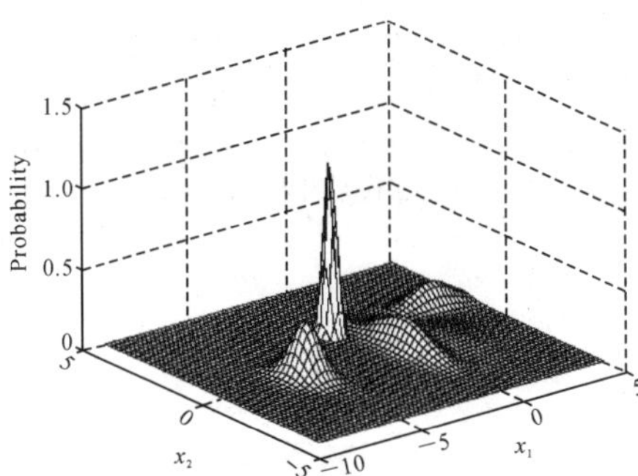

Fig. 1.2. An illustration of distribution-based classifications (also known as the Bayes optimal decision theory). Two Gaussian mixtures are engaged to model the distribution of two classes of data respectively. The distribution can then be used to construct the decision plane

and more difficult to obtain fast and valuable suggestions from experts. A further question is thus proposed, i.e. what is the next step in the community of machine learning, after experiencing a migration from rule-based models to probabilistic global models? Recent progress in machine learning seems to imply local learning as a solution.

1.2 Learning and Local Modeling

Global modeling addresses describing phenomena, no matter whether the summarized information from the observations is applicable to specific tasks or not. Moreover, the hidden principle under global learning is that information can be accurately extracted from data. On the other hand, local learning [10, 27, 28] which recently attracts active attention in the machine learning community, usually regards that a general and accurate global learning is an impossible mission. Therefore, local learning focuses on capturing only local yet useful information from data. Furthermore, recent research progress and empirical study demonstrate that this much different learning paradigm is superior to global learning in many facets.

In further details, instead of globally modeling data, local learning is more task-oriented. It does not aim to estimate a density from data as in global learning, which is usually an intermediate step for many tasks such as pattern recognitions (note that the distribution or density obtained by global learning actually is not directly related to the classification itself); it also does not intend to build an accurate model to fit the observations of data globally. Differently, it only extracts useful information from data and directly optimizes the learning goal. For example, when used in learning classifiers from data, only those observations of data around the separating plane need to be accurate, while inaccurate modeling over other data is certainly acceptable for the classification purpose. Fig. 1.3 illustrates such a problem. In this figure, the decision boundary is constructed only based on those filled points, while other points make no contributions to the classification plane (the decision boundary is given based on the Gabriel Graph method [1, 18, 34]).

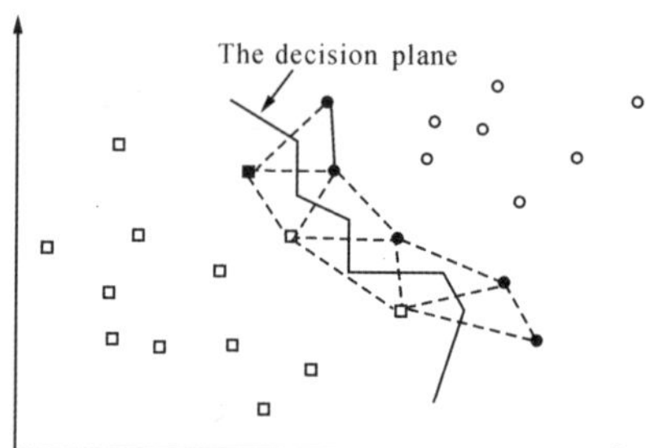

Fig. 1.3. An illustration of local learning (also known as the Gabriel Graph classification). The decision boundary is just determined by some local points indicated as filled points

However, although containing promising performance, local learning appears to locate itself at another extreme end to global learning. Employing only local information may lose the global view of data. Consequently, sometimes, it cannot grasp the data trend, which is critical for guaranteeing better performance for future data. This can be seen in the example as illustrated in Fig. 1.4. In this figure, the decision boundary (also constructed by the Gabriel Graph classification) is still determined by some local points indicated as filled points. Clearly, this boundary does not grasp the data trend.

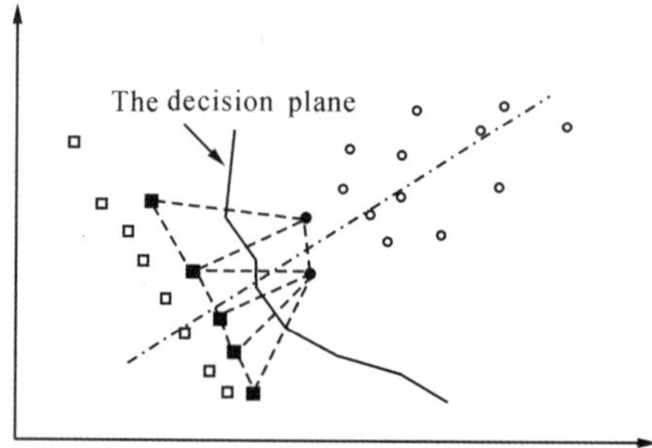

Fig. 1.4. An illustration on that local learning cannot grasp data trend. The decision boundary (constructed by the Gabriel Graph classification) is determined by some local points indicated as filled points. It, however, loses the data trend. The decision plane should be obviously closer to the filled squares rather than locating itself in the middle of filled □'s and o's

More specifically, the class associated with o's is obviously more scattered than the class
associated with □'s on the axis indicated as dashed line. Therefore, a more promising decision boundary should lie closer to filled □'s than those filled o's instead of lying midway between filled points. A similar example can also be seen in Chapter 2 on a more principled local learning model, i.e. the current state-of-the-art classifier, Support Vector Machines (SVM) [31]. Targeting this problem, we then suggest a hybrid learning in this book.

1.3 Hybrid Learning

There are complementary advantages for both local learning and global learning. Global learning summarizes data and provides practitioners with knowledge on the structure, independence, and trend of data, since with the precise modeling of phenomena, the observations can be accurately regenerated and therefore can be studied or analyzed thoroughly. However, this also presents difficulties in how to choose a valid model to describe all the information (also called the problem of model selection). In comparison, local learning directly employs part of information, critical for the specific oriented tasks, and does not assume models to re-synthesize/restore the whole road-map of data. Although demonstrated to be superior to global learning in many facets of machine learning, it may lose some important global information. The question here is thus, can reliable global information, independent of specific model assumptions, be combined into local learning? This question clearly motivates a hybrid learning of two largely different schools of approaches, which is also the focus of this book.

1.4 Major Contributions

In this book, we aim to describe a hybrid learning scheme to combine two different paradigms, namely global learning and local learning. Within this scheme, we propose a hybrid model, named the Maxi-Min Margin Machine (M^4), demonstrated to contain both the merits of global learning in representing data and the advantages of local learning in handling tasks directly and effectively. Moreover, adopting the viewpoint of local learning, we also introduce a global learning model, called the Minimum Error Minimax Probability Machine (MEMPM), which does not assume specific distributions on data and thus distinguishes itself from traditional global learning approaches. The main models discussed in this book are briefly described as follows.

- *The Maxi-Min Margin Machine model, a hybrid learning framework successfully combining global learning and local learning*

  ◇ *A unified framework of many important models*
  As will be demonstrated, our proposed hybrid model successfully unifies both important models in local learning, e.g. the Support Vector Machines [4], and significant models in global learning, such as the Minimax Probability Machine (MPM) [19] and the Fisher Discriminant Analysis (FDA) [9].

  ◇ *With the generalization Guarantee*
  Various statements from many views such as the sparsity and Marshall and Olkin Theory [20, 23] will be presented for providing the generalization bound for the combined approach.

  ◇ *A sequential Conic Programming solving method*
  Besides the theoretic advantages of the proposed hybrid learning, we also tailor a sequential Conic Programming method [24, 29] to solve the corresponding optimization problem. The computational cost is shown to be polynomial and thus the proposed M^4 model can be solved practically.

- *The Minimum Error Minimax Probability Machine, a general global learning model*

  ◇ *A worst-case distribution-free Bayes optimal classifier*
  Different from traditional Bayes optimal classifiers, MEMPM does not assume distributions for the data. Starting with the Marshall and Olkin theory, this model attempts to model data under the minimax schemes. It does not intend to extract exact information but the worst-case information from data and thus presents an important progress in global learning.

  ◇ *Derive an explicit error bound for future data*
  Inheriting the advantages of global learning, the proposed general global learning method contains an explicit worst-case error bound for future data under a mild condition. Moreover, the experimental results suggest that this bound is reliable and accurate.

  ◇ *Propose a sequential Fractional Programming optimization*
  We have proposed a Fractional Programming optimization method for the MEMPM model. In each iteration, the optimization is shown to be a pseudo-concave problem, which thus guarantees that each local solution will be the global solution in this step.

- *The Biased Minimax Probability Machine (BMPM), a global learning method for biased or imbalanced learning*

  ◇ *Present a rigorous and systematic treatment for biased learning tasks*
  Although being a special case of our proposed general global learning model, MEMPM, this model provides a quantitative and rigorous approach for biased learning tasks, where one class of data is always more important than the other class. Importantly, with explicitly controlling the accuracy of one class, this branch model can precisely impose biases on the important class.

◇ *Containing explicit generalization bounds for both classes of data*
Inheriting the good feature of the MEMPM model, this model also contains explicit generalization bounds for both classes of data. This therefore guarantees a good prediction accuracy for future data.

- *The Local Support Vector Regression (LSVR), a novel regression model*
  - ◇ *Provide a systematic and automatic treatment in adapting margins*
  Motivated from M^4, LSVR focuses on considering the margin setting locally. When compared to the regression model of SVM, i.e. the Support Vector Regression (SVR), this novel regression model is shown to be more robust with respect to the noise of data in that it contains the volatile margin setting.
  - ◇ *Incorporate special cases very much similar to the standard SVR*
  When considering a consistent trend for all data points, the LSVR can derive special cases very much similar to the standard SVR. We further demonstrate that in a meaningful assumption, the standard SVR is actually the special case of our LSVR model.

- *Support Vector Regression with Local Margin Variations*
  Motivated from the local view of data, another variation of SVR is proposed. It aims to adapt the margin in a more explicit way. This model is similar to LSVR in the sense that they both adapt margin locally.

We describe the relationship among our developed models in Fig. 1.5.

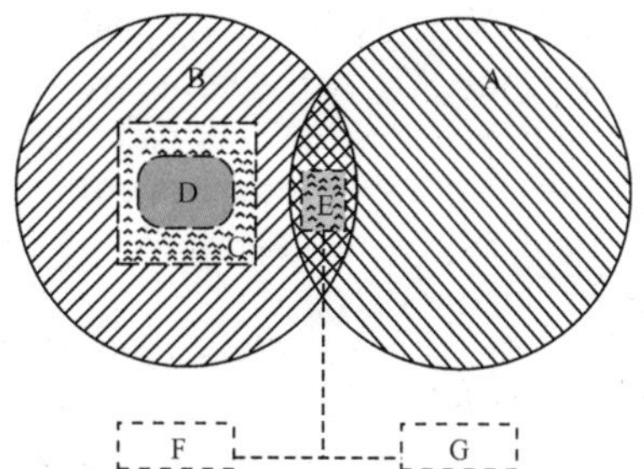

A:Local Learning
B:Global Learning
C:Minimum Error Minmax Probability Machine
D:Biased Minimax Probability Machine
E:Maxi-Min Margin Machine
F:Local Support Vector Regression
G:Support Vector Regression with Margin Variations

Fig. 1.5. The relationship among the developed models in this book

1.5 Scope

This book states and refers to the learning first as statistical learning, which appears to be the current main trend of learning approaches. We then further restrict the learning in the framework of classification, one of the main problems in machine learning. The corresponding discussions on different models including the conducted analysis of the computational and statistical aspects of machine learning are all subject to the classification tasks. Nevertheless, we will also extend the content of this book to regression problems, although it is not the focus of this book.

1.6 Book Organization

The rest of this book is organized as follows:

- Chapter 2
  We will review different learning paradigms in this chapter. We will establish a hierarchy graph attempting to categorize various models in the framework of local learning and global learning. We will then base this graph to describe and discuss these models. Finally, we motivate the Minimum Error Minimax Probability Machine and the Maxi-Min Margin Machine.
- Chapter 3
  We will develop a novel global learning model, called the Mininum Error Minimax Probability Machine. We will demonstrate how this new model represents the worst-case Bayes optimal classifier. We will detail its model definition, provide interpretations, establish a robust version, extend to nonlinear classifications, and present a series of experiments to demonstrate the advantages of this model.
- Chapter 4
  We will present the Maxi-Min Margin Machine, which successfully combines two different but complementary learning paradigms, i.e. local learning and global learning. We will show how this model incorporates the Support Vector Machine, the Minimax Probability Machine, and the Fisher Discriminant Analysis as special cases. We will also demonstrate the advantages of Maxi-Min Margin Machine by providing theoretical, geometrical, and empirical investigations.
- Chapter 5
  An extension of the proposed MEMPM model will be discussed in this chapter. More specifically, the Biased Minimum Minimax Probability Machine will be discussed and applied into the imbalanced learning tasks. We will review different criteria for evaluating imbalanced learning approaches. We will then base these criteria to tailor BMPM into this type of learning. Both illustrations on toy datasets and evaluations on real world imbalanced and medical datasets will be provided in this chapter.

- Chapter 6
  A novel regression model called the Local Support Vector Regression, which can be regarded as an extension from the Maxi-Min Margin Machine, will be introduced in detail in this chapter. We will show that our model can vary the tube (margin) systematically and automatically according to the local data trend. We will show that this novel regression model is more robust with respect to the noise of data. Empirical evaluations on both synthetic data and real financial time series data will be presented to demonstrate the merits of our model with respect to the standard Support Vector Regression.
- Chapter 7
  In this Chapter, we show how to adapt the margin settings locally for the Support Vector Regression differently from the LSVR. We demonstrate how the local view of data can be widely used in various models or even differently applied in the same model. Empirical evaluations are also presented in comparison with other competitive models on financial data.
- Chapter 8
  We will then summarize this book and conduct discussions on future work.

We try to make each of these chapters self-contained. Therefore, in several chapters, some critical contents, e.g. model definitions or illustrative figures, having appeared in previous chapters, may be briefly reiterated.

References

1. Barber CB, Dobkin DP, Huhanpaa H (1996) The quickhull algorithm for convex hulls. ACM Transactions on Mathematical Software 22(4):469–483
2. Baum LE, Egon JA (1967) An inequality with applications to statistical estimation for probabilistic functions of a Markov process and to a model for ecology. Bull. Amer. Meteorol. Soc. 73:360C-363
3. Bozdogan H (2004) Statistical Data Mining and Knowledge Discovery. Boca Raton, Fla.: Chapman & Hall/CRC
4. Christopher J, Burges C (1998) A tutorial on support vector machines for pattern recognition. Data Mining and Knowledge Discovery 2(2):121–167
5. Chow CK, Liu CN (1968) Approximating discrete probability distributions with dependence trees. IEEE Trans. on Information Theory 14:462–467
6. Duda R, Hart P(1973) Pattern Classification and Scene Analysis. New York, NY: John Wiley & Sons
7. Forsyth DA, Ponce J (2003) Computer Vision: A Modern Approach. Upper Saddle River, N.J. : Prentice Hall
8. Friedman N, Geiger D, Goldszmidt M (1997) Bayesian network classifiers. Machine Learning 29:131–161
9. Fukunaga K (1990) Introduction to Statistical Pattern Recognition. San Diego, Academic Press, 2nd edition

10   References

10. Girosi F (1998) An equivalence between sparse approximation and support vector machines. Neural Computation 10(6):1455–1480
11. Gonzalez MG, Thomason RC (1978) Syntactic Pattern Recognition: An Introduction. Reading, Mass. : Addison-Wesley Pub. Co., Advanced Book Program
12. Grzegorzewski P, Hryniewicz O, Gil M (2002) Soft Methods in Probability, Statistics and Data Analysis. Heidelberg; New York: Physica-Verlag
13. Hackman D, Meek C, Cooper G (1995) A tutorial on learning bayesian networks. In Tech Report MSR-TR-95-06. Microsoft Research
14. Huang K, King I, Lyu MR (2003) Discriminative training of Bayesian chow-liu tree multinet classifiers. In Proceedings of International Joint Conference on Neural Network (IJCNN-2003), Oregon, Portland, U.S.A. 1: 484–488
15. Jaakkola TS, Haussler D (1998) Exploiting generative models in discriminative classifiers. In Advances in Neural Information Processing Systems (NIPS)
16. Jebara T (2002) Discriminative, Generative and Imitative Learning. PhD thesis, Massachusetts Institute of Technology
17. Jordan MI (1998) Learning in Graphical Models. Kluwer Academic Publishers
18. Toussaint GT, Jaromczyk JW (1992) Relative neighborhood graphs and their relatives. Proceedings IEEE 80(9):1502–1517
19. Lanckriet GRG, Ghaoui LE, Bhattacharyya C, Jordan MI (2002) A robust minimax approach to classification. Journal of Machine Learning Research 3:555–582
20. Marshall AW, Olkin I (1960) Multivariate Chebyshev inequalities. Annals of Mathematical Statistics 31(4):1001–1014
21. McLachlan GJ, Basford KE (1988) Mixture Models: Inference and Applications to Clustering. New York, NY: Marcel Dekker Inc
22. Pearl J (1988) Probabilistic Reasoning in Intelligent Systems: Networks of Plausible Inference. San Francisco, CA: Morgan Kaufmann
23. Popescu I, Bertsimas D (2001) Optimal inequalities in probability theory: A convex optimization approach. Technical Report TM62, INSEAD
24. Pruessner A (2003) Conic programming in GAMS. In Optimization Software– The State of the Art. INFORMS Atlanta, http://www.gamsworld.org/cone/links.htm
25. Rabiner LR (1989) A tutorial on hidden Markov models and selected applications in speech recognition. Proceedings of the IEEE 77(2):257-286
26. Russell SJ, Norvig P (1995) Artificial Intelligence : A Modern Approach. Englewood Cliffs, N.J. : Prentice Hall
27. Schölkopf B, Smola A (2002) Learning with Kernels. Cambridge, MA: The MIT Press
28. Smola AJ, Bartlett PL, Scholkopf B, Schuurmans D (2000) Advances in Large Margin Classifiers. MA: The MIT Press
29. Sturm JF(1999) Using sedumi 1.02, a matlab toolbox for optimization over symmetric cones. Optimization Methods and Software 11:625–653
30. Thiesson B, Meek C, Heckman D (1998). Learning mixtures of Bayesian networks. In Technique Report, MSR-TR-97-30. Microsoft Research
31. Vapnik VN (1998). Statistical Learning Theory. John Wiley & Sons
32. Weizenbaum J (1966). Eliza—a computer program for the study of natural language communication between man and machine. Communications of the Association for Computing Machinery
33. Yedidia J, Freeman WT, Weiss Y (2000). Generalized belief propogation. In Neural Information Processing Systems 13

34. Zhang W, King I (2002) A study of the relationship between support vector machine and Gabriel Graph. In Proceedings of IEEE World Congress on Computational Intelligence—International Joint Conference on Neural Networks

Global Learning vs. Local Learning

In this chapter, we conduct a more detailed and more formal review on two different schools of learning approaches, namely, the global learning and local learning. We first provide a hierarchy graph as illustrated in Fig. 2.1 in which we try to classify many statistical models into their proper categories, either global learning or local learning. Our review will also be conducted based on this hierarchy structure. To make it clear, we use filled shapes to highlight our own work in the graph.

Global learning fits a distribution over data. If a specific mathematical model, e.g. a Gaussian model, is assumed on the distribution, this is often called generative learning, whose name implies that the mathematical formulation of the assumed model governs the generation of data in the learning task. To learn the parameters from the observations of data for the specific model, several schemes have been proposed. This includes Maximum Likelihood (ML) learning, which is easy to conduct but is less accurate, Conditional Likelihood (CL) learning, which is usually hard to perform optimization but is more effective, and Bayesian Average (BA) learning, which has a comparatively short history but is more promising. As generative learning pre-assigns a specific model before learning, it often lacks the generality and thus may be invalid in many cases. This thus motivates the non-parametric learning, which still estimates a distribution on data but assumes no specific mathematical generative models. The common way in this type of learning is to locally fit over each observation a simple density and then sums all the local densities as the final distribution for data. Although in some circumstances, this approach is successful, it is criticized for requiring a huge quantity of training points and containing a large space complexity. Differently, in this book, we will demonstrate a novel global learning method, named Minimum Error Minimax Probability Machine (MEMPM). Although still in the framework of global learning, it does not belong to non-parametric learning, therefore requiring no extremely heavy storage spaces. Moreover, it does not assume any specific distribution on data, which hence distinguishes itself

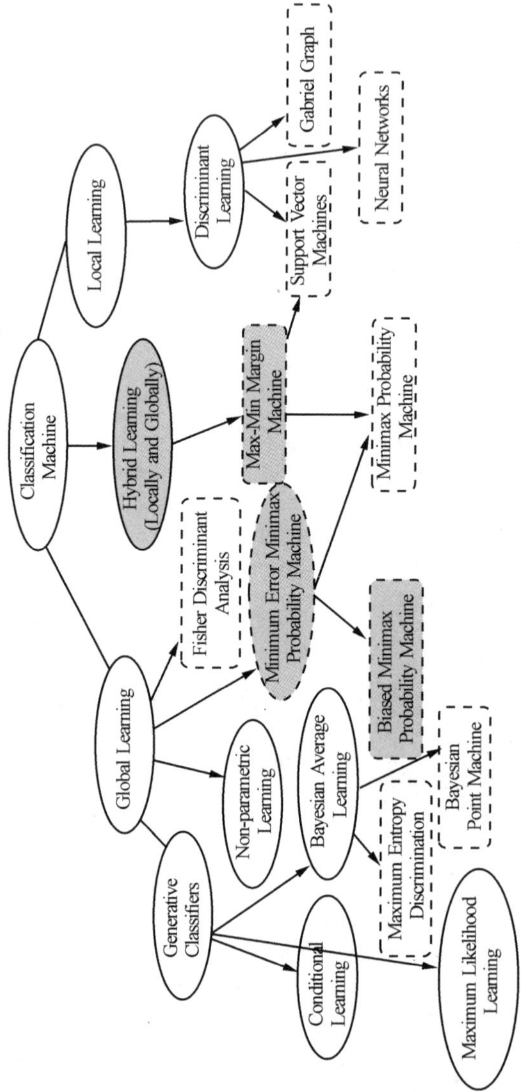

Fig. 2.1. A hierarchy graph of statistical learning models

from the traditional global generative learning. As a critical contribution, MEMPM represents a distribution-free Bayes optimal classifier in a worst-case scenario. Furthermore, we will show that this model incorporates two important global learning approaches, Biased Minimax Probability Machine (BMPM) and Minimax Probability Machine (MPM) [29, 30]. Since all approaches within the paradigm of global learning require summarizing the data information completely and globally, it thus may waste computational resources and is widely argued to be less direct. This motivates the local learning which makes no attempt to model the data globally, but focuses on extracting only those information directly related to the task. This type of learning is often refereed to as discriminative learning in the context of classifications. One famous model among them is Support Vector Machine (SVM). With the task-oriented, robust, computationally tractable properties, SVM has achieved a great success and is considered as the current state-of-the-art classifier. Although local learning demonstrates superior performance to traditional global learning, it appears to situate itself at another extreme end, which totally discards the useful global information, e.g. the structure information of data.

Our suggestion is that we should combine these two different but complementary paradigms. Towards this end, we then propose a new model called Maxi-Min Margin Machine (M^4), which not only successfully employs the global structure information from data but also holds merits of local learning such as robustness and superior classification accuracies. As a critical contribution, M^4, the hybrid learning model represents a general model successfully shown to contain both local learning models and global learning models as special cases. More specifically, it contains two significant and popular global learning models, i.e. Fisher Discriminant Analysis (FDA) [13] and Minimax Probability Machine [28, 29, 30] as special cases. Meanwhile, SVM, the local learning model can also be considered as one of its branches. In addition, M^4 also demonstrates a strong connection with MEMPM, the novel general global learning model.

In the following, we first present the problem definition which will be used throughout this book. We then base Fig. 2.1 to provide introductions and comments for each type of learning model sequently. Finally, we summarize the review and conclude with the proposition of the hybrid framework, the objective of this book.

2.1 Problem Definition

Given a dataset D consisting of N observations, where each observation is of the form $(z_1, z_2, \ldots, z_n, c)$ $(z_i \in \mathbb{R}$, for $1 \leq i \leq n$, $c \in \mathbb{F}$, where $\mathbb{F}$ is a finite set), the basic learning problem is to construct a mapping rule or a function f from $\{z_1, z_2, \ldots, z_n\}$ called features or attributes to the output c, denoted as the class variable, namely $f(z_1, z_2, \ldots, z_n, \Theta, D) \rightarrow c$, where Θ means the function parameters. The function f should be not only as accurate as possible to fit the observations D, but also can robustly predict the class for the new data. Sometimes, we also use Θ to denote the mapping model f and its associated parameters. For simplicity, we often use z to denote the n-dimensional variable $\{z_1, z_2, \ldots, z_n\}$. If we use z_j, we refer it to the j-th observation in D. Throughout this book, unless we provide statements explicitly, and bold typeface will indicate a vector or matrix, while normal typeface will refer to a scale variable or the component of the vectors.

2.2 Global Learning

Global learning often describes the data by attempting to estimate a distribution over variables $(z_1, z_2, \ldots, z_n, c)$, denoted as $p(\boldsymbol{z}, c, \Theta|D)$. The estimated distribution can then be used to make predictions by calculating the probability that a specific value of c will occur, when given an instance of features $\boldsymbol{z}$. In more details, the decision rule or the mapping function can be described as:

$$c = \arg\max_{c_k \in \mathbb{F}} p(c_k|D, \boldsymbol{z}) = \arg\max_{c_k \in \mathbb{F}} \int p(c_k, \Theta|D, \boldsymbol{z}) \mathrm{d}\Theta \ . \tag{2.1}$$

By employing Bayes theory, one can transform the above joint probability (the item inside the integral) into the following equivalent forms:

$$p(c_k, \Theta|D, \boldsymbol{z}) = \frac{p(c_k, \boldsymbol{z}|D, \Theta)p(\Theta|D)}{\sum_{c_k \in \mathbb{F}} \int p(c_k, \boldsymbol{z}|D, \Theta)p(\Theta|D)\mathrm{d}\Theta} \ . \tag{2.2}$$

Since the denominator in the above does not influence the decision in practice, the decision rule of Eq.(2.1) can be written into a relatively easily-calculated form:

$$c = \arg\max_{c_k \in \mathbb{F}} \int p(c_k, \boldsymbol{z}|D, \Theta)p(\Theta|D)\mathrm{d}\Theta \ . \tag{2.3}$$

Depending on how the model Θ is assumed on D, global learning can be further divided into generative learning and non-parametric learning as elaborated in the following subsections.

2.2.1 Generative Learning

Generative learning often assumes a specific model on data D. For example, a Gaussian distribution is assumed to be the underlying model to generate D. In this case, the parameters Θ refer to the mean and covariance for the Gaussian distribution. There are many models which belong to this type of learning. Among them are Naive Bayes model [9, 26, 32], Gaussian Mixture Model [4, 15, 16, 33], Bayesian Network [19, 20, 21, 31, 40], Hidden Markov Model [2, 48], Logistic Regression [23], Bayes Point Machine [18, 36, 44], Maximum Entropy Estimations [22], etc. The key problem for generative learning is how to learn the parameters Θ from data. Generally, in the literature of machine learning, three schemes, Maximum Likelihood learning, Conditional Likelihood learning and Bayesian Average learning, are engaged for estimating the parameters. We state these approaches one by one in the following.

2.2.1.1 Maximum Likelihood Learning & Maximum A Posterior Learning

Considering that it is not always easy to calculate the integral in Eq.(2.3), earlier researchers often try to compute some approximations of Eq.(2.3) instead. This motivates the Maximum Likelihood learning and Maximum A Posterior (MAP) learning [9, 40].

These learning methods replace Eq.(2.3) with the formulation below:

$$c = \arg\max_{c_k \in \mathbb{F}} p(c_k, \boldsymbol{z}|D, \Theta_*) \, . \tag{2.4}$$

In the above, how Θ_* are estimated, thus discriminates MAP from ML. In MAP, Θ_* are estimated as:

$$\Theta_* = \arg\max p(\Theta|D) \, , \tag{2.5}$$

while in ML, the parameters are given as:

$$\Theta_* = \arg\max p(D|\Theta) \, . \tag{2.6}$$

Observing Eq.(2.3), one can see that MAP actually enforces the approximated conditional distribution over parameters as a delta function situating itself at the most prominent Θ. Namely,

$$\widehat{p}(\Theta|D) = \begin{cases} 1, \text{ if } \quad \Theta = \arg\max p(\Theta|D) \\ 0, \text{ otherwise} \end{cases} . \tag{2.7}$$

For ML, it is even simpler. This can be observed by looking into the relationship between MAP and ML:

$$\arg\max p(\Theta|D) = \arg\max p(D|\Theta)p(\Theta) \, . \tag{2.8}$$

Thus, compared to MAP, ML omits the item $p(\Theta)$, the prior probability over the parameters. In practice, a model with a more complex structure may be more possible to cause over-fitting, which means the model can fit the training data perfectly while having a bad prediction ability on the test or future data. In this sense, discarding the prior probability, ML lacks the flexibility to favor simple models by conditioning the prior probability [5, 49]. On the other hand, MAP permits a regularization on the prior probability and thus contains potentials to resist over-fitting problems.

When applied in practice, under independent, identically distributional data (i.i.d.) conditions, rather than directly optimizing the original form, ML estimations usually take the maximization on the log-likelihood, which can transform the multiplication form into an easily-solved additional one:

$$\Theta_* = \arg\max p(D|\Theta) = \arg\max \log p(D|\Theta) = \arg\max \sum_{j=1}^{N} \log p(\boldsymbol{z}_j|\Theta). \tag{2.9}$$

2.2.1.2 Maximum Conditional Learning

Rather than computing the integral form, both the above ML learning and MAP learning seek to use one specific point Θ_* to calculate Eq.(2.3). The difference between them lies in how they estimate the specific parameter Θ_*. Compared with the long history in using ML and MAP estimations, Maximum Conditional (MC) learning enjoys a short span of time but has achieved state-of-the-art performance in many domains such as speech recognition [4, 42, 53].

Maximum Conditional learning also focuses on adopting one certain Θ_* to simplify the computation of Eq.(2.3). Differently, the selection of Θ_* is based on maximizing a conditional likelihood defined as follows:

$$\Theta_* = \arg\max p(\boldsymbol{C}|\Theta, \boldsymbol{Z}) \,, \tag{2.10}$$

where $\boldsymbol{C} = \{c^1, c^2, \ldots, c^N\}$ is the vector formed by the class label of each observation in D, and $\boldsymbol{Z} = \{z^1, z^2, \ldots, z^N\}$ corresponds to the data of the attributes (or features) in D. Similar to the relation between ML and MAP, MC can also plug in a prior probability into the above formulae for resisting over-fitting problems, i.e.

$$\Theta_* = \arg\max p(\boldsymbol{C}|\Theta, \boldsymbol{Z})p(\Theta) \,. \tag{2.11}$$

By maximizing the conditional likelihood, MC is thus more direct and classification–oriented. Note that only the conditional probability which is maximized above is directly related to the classification purpose. Maximizing other quantities as done in ML or MAP, possibly optimizes unnecessary information for classifications, which is wasteful and imprecise. However, although MC appears to be more precise, it is usually hard to conduct the optimization due to the involvement of the conditional item. Such an example can be seen in optimizing a tree-based Bayesian network [12]. Moreover, when there is missing information, the optimization of MC may even present a more tough problem in general, while in such circumstances, powerful Expectation Maximization (EM) techniques [27, 35] can easily be applied in ML.

2.2.1.3 Bayesian Average Learning

It is noted that in ML, MAP and MC, for the easy calculation of Eq.(2.3) one certain Θ_* is adopted for approximations. However, although one point estimation enjoys computational advantages in approximating Eq.(2.3), in practice it may be very inaccurate and in this sense may impair the prediction ability of global learning. Aiming to solve this problem, recent researches have suggested to use the Bayesian Average learning approaches. This type of approaches facilitates the computation of Eq.(2.3) by changing the integral into a summation form based on sampling methods, e.g. Markov Chain Monte Carlo methods [14, 25, 37, 38, 41].

Following this trend, many models are proposed. Among them are Bayesian Point Machine [18, 36, 44] and Maximum Entropy Estimation [22]. Bayes Point Machine restricts the averaging of the parameters in the version space which denotes the space where the training data can be perfectly classified. This proposed method is reported to contain a better generalization ability within the global learning framework. But it is challenged to lack systematic ways to extend its applications into non-separable datasets, where the version space may include no candidate solutions. Maximum Entropy Estimation, on the other hand, seems to provide a more flexible and more systematic scheme to perform the averaging of models. By trying to maximize an entropy-like objective, Maximum Entropy Estimation demonstrates some characteristics of both global learning and local learning. However, only two small datasets are used to evaluate its performance. Moreover, the prior, usually unknown, plays an important role in this model, but has to be assumed beforehand.

2.2.2 Non-parametric Learning

In contrast with generative learning discussed in the above, non-parametric learning does not assume any specific global models before learning. Therefore, no risk will be taken on possible wrong assumptions on data. Consequently, non-parametric learning appears to set a more valid foundation than generative learning models. Typical non-parametric learning models in the context of classifications consist of Parzen Window estimation [10] and the widely used k-Nearest-Neighbor model [7, 43]. We will discuss these two models in the following.

The Parzen Window estimation also attempts to estimate a density among the training data. However it employs a totally different way. Parzen Window first defines an n-dimensional cell hypercube region R_N over each observation. By defining a window function:

$$w(u) = \begin{cases} 1, & |u_j| \leq 1/2, \quad j = 1, 2, \ldots, n \\ 0, & \text{otherwise} \end{cases} , \tag{2.12}$$

the density is then estimated as:

$$p_N(z) = \frac{1}{N} \sum_{i=1}^{N} \frac{1}{h_N} w\left(\frac{z - z_i}{h_N}\right) , \tag{2.13}$$

where h_N is defined as the length of the edge of R_N.

From the above, one can observe that Parzen Window puts a local density over each observation, the final density is then the statistical result of averaging all local densities. In practice, the window function can actually be general functions including the most commonly-used Gaussian function. Fig. 2.2 illustrates a density estimated by the Parzen Window algorithm.

The k-Nearest-Neighbor method can be cast as designing a special cell over each observation and then averages all the cell densities as the overall

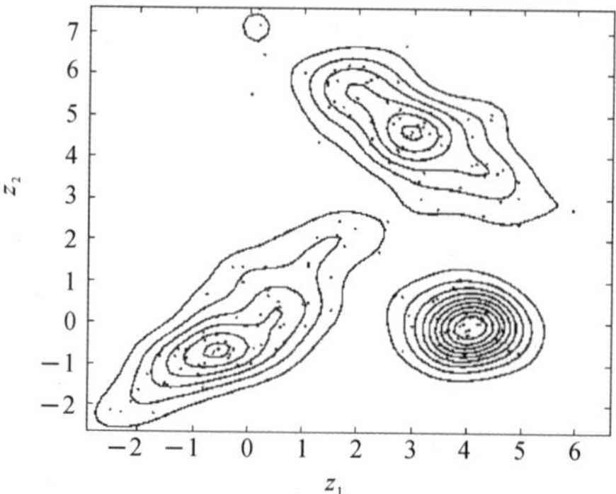

Fig. 2.2. An illustration of Parzen Window estimation

density for data. More specifically, the cell volume V_N is designed as follows: let the cell volume be a function of the training data, by centering a cell around each point z^j and increasing the volume until k_N samples are contained, where k_N depends on N. The local density for each observation is then defined as

$$p_N(z_j) = \frac{k_N/N}{V_N} \; .$$

(2.14)

When used for classifications, the prediction is given by the class with the maximum posterior probability, i.e.

$$c = \arg\max_{c_i \in \mathbb{F}} p_N(c_i|z) \; .$$

(2.15)

Further, the posterior probability can be calculated as below:

$$p_N(c_i|z) = \frac{p_N(c_i, z)}{\sum_{i \in \mathbb{F}} p_N(z, c_i)} = \frac{(k_i/N)/V}{\sum_{i \in \mathbb{F}} (k_i/N)/V} = \frac{k_i}{k} \; .$$

(2.16)

Therefore, the prediction result is just the class with the maximum fraction of the samples in a cell.

These non-parametric methods make no underlying assumptions on data and appear to be more general in real cases. However, using no parameters actually means using many parameters so that each parameter would not dominate other parameters (in the discussed models, the data points can be in fact considered as the "parameters"). In such a way, if one parameter fails to work, it will not influence the whole system globally and statistically. However, using many parameters also results in serious problems. One of the main problems is that the density is overwhelmingly dependent on the training samples. Therefore, to generate an accurate density, the number of samples needs to be very large (much larger than would be required if we perform the estimation by generative learning approaches). What is even worse is that the number of data will unfortunately increase exponentially with the dimension of data. Another disadvantage caused is its severe requirement for the storage, since all the samples need to be saved beforehand in order to predict new data.

2.2.3 The Minimum Error Minimax Probability Machine

Within the context of global learning, a dilemma seems existing: If we assume a specific model as in generative learning, it loses the generality; if we use instead non-parametric learning, it is impractical for high-dimension data. One question is then proposed, can we have an approach which does not require a large number of training samples for reducing complexities and also does not assume specific models for maintaining the generality? Towards this end, we propose Minimum Error Minimax Probability Machine (MEMPM) in this book.

Unlike generative learning or non-parametric learning, Minimum Error Minimax Probability Machine does not try to estimate a distribution over data. Instead, it attempts to extract reliable global information from data and estimates parameters for maximizing the minimal possibility that a future data will fall into the correct class. More precisely, rather than seeking to find an accurate distribution, MEMPM focuses on studying the worst-case probability (which is relatively robust) to predict data. In terms of the style in making decisions, MEMPM is more like a local learning method due to its direct optimization for classification and the task-oriented characteristic. However, because MEMPM only summarizes global information from data (not a distribution) as well, we still locate it in the framework of global learning.

The proposed MEMPM contains many appealing features. Firstly, it represents a distribution-free Bayes optimal classifier in the worst-case scenario. A perfect balance is achieved by MEMPM in this way: No specific model is assumed on data, since it is distribution-free. At the same time, although in the worst-case scenario, it is also the Bayes optimal classifier which is only originally applicable in the cases with a known distribution. Another critical feature of MEMPM is that under a mild condition, it contains an explicit generalization bound. Furthermore, by exploring the bound, the recently-proposed promising model, Minimax Probability Machine is clearly demonstrated to be its special case. Importantly, based on specifying a bound for one class of data, a Biased Minimax Probability Machine is branched out from MEMPM, which will be shown to provide a rigorous and systematic treatment for biased classifications. We will detail the MEMPM model and BMPM model in the next chapter.

2.3 Local Learning

Local learning adopts a largely different way to construct classifiers. This type of learning is even more task-oriented than Minimum Error Minimax Probability Machine and Maximal Conditional learning. In the context of classifications, only the final mapping function from the features z to c is crucial. Therefore, describing global information from data or explicitly summarizing a distribution whatever is conditional or joint, is a roundabout or intermediate step and therefore may be deemed wasteful or imprecise especially when the global information cannot be estimated accurately.

Alternatively, recent progress has suggested a local learning method, or well known as the discriminative learning method. The family of approaches directly pin-points the most critical quantities for classifications, while all other information less irrelevant to this purpose is simply omitted. Compared to global learning, no model is assumed and also no explicit global information will be engaged in this scheme. Among this school of methods are Neural Networks [1, 11, 17, 34, 39, 43], Gabriel Graph methods [3, 24, 54], large margin classifiers [8, 45, 46, 47] including Support Vector Machine (SVM), a state-of-the-art classifier which achieves superior performance in various pattern recognition fields. In the following, we will focus on introducing SVM in details.

Support Vector Machines

Support Vector Machine is established based on minimizing the expected classification risk as defined as follows:

$$R(\Theta) = \int_{z,c} l(z, c, \theta) \mathrm{d}(p(z, c)) \,, \tag{2.17}$$

where $l(z, c, \Theta)$ is the loss function. Similar problems occur in the global learning, since generally $p(z, c)$ is unknown. Therefore, in practice, the above expected risk is often approximated by the so-called empirical risk:

$$R_{\mathrm{emp}}(\Theta) = \frac{1}{N} \sum_{j=1}^{N} l(z^j, c^j, \Theta) \,. \tag{2.18}$$

The above loss function describes the extent on how close the estimated class disagrees with the real class for the training data. Various metrics can be used for defining this loss function, including the $0-1$ loss and the quadratic loss [50].

However, considering only the training data may lead to the over-fitting problem again. In SVM, one big step in dealing with the over-fitting problem has been made, i.e. the margin between two classes should be pulled away in order to reduce the over-fitting risk. Fig. 2.3 illustrates the idea of SVM.

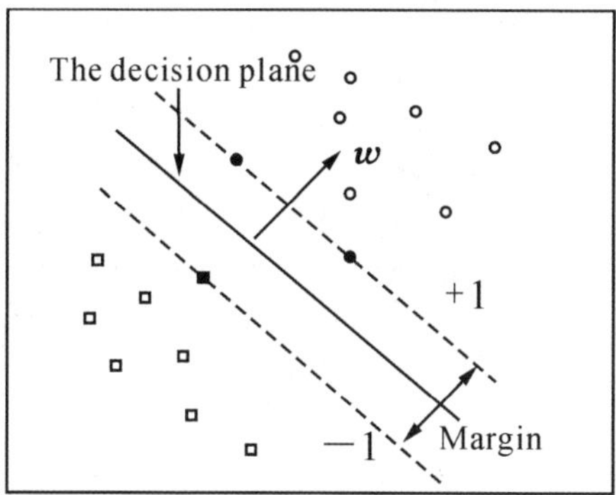

Fig. 2.3. An illustration of Support Vector Machine

Two classes of data depicted as circles and solid dots are presented in this figure. Intuitively observed, there are many decision hyperplanes which can be adopted for separating these two classes of data. However, the one plotted in this figure is selected as the favorable separating plane, because it contains the maximum margin between two classes. Therefore, in the objective function of SVM, a regularization term representing the margin shows up. Moreover, as seen in this figure, only those filled points called support vectors mainly determine the separating plane, while other points do not contribute to the margin at all. In another word, only several local points are critical for the classification purpose in the framework of SVM and thus should be extracted.

Actually, a more formal explanation and theoretical foundation can be obtained from the Structure Risk Minimization criterion [6, 52]. Therein, maximizing the margin between different classes of data is minimizing an upper bound of the expected risk, i.e. the VC dimension bound [52]. However, since the focus of this book does not lie in the theory of SVM, we will not go further to discuss the details about this. Interested readers can refer to [51, 52].

2.4 Hybrid Learning

Local learning (or simply regarded as SVM) has demonstrated its advantages, such as its state-of-the-art performance (the lower generalization error), the optimal and unique solution, and the mathematical tractability. However, it does discard many useful information from data, e.g. the structure information from data.

An illustrative example has been seen in Fig. 1.4. In the current state-of-the-art classifier, i.e. SVM, similar problems also occur. This can be seen in Fig. 2.4. In this figure, the purpose is to separate two catergories of data x and y. As observed, the classification boundary is intuitively observed to be mainly determined by the dotted axis, i.e. the long axis of the y data (represented by $\square$'s) or the short axis of the x data (represented by o's). Moreover, along this axis, the y data are more possible to scatter than the x data, since y contains a relatively larger variance in this direction. Noting this "global" fact, a good decision hyperplane seems reasonable to lie closer to the x side (see the dash-dot line). However, SVM ignores this kind of "global" information, i.e. the statistical trend of data occurrence. The derived SVM decision hyperplane (the solid line) lies unbiasedly right in the middle of two "local" points (the support vectors).The above considerations directly motivate Maxi-Min Margin Machine.

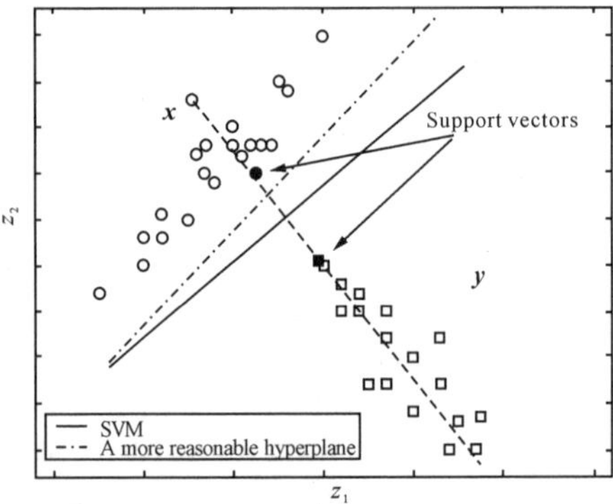

Fig. 2.4. A decision hyperplane with considerations of both local and global information

2.5 Maxi-Min Margin Machine

After examining the road-map of the learning models, especially the global learning and local learning, we have seen a strong motivation for combining two different but complementary schemes. More specifically, borrowing the idea from local learning by assuming no distribution on data would set a valid foundation for the learning models. Meanwhile, fusing robust global information, e.g. structure information, into learning models appears to benefit more on refining decisions in separating data.

Our effort will be made in this direction. As will be detailed in Chapter 4, the hybrid learning model, Maxi-Min Margin Machine successfully plugs the global information into the learning and enjoys good features from both local learning and global learning. As seen in Fig. 2.1, the Maxi-Min Margin Machine model has built up various connections with many models in the literature; it incorporates Support Vector Machine as a special case, which lies in the framework of local learning; it also includes Minimax

Probability Machine and Fisher Discriminant Analysis as direct spin-offs. Moreover, a strong link has been established between this model and Minimum Error Minimax Probability Machine. Moreover, empirical investigations have shown that this combined model outperforms both local learning model such as SVM and global learning models, e.g. MPM.

In the next chapter, we will first present the Minimum Error Minimax Probability Machine which is a general global learning model. Following that, we then introduce the Maxi-Min Margin Machine and demonstrate its merits both theoretically and empirically.

References

1. Anand R, Mehrotram GK, Mohan KC, Ranka S (1993) An improved alogrithm for neural network classification of imbalance training sets. IEEE Transactions on Neural Networks 4(6):962–969
2. Bahl LR, Brown PF, de Souza PV, Mercer RL (1993) Estimating hidden Markov model parameters so as to maximize speech recognition accuracy. IEEE Transactions on Speech and Audio Processing 1:77–82
3. Barber CB, Dobkin DP, Huhanpaa H (1996) The quickhull algorithm for convex hulls. ACM Transactions on Mathematical Software 22(4):469–483
4. Beaufays F, Wintraub M, Konig Y (1999) Discriminative mixture weight estimation for large Gaussian mixture models. In Proceedings of the International Conference on Acoustics, Speech and Signal Processing 337–340
5. Brand M (1998) Structure discovery via entropy minimization. In Neural Information Processing System 11
6. J Christopher, Burges C (1998) A tutorial on support vector machines for pattern recognition. Data Mining and Knowledge Discovery 2(2):121–167
7. Cover TM, Hart PE (1967) Nearest neighbor pattern classification. IEEE Transactions on Information Theory IT-13(1):21–27
8. Cristianini N, Shawe-Taylor J (2000) An Introduction to Support Vector Machines(and Other Kernel-based Learning Methods). Cambridge, U.K.; New York, NY: Cambridge University Press
9. Duda R, Hart P (1973) Pattern Classification and Scene Analysis. New York, NY: John Wiley & Sons
10. Duda RO, Hart PE, Stork DG (2000) Pattern Classification. New York, NY: John Wiley & Sons
11. Fausett L (1994) Fundamentals of Neural Networks. New York, NY: Prentice Hall
12. Friedman N, Geiger D, Goldszmidt M (1997) Bayesian network classifiers. Machine Learning 29:131–161
13. Fukunaga K (1990) Introduction to Statistical Pattern Recognition. San Diego, Academic Press, 2nd edition
14. Gilks WR, Richardson S, Spiegelhalter DJ (1996) Markov Chain Monte Carlo in Practice. London: Chapman & Hall
15. Grzegorzewski P, Hryniewicz O, Gil M (2002) Soft Methods in Probability, Statistics and Data Analysis. Heidelberg; New York: Physica-Verlag

16. Hastie T, Tibshirani R (1996) Discriminant analysis by Gaussian mixtures. Journal of the Royal Statistical Society(B) 58:155–176

17. Haykin S (1994) Neural Networks: A Comprehensive Foundation. New York, NY: Macmillan Publishing

18. Herbrich R, Graepel T (2001) Large scale Bayes point machines. In Advances in Neural Information Processing Systems (NIPS)

19. Huang K, King I, Chan L, Yang H (2004) Improving Chow-Liu tree performance based on association rules. In J. C. Rajapakse and L. Wang, editors, Neural Information Processing: Research and Development, Studies in Fuzziness and Soft Computing, 152: 94–112. Heidelberg; New York: Springer-Verlag

20. Huang K, King I, Lyu MR (2002). Learning maximum likelihood semi-naive Bayesian network classifier. In Proceedings of IEEE International Conference on Systems, Man and Cybernetics (SMC2002). Hammamet, Tunisia TA1F3

21. Huang K, King I, Lyu MR (2003) Finite mixture model of bound semi-naive Bayesian network classifier. In Proceedings of the International Conference on Artificial Neural Networks (ICANN-2003), Lecture Notes in Artificial Intelligence, Long Paper. Heidelberg: Springer-Verlag 2714: 115–122

22. Jebara T (2002) Discriminative, Generative and Imitative Learning. PhD thesis, Massachusetts Institute of Technology

23. Jordan MI (1995) Why the logistic function? A tutorial discussion on probabilities and neural networks. Technical Report 9503, MIT Computational Cognitive Science Report

24. Toussaint GT, Jaromczyk JW(1992) Relative neighborhood graphs and their relatives. Proceedings IEEE 80(9):1502–1517

25. Kass RE, Carlin BP, Gelman A, Neal RM (1998) Markov chain Monte Carlo in practice: A roundtable discussion. The American Statistician 52:93–100

26. Kohavi R, Becker B, Sommerfield D (1997) Improving simple Bayes. In Technique Report. Mountain View, CA: Data Mining and Visualization Group, Silicon Graphics Inc

27. Laird NM, Dempster AP, Rubin DB (1977) Maximum likelihood from incomplete data via the EM algorithm. J. Royal Statist. Society B39:1–38

28. Lanckriet GRG, Ghaoui LE, Bhattacharyya C, Jordan MI (2001) Minimax probability machine. In Advances in Neural Information Processing Systems (NIPS)

29. Lanckriet GRG, Ghaoui LE, Bhattacharyya C, Jordan MI (2002) A robust minimax approach to classification. Journal of Machine Learning Research 3:555–582

30. Lanckriet GRG, Ghaoui LE, Jordan MI (2002) Robust novelty detection with single-class MPM. In Advances in Neural Information Processing Systems (NIPS)

31. Langley P (1993) Introduction of recursive Bayesian classifiers. In Proceedings of the 1993 European Conference on Machine Learning 153–164

32. Langley P, Iba W, Thompson K (1992) An analysis of Bayesian classifiers. In Proceedings of National Conference on Artificial Intelligence 223–228

33. McLachlan GJ, Basford KE (1988) Mixture Models: Inference and Applications to Clustering. New York, NY: Marcel Dekker Inc

34. Pankaj Mehra, Benjamin W Wah (1992) Artificial Neural Networks : Concepts and Theory. Los Alamitos, California: IEEE Computer Society Press

35. Meng XL, Rubin DB (1993) Maximum likelihood estimation via the ECM algorithm: A general framework. Biometrika 80(2)

36. Minka T (2001) A family of Algorithms for Approximate Inference. PhD thesis, Massachusetts Institute of Technology
37. Neal RM (1993) Probabilistic inference using Markov chain Monte Carlo methods. Technical Report CRG-TR-93-1, Dept. of Computer Science, University of Toronto
38. Neal RM (1998). Suppressing random walks in Markov chain Monte Carlo using ordered overrelaxation M. I. Jordan (editor) Learning in Graphical Models, Dordrecht: Kluwer Academic Publishers 205–225
39. Patterson D (1996) Artificial Neural Networks. Singapore: Prentice Hall
40. Pearl J (1988) Probabilistic Reasoning in Intelligent Systems: Networks of Plausible Inference. San Francisco, CA: Morgan Kaufmann
41. Pinto RL, Neal RM (2001) Improving Markov chain Monte Carlo estimators by coupling to an approximating chain. Technical Report No. 0101, Dept. of Statistics, University of Toronto
42. Rathinavelu C, Deng L (1996) The trended HMM with discriminative training for phonetic classification. In Proceedings of ICSLP
43. Ripley BD (1996) Pattern Recognition and Neural Networks. Press Syndicate of the University of Cambridge
44. Rujam R (1997) Preceptron learning by playing billiards. Neural Computation 9:99–122
45. Schölkopf B, Burges C, Smola A (1999) Advances in Kernel Methods: Support Vector Learning. Cambridge, MA: The MIT Press
46. Schölkopf B , Smola A (2002) Learning with Kernels: Support Vector Machines, Regularization, Optimization and Beyond. Cambridge, MA: The MIT Press
47. Smola AJ, Bartlett PL, Scholkopf B, Schuurmans D (2000). Advances in Large Margin Classifiers. Cambridge, MA: The MIT Press
48. Stolcke A, Omohundro S (1993) Hidden Markov model induction by Bayesian model merging. In NIPS 5: 11–18
49. Tipping M(1999) The relevance vector machine. In Advances in Neural Information Processing Systems 12 (NIPS)
50. Trivedi PK (1978) Estimation of a distributed lag model under quadratic loss. Econometrica 46(5):1181–1192
51. Vapnik VN (1998) Statistical Learning Theory. New York, NY: John Wiley & Sons
52. Vapnik VN (1999) The Nature of Statistical Learning Theory. New York, NY: Springer, 2nd edition
53. Woodland P, Povey D (2000) Large scale discriminative training for speech recognition. In Proceedings of ASR 2000
54. Zhang W, King I (2002) A study of the relationship between support vector machine and Gabriel Graph. In Proceedings of IEEE World Congress on Computational Intelligence—International Joint Conference on Neural Networks

3

A General Global Learning Model: MEMPM

Traditional global learning, especially generative learning, enjoys a long and distinguished history, holding a lot of merits, e.g. a relatively simple optimization, and the flexibility in incorporating global information such as structure information and invariance, etc. However, it is widely argued that this model lacks the generality for having to assume a specific model beforehand. Assuming a specific model over data is useful in some cases. However, the assumption may not always coincide with the true data distribution in general and thus may be invalid in many circumstances. In this chapter, we propose a novel global learning model, named Minimum Error Minimax Probability Machine (MEMPM), which is directly motivated from Marshall and OlKin Probability Theory [20, 24]. For classifying data correctly, this model focuses on estimating the worse-case probability, which is not only more reliable, but also more importantly provides no need for assuming specific models. Furthermore, this new model consists of several appealing features.

First, MEMPM acutally presents a novel general framework for classifications. As demonstrated later, MEMPM includes a recently-proposed promising model Minimax Probability Machine as its special case, which is reported to achieve comparable performance to SVM. Interpretations from both viewpoints of the optimal thresholding problem and the geometry will be provided to show the advantages of MEMPM. Moreover, this novel model branches out another promising special case, named Biased Minimax Probability Machine (BMPM) [12] and extends its application into a type of important classifications, i.e. biased classifications.

Second, this model derives a distribution-free Bayes optimal classifier in the worst-case scenario. It thus distinguishes itself from the traditional global learning methods, or more particularly, the traditional Bayes optimal classifiers which have to assume a distribution on data and thus lack the generality in real cases. Furthermore, we will show that under some conditions, e.g. when a Gaussian distribution is assumed on data, the worst-case Bayes optimal classifier becomes the true Bayes optimal hyperplane.

Third, the MEMPM model contains an explicit performance indicator, namely an explicit upper bound on the probability of misclassification of future data. Moreover, we will demonstrate theoretically and empirically that MEMPM attains a smaller upper bound of the probability of misclassification than MPM, which thus implies the advantages of MEMPM over MPM.

Fourth, although in general the optimization of MEMPM is shown to be a non-concave problem, empirically, it demonstrates a good concavity in the main "interest" region and thus can be solved practically. Furthermore, we will show that the final optimization problem involves solving a one-dimensional line search problem and thus results in a satisfactory solving method.

This chapter is organized as follows. In the next section, we will first introduce the Marshall and Olkin Theory. We then present the main content of this chapter, the MEMPM model, including its definition, interpretations, the practical solving method, and the sufficient conditions for the convergence into the true Bayes decision hyperplane. Following that, we demonstrate a robust version of MEMPM. In Section 3.4, we seek to kernelize the MEMPM model to attack nonlinear classification problems. We then, in Section 3.5, present a series of experiments on synthetic datasets and real-world benchmark data sets. In Section 3.6, we analyze the tightness of the worst-case accuracy bound. In Section 3.7, we show that empirically MEMPM is often concave in the main "interest" region. In Section 3.8, we present the limitations of MEMPM and envision the possible future work. Finally, we summarize this chapter in Section 3.9.

3.1 Marshall and Olkin Theory

The Marshall and Olkin Theory can be described as follows:

Theorem 3.1. [Marshall and Olkin Theory] *The probability that a random vector $\boldsymbol{y}$ belongs to a convex set S can be bounded by the following formulation:*

$$\sup_{\boldsymbol{y} \sim (\overline{\boldsymbol{y}}, \boldsymbol{\Sigma_y})} Pr\{\boldsymbol{y} \in S\} = \frac{1}{1 + d^2}, \text{ with } d^2 = \inf_{\boldsymbol{y} \in S} (\boldsymbol{y} - \overline{\boldsymbol{y}})^{\mathrm{T}} \boldsymbol{\Sigma_y}^{-1} (\boldsymbol{y} - \overline{\boldsymbol{y}}) \, , (3.1)$$

where the supremum is taken over all distributions for $\boldsymbol{y}$ containing the mean as $\overline{\boldsymbol{y}}$ and the covariance matrix as $\boldsymbol{\Sigma_y}$ [1].

The theory provides us with a possibility to assume no model, but bound the probability of misclassifying a point and consequently develop a novel classifier within the framework of global learning. More specifically, one can design a linear separating plane by replacing S with a half space associated

---

[1] We assume $\boldsymbol{\Sigma_y}$ to be positive definite for simplicity. Otherwise, we can always add a small positive amount to its diagonal elements to force its positive definition.

with this linear plane. To take the supremum can then be considered to bound the misclassification rate for one class of data. We in the following, first introduce the model definition and then show how this theory can be applied therein for deriving a distribution-free classifier.

3.2 Minimum Error Minimax Probability Decision Hyperplane

In this section, we first present the model definition of MEMPM while reviewing the original MPM model. We then in Section 3.2.2 interpret MEMPM with respect to MPM. In Section 3.2.3, we specialize the MEMPM model for dealing with biased classifications. In Section 3.2.4, we analyze the MEMPM optimization problem and propose a practical solving method. In Section 3.2.5, we address the sufficient conditions when the worst-case Bayes optimal classifier derived from MEMPM becomes the true Bayes optimal classifier. In Section 3.2.6, we provide a geometrical interpretation for BMPM and MEMPM.

3.2.1 Problem Definition

The notation in this chapter will largely follow that of [16]. Let x and y denote two random vectors representing two classes of data with means and covariance matrices as $\{\overline{x}, \Sigma_x\}$ and $\{\overline{y}, \Sigma_y\}$, respectively, in a two-category classification task, where $x, y, \overline{x}, \overline{y} \in \mathbb{R}^n$, and $\Sigma_x, \Sigma_y \in \mathbb{R}^{n \times n}$.

Assuming $\{\overline{x}, \Sigma_x\}$, $\{\overline{y}, \Sigma_y\}$ for two classes of data are reliable, MPM attempts to determine the hyperplane $w^T z = b$ ($w \in \mathbb{R}^n \backslash \{0\}$, $z \in \mathbb{R}^n$, $b \in \mathbb{R}$, and superscript T denotes the transpose) which can separate two classes of data with the maximal probability. The formulation for the MPM model is written as follows:

$$\max_{\alpha, \beta, w \neq 0, b} \{\theta\alpha + (1 - \theta)\beta\} , \tag{3.2}$$

$$\text{s.t.} \quad \inf_{x \sim (\overline{x}, \Sigma_x)} Pr\{w^T x \geq b\} \geq \alpha , \tag{3.3}$$

$$\inf_{y \sim (\overline{y}, \Sigma_y)} Pr\{w^T y \leq b\} \geq \beta , \tag{3.4}$$

where α and β indicate the worst-case classification accuracies of future data points for the class x and y, respectively, namely, the worst-case accuracy for classifying x data and y data. Future points z for which $w^T z \geq b$ are then classified as the class x; otherwise they are judged as the class y. $\theta \in [0, 1]$ is the prior probability of the class x and $1 - \theta$ is thus the prior probability of the class y. Intuitively, maximizing $\theta\alpha + (1 - \theta)\beta$ can be naturally considered as maximizing the expected worst-case accuracy for future data. In other words, this optimization leads to minimizing the expected upper bound of the error rate. More precisely, if we change $\max\{\theta\alpha + (1-\theta)\beta\}$ to $\min\{\theta(1-\alpha) + (1-\theta)(1-\beta)\}$ and consider $1-\alpha$ as the upper bound probability that an $\boldsymbol{x}$ data is classified into class $\boldsymbol{y}$ ($1-\beta$ is similarly considered), the MEMPM model exactly minimizes the maximum Bayes error and thus derives the Bayes optimal hyperplane in the worst-case scenario. In comparison, MPM assumes the equal worst-case probability for both classes, i.e. it forces $\alpha = \beta$. Obvisouly, this is inappropriate since it is unnecessary that the worst-case accuracies are presumed equal. However, even in such a constrained way, MPM is reported to achieve comparable performacne to SVM, a current state-of-the-art classifier. Therefore, the generalized case of MPM, namely, MEMPM may be expected to be more pomising. This will be empirically demonstrated in the experimental part of this chapter.

3.2.2 Interpretation

We interpret MEMPM with respect to MPM in this section. First, it is evident that if we presume $\alpha = \beta$, the optimization of MEMPM degrades to the MPM optimization. This would mean that MPM is actually a special case of MEMPM.

An analogy to illustrate the difference between MEMPM and MPM can be seen in the optimal thresholding problem. Fig. 3.1 illustrates this analogy. To separate two classes of one-dimensional data with density functions as p_1 and p_2, respectively, the optimal thresholding is given by the decision plane in Fig. 3.1(a) (assuming that the prior probabilities for two classes of data are equal). This optimal thesholding corresponds to the point minimizing the

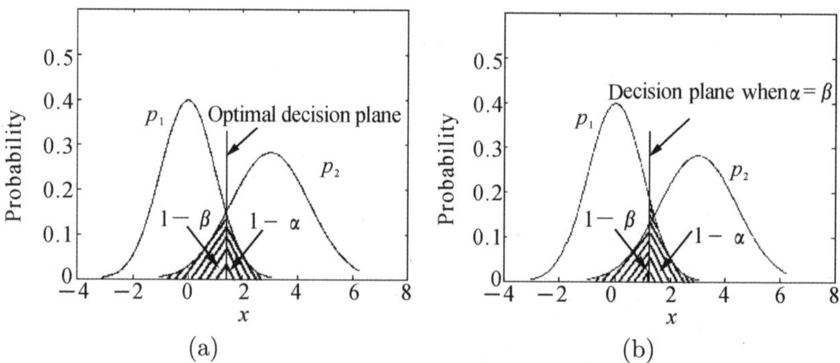

Fig. 3.1. An analogy to illustrate the difference between MEMPM and MPM with equal prior probabilities for two classes. The optimal decision plane corresponds to the intersection point, where the error $(1-\alpha) + (1-\beta)$ is minimized (or the accuracy $\alpha + \beta$ is maximized) as implied by MEMPM, rather than the one where α is equal to β as implied by MPM

error rate $(1-\alpha)+(1-\beta)$ or maximizing the accuracy $\alpha+\beta$, which is exactly the intersection point of two density functions ($1-\alpha$ represents the area of $135°$-line filled region and $1-\beta$ represents the area of $45°$-line filled region). On the other hand, the thresholding point to force $\alpha = \beta$ is not necessarily the optimal point to separate these two classes.

It should be clarified that the MEMPM model assumes no distributions. This distinguishes the MEMPM model from the traditional Bayes optimal thresholding method which has to make specific assumptions on data distribution. On the other hand, although MEMPM minimizes the upper bound of the Bayes error rate of future data points, as shown later in Section 3.2.5, it will represent the true Bayes optimal hyperplane under some conditions, e.g. when a Gaussian distribution is assumed on data.[2]

3.2.3 Special Case for Biased Classifications

The above discussion only covers the unbiased classification tasks, which does not favor one class over the other class intentionally. However, another important type of pattern recognition tasks, namely biased classification, arises very often in practice. In this scenario, one class is usually more important than the other class. Thus a bias should be imposed towards the important class. Such typical example can be seen in the diagnosis of epidemical disease. Classifying a patient who is infected with a disease into an opposite class results in serious consequence. Thus in this problem, the classification accuracy should be biased towards the class with disease. In other words, we would prefer to diagnose the person without the disease to be the infected case rather than the other way round.

We in the following demonstrate that MEMPM actually contains a special case we call Biased Minimax Probability Machine for biased classifications. We formulate this special case as:

$$\max_{\alpha,\beta,\boldsymbol{w}\neq\boldsymbol{0},b} \alpha \, ,$$

$$\text{s.t.} \quad \inf_{\boldsymbol{x}\sim(\overline{\boldsymbol{x}},\boldsymbol{\Sigma}_x)} Pr\{\boldsymbol{w}^{\mathrm{T}}\boldsymbol{x} \geq b\} \geq \alpha \, ,$$

$$\inf_{\boldsymbol{y}\sim(\overline{\boldsymbol{y}},\boldsymbol{\Sigma}_y)} Pr\{\boldsymbol{w}^{\mathrm{T}}\boldsymbol{y} \leq b\} \geq \beta_0 \, ,$$

---

[2]Another interpretation of the difference between MEMPM and MPM can be stated from the viewpoint of Game Theory. MPM can be regarded as a non-cooperative competitive game. In this game, each player (class) tries to maximize its individual benefit, i.e. α. The competition leads to each class obtaining the same benefit when all classes fulfill a kind of equilibrium. However, in the game theory, many models, e.g. the prisoners' dilemma, Counot Model and the tragedy of the commons [21], have stated that maximizing individual benefit does not lead to maximizing the global optimum. Our model, on the contrary, can be considered as a kind of cooperative game. It achieves the global optimum through cooperation.

where β_0 is a pre-specified positive constant, which represents an acceptable accuracy level for the less important class $\boldsymbol{y}$.

The above optimization utilizes a typical setting in biased classifications, i.e. the accuracy for the important class (associated with $\boldsymbol{x}$) should be as high as possible, if only the accuracy for the less important class (associated with $\boldsymbol{y}$) maintains at an acceptable level specified by the lower bound β_0 (which can be set by users).

With quantitatively plugging a specified bias β_0 into classifications and also containing an explicit accuracy bound α for the important class, BMPM provides a more direct and elegant way for biased classifications. Comparatively, to achieve a specified bias, traditional biased classifiers such as the Weighted Support Vector Machine [23] and the Weighted k-Nearest Neighbor method [18] usually adapt different costs for different classes. However, due to the difficulties in building up quantitative connections between the cost and the accuracy,[3] for imposing a specified bias, these methods need resort to the trial and error procedure to attain suitable costs which are generally indirect and lack rigorous treatments.

3.2.4 Solving the MEMPM Optimization Problem

In this section, we will propose to solve the MEMPM optimization problem. As will be demonstrated shortly, the MEMPM optimization can be transformed into a one-dimensional line search problem. More specifically, the objective function of the line search problem is implicitly determined by dealing with a BMPM problem. Therefore, solving the line search problem corresponds to solving a Sequential Biased Minimax Probability Machine (SBMPM) problem. Before we proceed, we first introduce how to solve the BMPM optimization problem.

3.2.4.1 Solving the BMPM Optimization Problem

First, we describe Lemma 3.2 which is developed in [16].

Lemma 3.2. *Given* $\boldsymbol{w} \neq \boldsymbol{0}$ *and* b, *such that* $\boldsymbol{w}^{\mathrm{T}}\boldsymbol{y} \leq b$ *and* $\beta \in [0,1)$, *the condition:*

$$\inf_{\boldsymbol{y} \sim (\overline{\boldsymbol{y}}, \boldsymbol{\Sigma_y})} Pr\{\boldsymbol{w}^{\mathrm{T}}\boldsymbol{y} \leq b\} \geq \beta$$

holds if and only if $b - \boldsymbol{w}^{\mathrm{T}}\overline{\boldsymbol{y}} \geq \kappa(\beta)\sqrt{\boldsymbol{w}^{\mathrm{T}}\boldsymbol{\Sigma_y}\boldsymbol{w}}$ *with* $\kappa(\beta) = \sqrt{\frac{\beta}{1-\beta}}$.

The lemma can be proved according to the Marshall and Olkin Theory and the Lagrangian Multiplier theory.

---

[3] Although cross validations could be used to provide empirical connections, they are problem-dependent and are usually slow procedures as well.

Proof. In Marshall and Olkin Theory, if we define $\mathcal{S} = \{\boldsymbol{w}^{\mathrm{T}}\boldsymbol{y} \geq b\}$, the theorem is changed to:

$$\sup_{\boldsymbol{y} \sim \{\overline{\boldsymbol{y}}, \boldsymbol{\Sigma}_{\boldsymbol{y}}\}} Pr\{\boldsymbol{w}^{\mathrm{T}}\boldsymbol{y} \geq b\} = \frac{1}{1+d^2}, \quad \text{with} \quad d^2 = \inf_{\boldsymbol{w}^{\mathrm{T}}\boldsymbol{y} \geq b} (\boldsymbol{y} - \overline{\boldsymbol{y}})^{\mathrm{T}} \boldsymbol{\Sigma}_{\boldsymbol{y}}^{-1} (\boldsymbol{y} - \overline{\boldsymbol{y}}) .$$

We next show that d can be obtained as follows:

$$d^2 = \inf_{\boldsymbol{w}^{\mathrm{T}}\boldsymbol{y} \geq b} (\boldsymbol{y} - \overline{\boldsymbol{y}})^{\mathrm{T}} \boldsymbol{\Sigma}_{\boldsymbol{y}}^{-1} (\boldsymbol{y} - \overline{\boldsymbol{y}}) = \frac{\max(b - \boldsymbol{w}^{\mathrm{T}}\overline{\boldsymbol{y}}, 0)^2}{\boldsymbol{w}^{\mathrm{T}} \boldsymbol{\Sigma}_{\boldsymbol{y}} \boldsymbol{w}} .$$

This can be proved by using the Lagrangian multiplier method as follows:

(1) If $\boldsymbol{w}^{\mathrm{T}}\overline{\boldsymbol{y}} \leq b$.

Denoting $\boldsymbol{p}^{\mathrm{T}} = \boldsymbol{w}^{\mathrm{T}} \boldsymbol{\Sigma}_{\boldsymbol{y}}^{1/2}$, $\boldsymbol{g} = \boldsymbol{\Sigma}_{\boldsymbol{y}}^{-1/2}(\boldsymbol{y} - \overline{\boldsymbol{y}})$, and $q = b - \boldsymbol{w}^{\mathrm{T}}\overline{\boldsymbol{y}}$, one can write $d^2 = \inf_{\boldsymbol{p}^{\mathrm{T}}\boldsymbol{w} \geq q} \boldsymbol{g}^{\mathrm{T}}\boldsymbol{g}$. One can obtain $\boldsymbol{g}$ by introducing Lagrangian multiplier:

$$\{\boldsymbol{g}, \lambda\} = \arg\min_{\boldsymbol{g}} \arg\max_{\lambda} \{\boldsymbol{g}^{\mathrm{T}}\boldsymbol{g} + \lambda(q - \boldsymbol{p}^{\mathrm{T}}\boldsymbol{g})\},$$

where the multiplier $\lambda \geq 0$. Therefore, one can get the following equalities:

$$\boldsymbol{g} = \frac{\lambda \boldsymbol{p}}{2}, \quad q = \boldsymbol{p}^{\mathrm{T}}\boldsymbol{g}.$$

Since $\boldsymbol{w}^{\mathrm{T}}\overline{\boldsymbol{y}} \leq b$, one can easily obtain $q \geq 0$. One can further obtain:

$$\lambda = \frac{2q}{\boldsymbol{p}^{\mathrm{T}}\boldsymbol{p}}, \quad \boldsymbol{g} = \frac{d\boldsymbol{p}}{\boldsymbol{p}^{\mathrm{T}}\boldsymbol{p}}.$$

Finally, this leads to the following equation:

$$d^2 = \inf_{\boldsymbol{w}^{\mathrm{T}}\boldsymbol{y} \geq b} (\boldsymbol{y} - \overline{\boldsymbol{y}})^{\mathrm{T}} \boldsymbol{\Sigma}_{\boldsymbol{y}}^{-1} (\boldsymbol{y} - \overline{\boldsymbol{y}}) = \frac{(b - \boldsymbol{w}^{\mathrm{T}}\overline{\boldsymbol{y}})^2}{\boldsymbol{w}^{\mathrm{T}} \boldsymbol{\Sigma}_{\boldsymbol{y}} \boldsymbol{w}} .$$

(2) If $\boldsymbol{w}^{\mathrm{T}}\overline{\boldsymbol{y}} \geq b$.

In this case, we can only have $\boldsymbol{y} = \overline{\boldsymbol{y}}$. Therefore, $d = 0$.

By integrating the above, we thus complete the proof of this theorem.

By using Lemma 3.2 we can transform the BMPM optimization problem as follows:

$$\max_{\alpha, \boldsymbol{w} \neq \boldsymbol{0}, b} \alpha , \tag{3.5}$$

$$\text{s.t.} \quad -b + \boldsymbol{w}^{\mathrm{T}}\overline{\boldsymbol{x}} \geq \kappa(\alpha)\sqrt{\boldsymbol{w}^{\mathrm{T}}\boldsymbol{\Sigma}_{\boldsymbol{x}}\boldsymbol{w}} , \tag{3.6}$$

$$b - \boldsymbol{w}^{\mathrm{T}}\overline{\boldsymbol{y}} \geq \kappa(\beta_0)\sqrt{\boldsymbol{w}^{\mathrm{T}}\boldsymbol{\Sigma}_{\boldsymbol{y}}\boldsymbol{w}} , \tag{3.7}$$

where $\kappa(\alpha) = \sqrt{\frac{\alpha}{1-\alpha}}$, $\kappa(\beta_0) = \sqrt{\frac{\beta_0}{1-\beta_0}}$. Eq.(3.7) is directly obtained from Eq.(3.4) by using Lemma 3.2. Similarly, by changing $\boldsymbol{w}^{\mathrm{T}}\boldsymbol{x} \geq b$ to $\boldsymbol{w}^{\mathrm{T}}(-\boldsymbol{x}) \leq -b$, Eq.(3.6) can be obtained from Eq.(3.3).

From Eqs.(3.6) and (3.7), we get

$$\boldsymbol{w}^{\mathrm{T}}\overline{\boldsymbol{y}} + \kappa(\beta_0)\sqrt{\boldsymbol{w}^{\mathrm{T}}\boldsymbol{\Sigma}_y\boldsymbol{w}} \leq b \leq \boldsymbol{w}^{\mathrm{T}}\overline{\boldsymbol{x}} - \kappa(\alpha)\sqrt{\boldsymbol{w}^{\mathrm{T}}\boldsymbol{\Sigma}_x\boldsymbol{w}} \ . \tag{3.8}$$

If we eliminate b from this inequality, we obtain:

$$\boldsymbol{w}^{\mathrm{T}}(\overline{\boldsymbol{x}} - \overline{\boldsymbol{y}}) \geq \kappa(\alpha)\sqrt{\boldsymbol{w}^{\mathrm{T}}\boldsymbol{\Sigma}_x\boldsymbol{w}} + \kappa(\beta_0)\sqrt{\boldsymbol{w}^{\mathrm{T}}\boldsymbol{\Sigma}_y\boldsymbol{w}} \ . \tag{3.9}$$

We observe that the magnitude of $\boldsymbol{w}$ does not influence the solution of Eq.(3.9). Moreover, we can assume $\overline{\boldsymbol{x}} \neq \overline{\boldsymbol{y}}$; otherwise, if $\overline{\boldsymbol{x}} = \overline{\boldsymbol{y}}$, the minimax machine does not have a physical meaning. In this case, Eq.(3.9) may even have no solution for every $\beta_0 \neq 0$, since the right hand side would be always positive provided that $\boldsymbol{w} \neq 0$. Thus in the extreme case, β and α have to be zero, which means the worst-case misclassification are always zero.

Without loss of generality, we can set $\boldsymbol{w}^{\mathrm{T}}(\overline{\boldsymbol{x}} - \overline{\boldsymbol{y}}) = 1$. Thus the problem can be further changed as:

$$\max_{\alpha, \boldsymbol{w} \neq \boldsymbol{0}} \ \alpha \ , \tag{3.10}$$

$$\text{s.t.} \quad 1 \geq \kappa(\alpha)\sqrt{\boldsymbol{w}^{\mathrm{T}}\boldsymbol{\Sigma}_x\boldsymbol{w}} + \kappa(\beta_0)\sqrt{\boldsymbol{w}^{\mathrm{T}}\boldsymbol{\Sigma}_y\boldsymbol{w}} \ , \tag{3.11}$$

$$\boldsymbol{w}^{\mathrm{T}}(\overline{\boldsymbol{x}} - \overline{\boldsymbol{y}}) = 1 \ . \tag{3.12}$$

Since $\boldsymbol{\Sigma}_x$ can be assumed as positive definite (otherwise, we can always add a small positive amount to its diagonal elements and make it positive definite), from Eq.(3.11) we can obtain:

$$\kappa(\alpha) \leq \frac{1 - \kappa(\beta_0)\sqrt{\boldsymbol{w}^{\mathrm{T}}\boldsymbol{\Sigma}_y\boldsymbol{w}}}{\sqrt{\boldsymbol{w}^{\mathrm{T}}\boldsymbol{\Sigma}_x\boldsymbol{w}}} \ . \tag{3.13}$$

Because $\kappa(\alpha)$ increases monotonically with α, maximizing α is equivalent to maximizing $\kappa(\alpha)$, which further leads to:

$$\max_{\boldsymbol{w} \neq \boldsymbol{0}} \frac{1 - \kappa(\beta_0)\sqrt{\boldsymbol{w}^{\mathrm{T}}\boldsymbol{\Sigma}_y\boldsymbol{w}}}{\sqrt{\boldsymbol{w}^{\mathrm{T}}\boldsymbol{\Sigma}_x\boldsymbol{w}}} \ ,$$

$$\text{s.t.} \quad \boldsymbol{w}^{\mathrm{T}}(\overline{\boldsymbol{x}} - \overline{\boldsymbol{y}}) = 1 \ .$$

This kind of optimization is called Fractional Programming (FP) problem [13, 19, 26]. To elaborate further, this optimization is equivalent to solving the following fractional problem:

$$\max_{\boldsymbol{w} \neq \boldsymbol{0}} \frac{f(\boldsymbol{w})}{g(\boldsymbol{w})} \ , \tag{3.14}$$

subject to $\boldsymbol{w} \in A = \{\boldsymbol{w} | \boldsymbol{w}^{\mathrm{T}}(\overline{\boldsymbol{x}} - \overline{\boldsymbol{y}}) = 1\}$, where $f(\boldsymbol{w}) = 1 - \kappa(\beta_0)\sqrt{\boldsymbol{w}^{\mathrm{T}} \boldsymbol{\Sigma}_y \boldsymbol{w}}$, $g(\boldsymbol{w}) = \sqrt{\boldsymbol{w}^{\mathrm{T}} \boldsymbol{\Sigma}_x \boldsymbol{w}}$.

Theorem 3.3. *The Fractional Programming problem Eq.(3.14) associated with the BMPM optimization is a pseudo-concave problem whose every local optimum is the global optimum.*

Proof. It is easy to see that the domain A is a convex set on $\mathbb{R}^n$, $f(\boldsymbol{w})$ and $g(\boldsymbol{w})$ are differentiable on A. Moreover, since $\boldsymbol{\Sigma}_x$ and $\boldsymbol{\Sigma}_y$ can be both considered as positive definite matrices, $f(\boldsymbol{w})$ is a concave function on A and $g(\boldsymbol{w})$ is a convex function on A. Then $f(\boldsymbol{w})/g(\boldsymbol{w})$ is a concave-convex FP problem. Hence it is a pseudo-concave problem [26]. Therefore, every local maximum is the global maximum [26].

To handle this specific FP problem, many methods such as the parametric method [26], the dual FP method [7, 25], and the concave FP method [6] can be used. A typical Conjugate Gradient method [2] in solving this problem will have a worst-case $O(n^3)$ time complexity. Adding the time cost to estimate $\overline{\boldsymbol{x}}, \overline{\boldsymbol{y}}, \boldsymbol{\Sigma}_x$, and $\boldsymbol{\Sigma}_y$, the total cost for this method is $O(n^3 + Nn^2)$, where N is the number of data points. This complexity is in the same order as the linear Support Vector Machines [27] and the linear MPM [16].

In this chapter, the Rosen gradient projection method [2] is used to find the solution of this pseudo-concave FP problem, which is proved to converge to a local maximum with a worse-case linear convergence rate. Moreover, the local maximum will exactly be the global maximum in this problem.

3.2.4.2 Sequential BMPM Optimization Method for MEMPM

We now turn to solving the MEMPM problem. Similar to Section 3.2.4.1, we can base on Lemma 3.2 to transform the MEMPM optimization as follows:

$$\max_{\alpha, \beta, \boldsymbol{w} \neq \boldsymbol{0}, b} \{\theta\alpha + (1 - \theta)\beta\} \ , \tag{3.15}$$

$$\text{s.t.} \quad -b + \boldsymbol{w}^{\mathrm{T}}\overline{\boldsymbol{x}} \geq \kappa(\alpha)\sqrt{\boldsymbol{w}^{\mathrm{T}} \boldsymbol{\Sigma}_x \boldsymbol{w}} \ , \tag{3.16}$$

$$b - \boldsymbol{w}^{\mathrm{T}}\overline{\boldsymbol{y}} \geq \kappa(\beta)\sqrt{\boldsymbol{w}^{\mathrm{T}} \boldsymbol{\Sigma}_y \boldsymbol{w}} \ . \tag{3.17}$$

Using the similar analysis as in Section 3.2.4.1, we can further transform the above optimization into

$$\max_{\alpha, \beta, \boldsymbol{w} \neq \boldsymbol{0}} \{\theta\alpha + (1 - \theta)\beta\} \ , \tag{3.18}$$

$$\text{s.t.} \quad 1 \geq \kappa(\alpha)\sqrt{\boldsymbol{w}^{\mathrm{T}} \boldsymbol{\Sigma}_x \boldsymbol{w}} + \kappa(\beta)\sqrt{\boldsymbol{w}^{\mathrm{T}} \boldsymbol{\Sigma}_y \boldsymbol{w}} \ , \tag{3.19}$$

$$\boldsymbol{w}^{\mathrm{T}}(\overline{\boldsymbol{x}} - \overline{\boldsymbol{y}}) = 1 \ . \tag{3.20}$$

In the following we provide a lemma to show that the MEMPM solution is actually attained on the boundary of the set formed by the constraints of Eqs.(3.19) and (3.20).

Lemma 3.4. *The maximum value of $\theta\alpha + (1 - \theta)\beta$ under the constraints of Eqs.(3.19) and (3.20) is achieved when the right hand side of Eq.(3.19) is strictly equal to 1.*

Proof. Assume the maximum is achieved when

$$1 > \kappa(\beta)\sqrt{\boldsymbol{w}^{\mathrm{T}}\boldsymbol{\Sigma}_y\boldsymbol{w}} + \kappa(\alpha)\sqrt{\boldsymbol{w}^{\mathrm{T}}\boldsymbol{\Sigma}_x\boldsymbol{w}} \;.$$

A new solution constructed by increasing α or $\kappa(\alpha)$ by a small positive amount,[4] and maintaining β, $\boldsymbol{w}$ unchanged will satisfy the constraints and will be a better solution.

By applying Lemma 3.4 we can transform the optimization problem Eq.(3.18) under the constraints of Eqs.(3.19) and (3.20) as follows:

$$\max_{\beta,\boldsymbol{w}\neq\boldsymbol{0}} \quad \left\{ \frac{\theta\kappa^2(\alpha)}{\kappa^2(\alpha) + 1} + (1 - \theta)\beta \right\} \;, \tag{3.21}$$

$$\text{s.t.} \quad \boldsymbol{w}^{\mathrm{T}}(\overline{\boldsymbol{x}} - \overline{\boldsymbol{y}}) = 1 \;, \tag{3.22}$$

where

$$\kappa(\alpha) = \frac{1 - \kappa(\beta)\sqrt{\boldsymbol{w}^{\mathrm{T}}\boldsymbol{\Sigma}_y\boldsymbol{w}}}{\sqrt{\boldsymbol{w}^{\mathrm{T}}\boldsymbol{\Sigma}_x\boldsymbol{w}}}$$

In Eq.(3.22), if we fix β to a specific value within $[0, 1)$, the optimization is equivalent to maximizing $\kappa^2(\alpha)/\kappa^2(\alpha) + 1$ and further equivalent to maximizing $\kappa(\alpha)$, which is exactly the BMPM problem. We can then update β according to some rules and repeat the whole process until an optimal β is found. This is also the so-called line search problem [2, 1]. More precisely, if we denote the value of optimization as a function $f(\beta)$, the above procedure corresponds to finding an optimal β to maximize $f(\beta)$. Instead of using an explicit function as in traditional line search problems, the value of the function here is implicitly given by a BMPM optimization procedure.

Many methods can be used to solve the line search problem. In this chapter, we use the Quadratic Interpolation (QI) method [2]. As illustrated in Fig.3.2, QI finds the maximum point by updating a three-point pattern $(\beta_1, \beta_2, \beta_3)$ repeatedly. The new β denoted by β_{new} is given by the quadratic interpolation from the three-point pattern. Then a new three-point pattern is constructed by β_{new} and two of $\beta_1, \beta_2, \beta_3$. This method can be shown to converge superlinearly to a local optimum point [2]. Moreover, as shown in Section 3.7, although MEMPM generally cannot guarantee its concavity, empirically it is often a concave problem. Thus the local optimum will be often the global optimum in practice.

---

[4]Since $\kappa(\alpha)$ increases monotonically with α, increasing α by a small positive amount corresponds to increasing $\kappa(\alpha)$ by a small positive amount.

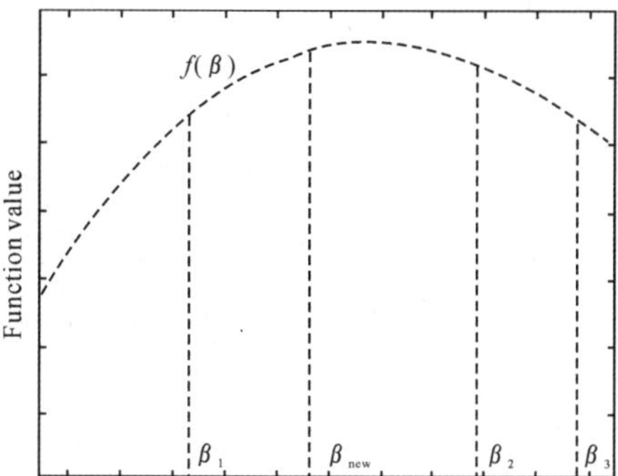

Fig. 3.2. A three-point pattern and quadratic line search method. A β_{new} is obtained and a new three-point pattern is constructed by β_{new} and two of β_1, β_2 and β_3

Until now, we do not mention how to calculate the intercept b. From Lemma 3.4, we can see that the inequalities Eqs.(3.16) and (3.17) will become equalities at the maximum point $(\boldsymbol{w}_*, b_*)$. The optimal b will thus be obtained by

$$b_* = \boldsymbol{w}_*^{\mathrm{T}}\overline{\boldsymbol{x}} - \kappa(\alpha_*)\sqrt{\boldsymbol{w}_*^{\mathrm{T}}\boldsymbol{\Sigma}_{\boldsymbol{x}}\boldsymbol{w}_*} = \boldsymbol{w}_*^{\mathrm{T}}\overline{\boldsymbol{y}} + \kappa(\beta_*)\sqrt{\boldsymbol{w}_*^{\mathrm{T}}\boldsymbol{\Sigma}_{\boldsymbol{y}}\boldsymbol{w}_*}\,. \qquad (3.23)$$

3.2.5 When the Worst-case Bayes Optimal Hyperplane Becomes the True One

As discussed, the MEMPM derives the worst-case Bayes optimal hyperplane, thus it is interesting to dig out on what conditions the worst-case optimal one changes into the true optimal one.

In the following we demonstrate two propositions: the first is that when data are assumed under some distributions, e.g. Gaussian distribution, the MEMPM leads to the Bayes optimal classifier; the second is that when applied into high-dimensional classification tasks, the MEMPM can be adapted to converge into the true Bayes optimal classifier under the Lyapunov condition.

To introduce the first proposition, we begin with assuming data distribution as a Gaussian distribution.

Assuming $\boldsymbol{x} \sim N(\overline{\boldsymbol{x}}, \boldsymbol{\Sigma}_{\boldsymbol{x}})$ and $\boldsymbol{y} \sim N(\overline{\boldsymbol{y}}, \boldsymbol{\Sigma}_{\boldsymbol{y}})$, Eq.(3.3) becomes:

$$\inf_{\boldsymbol{x}\sim N(\overline{\boldsymbol{x}},\boldsymbol{\Sigma}_{\boldsymbol{x}})} Pr\{\boldsymbol{w}^{\mathrm{T}}\boldsymbol{x} \geq b\} = Pr_{\boldsymbol{x}\sim N(\overline{\boldsymbol{x}},\boldsymbol{\Sigma}_{\boldsymbol{x}})}\{\boldsymbol{w}^{\mathrm{T}}\boldsymbol{x} \geq b\}$$

$$= Pr\left\{ N(0,1) \geq \frac{b - \boldsymbol{w}^{\mathrm{T}}\overline{\boldsymbol{x}}}{\sqrt{\boldsymbol{w}^{\mathrm{T}}\boldsymbol{\Sigma}_{\boldsymbol{x}}\boldsymbol{w}}} \right\}$$

$$= 1 - \Phi\left(\frac{b - \boldsymbol{w}^{\mathrm{T}}\overline{\boldsymbol{x}}}{\sqrt{\boldsymbol{w}^{\mathrm{T}}\boldsymbol{\Sigma}_{\boldsymbol{x}}\boldsymbol{w}}} \right)$$

$$= \Phi\left(\frac{-b + \boldsymbol{w}^{\mathrm{T}}\overline{\boldsymbol{x}}}{\sqrt{\boldsymbol{w}^{\mathrm{T}}\boldsymbol{\Sigma}_{\boldsymbol{x}}\boldsymbol{w}}} \right) \geq \alpha \, , \tag{3.24}$$

where $\Phi(z)$ is the cumulative distribution function for the standard normal Gaussian distribution defined as:

$$\Phi(z) = Pr\{N(0,1) \leq z\} = \frac{1}{\sqrt{2\pi}} \int_{-\infty}^{z} \exp\left(\frac{-s^2}{2} \right) \mathrm{d}s.$$

Due to the monotonic property of $\Phi(z)$, we can further write Eq.(3.24) as:

$$-b + \boldsymbol{w}^{\mathrm{T}}\overline{\boldsymbol{x}} \geq \Phi^{-1}(\alpha)\sqrt{\boldsymbol{w}^{\mathrm{T}}\boldsymbol{\Sigma}_{\boldsymbol{x}}\boldsymbol{w}} \, .$$

Constraint Eq.(3.4) can be reformulated to a similar form. The optimization Eq.(3.2) is thus changed as:

$$\max_{\alpha,\beta,\boldsymbol{w}\neq\boldsymbol{0},b} \{\theta\alpha + (1 - \theta)\beta\} \, , \tag{3.25}$$

$$\text{s.t.} \quad -b + \boldsymbol{w}^{\mathrm{T}}\overline{\boldsymbol{x}} \geq \Phi^{-1}(\alpha)\sqrt{\boldsymbol{w}^{\mathrm{T}}\boldsymbol{\Sigma}_{\boldsymbol{x}}\boldsymbol{w}} \, ,$$

$$b - \boldsymbol{w}^{\mathrm{T}}\overline{\boldsymbol{y}} \geq \Phi^{-1}(\beta)\sqrt{\boldsymbol{w}^{\mathrm{T}}\boldsymbol{\Sigma}_{\boldsymbol{y}}\boldsymbol{w}} \, . \tag{3.26}$$

The above optimization is nearly the same as Eq.(3.2) subject to the constraints of Eqs.(3.3) and (3.4) except that, $\kappa(\alpha)$ is equal to $\Phi^{-1}(\alpha)$, instead of $\sqrt{\frac{\alpha}{1-\alpha}}$. Thus, it can be similarly solved based on the Sequential Biased Minimax Probability Machine method.

On the other hand, the Bayes optimal hyperplane corresponds to the one, $\boldsymbol{w}^{\mathrm{T}}\boldsymbol{z} = b$, which minimizes the Bayes error:

$$\min_{\boldsymbol{w}\neq\boldsymbol{0},b} \theta Pr_{\boldsymbol{x}\sim N(\overline{\boldsymbol{x}},\boldsymbol{\Sigma}_{\boldsymbol{x}})}\{\boldsymbol{w}^{\mathrm{T}}\boldsymbol{x} \leq b\} + (1 - \theta)Pr_{\boldsymbol{y}\sim N(\overline{\boldsymbol{y}},\boldsymbol{\Sigma}_{\boldsymbol{y}})}\{\boldsymbol{w}^{\mathrm{T}}\boldsymbol{y} \geq b\} \tag{3.27}$$

The above is exactly the upper bound of $\theta\alpha + (1 - \theta)\beta$. From Lemma 3.4 we can know that Eq.(3.26) will eventually become equalities. Traced back to Eq.(3.24), the equalities imply that α and β will achieve their upper bounds respectively. Therefore, with the Gaussian distribution assumption on data, the MEMPM derives the optimal Bayes hyperplane.

We propose Proposition 3.5 to extend the above analysis to general distribution assumptions.

Proposition 3.5. *If the distribution of the normalized random variable*

$$\frac{\boldsymbol{w}^{\mathrm{T}}\boldsymbol{x} - \boldsymbol{w}^{\mathrm{T}}\overline{\boldsymbol{x}}}{\sqrt{\boldsymbol{w}^{\mathrm{T}}\boldsymbol{\Sigma}_{\boldsymbol{x}}\boldsymbol{w}}},$$

denoted as NS, is independent of $\boldsymbol{w}$, as the case in Gaussian distribution, the similar MEMPM version as in Gaussian distribution assumption will be easily derived, except that $\Phi(z)$ is changed as $Pr\{NS(0,1) \leq z\}$. In such case, minimizing the Bayes error bound will exactly minimize the true Bayes error.

Before presenting Proposition 3.7, we first introduce the Central Limit Theorem under the Lyapunov condition [5].

Theorem 3.6. *Let $\boldsymbol{x}_n$ be a sequence of independent random variables defined on the same probability space. Assume that $\boldsymbol{x}_n$ has finite expected value μ_n and finite standard deviation σ_n. We define $s_n^2 = \sum_{i=1}^{n} \sigma_i^2$. Assume that the third central moment $r_n^3 = \sum_{i=1}^{n} E(|\boldsymbol{x}_n - \mu_n|^3)$ is finite for every n, and that $\lim_{n \to \infty} (r_n/s_n) = 0$ (This is the Lyapunov condition). The sum $\boldsymbol{S}_n = \boldsymbol{x}_1 + ... + \boldsymbol{x}_n$ converges towards a Gaussian distribution.*

One interesting finding directly elicited from the above Central Limit Theorem is that, if the component variable $\boldsymbol{x}_i$ of a given n-dimensional random variable $\boldsymbol{x}$ satisfies the Lyapunov condition, the sum of weighted component variables $\boldsymbol{x}_i$, $1 \leq i \leq n$, namely, $\boldsymbol{w}^{\mathrm{T}}\boldsymbol{x}$ tends to be a Gaussian distribution, as n grows.[5] This shows that, under the Lyapunov condition, when the dimension n grows, the hyperplane derived by MEMPM with Gaussian assumption tends to be the true Bayes optimal hyperplane. In this case, the MEMPM using $\Phi^{-1}(\alpha)$, the inverse function of the normal cumulative distribution, instead of $\sqrt{\alpha/(1-\alpha)}$, will converge to the true Bayes optimal decision hyperplane in the high-dimensional space. We summarize the analysis into Proposition 3.7.

Proposition 3.7. *If the component variable $\boldsymbol{x}_i$ of a given n-dimensional random variable $\boldsymbol{x}$ satisfies the Lyapunov condition, the MEMPM hyperplane derived by using $\Phi^{-1}(\alpha)$ the inverse function of normal cumulative distribution, will converge to the true Bayes optimal one.*

The underlying justifications in the above two propositions root in the fact that the generalized MPM is exclusively determined by the first and second moments. These two propositions actually emphasize the dominance of the first and second moments in representing data. More specifically, Proposition 3.5 hints that the distribution is only decided by up to the second

---

[5]Some techniques such as Independent Component [8] can be applied to decorrelate the dependence among random variables beforehand.

moment. The Lyapunov condition in Proposition 3.7 also implies that the second order moment dominates the third order moment in the long run. It also deserves attention that with the fixed mean and covariance, the distribution of Maximum Entropy Estimation is the Gaussian distribution [14]. This would once again suggest the usage of $\Phi^{-1}(\alpha)$ in the high-dimensional space.

3.2.6 Geometrical Interpretation

In this section, we first provide a parametric solving method for BMPM, then demonstrate that this parametric method actually enables a nice geometrical interpretation for both BMPM and MEMPM.

3.2.6.1 A Parametric Method for BMPM

According to the parametric method, the fractional function can be iteratively optimized in two steps [26]:

Step 1. Find w by maximizing $f(w) - \lambda g(w)$ in the domain A, where $\lambda \in \mathbb{R}$ is the newly introduced parameter.

Step 2. Update λ by $f(w)/g(w)$.

The iteration of the above two steps will guarantee to converge to the local maximum which is also the global maximum in our problem. In the following, we adopt a method to solve the maximization problem in Step 1. Replacing $f(w)$ and $g(w)$, we expand the optimization problem as:

$$\max_{w \neq 0} \left\{ 1 - \kappa(\beta_0)\sqrt{w^{\mathrm{T}}\Sigma_y w} - \lambda\sqrt{w^{\mathrm{T}}\Sigma_x w} \right\}, \text{s.t. } w^{\mathrm{T}}(\overline{x} - \overline{y}) = 1. \quad (3.28)$$

Maximizing Eq.(3.28) is equivalent to $\min_w \kappa(\beta_0)\sqrt{w^{\mathrm{T}}\Sigma_y w} + \lambda\sqrt{w^{\mathrm{T}}\Sigma_x w}$ under the same constraint. By writing $w = w_0 + Fu$, where $w_0 = (\overline{x} - \overline{y})/\| \overline{x} - \overline{y} \|_2^2$ and $F \in \mathbb{R}^{n \times (n-1)}$ is an orthogonal matrix whose columns span the subspace of vectors orthogonal to $\overline{x} - \overline{y}$, an equivalent form (a factor $1/2$ over each term has been dropped) to remove the constraint can be obtained:

$$\min_{u, \eta > 0, \xi > 0} \left\{ \eta + \frac{\lambda^2}{\eta}\|\Sigma_x^{1/2}(w_0 + Fu)\|_2^2 + \xi + \frac{\kappa(\beta_0)^2}{\xi}\|\Sigma_y^{1/2}(w_0 + Fu)\|_2^2 \right\},$$
$$(3.29)$$

where $\eta, \xi \in \mathbb{R}$. This optimization form is very similar to the one in Minimax Probability Machine [15] and can also be solved by using an iterative least-squares approach.

3.2.6.2 A Geometrical Interpretation for BMPM and MEMPM

The parametric method actually enables a nice geometrical interpretation of BMPM and MEMPM in a fashion similar to that of MPM in [16]. Similarly, we assume $\overline{x} \neq \overline{y}$ for the meaningful classification and also assume that Σ_x and Σ_y are positive definite for the purpose of simplicity.

By using the 2-norm definition of a vector $z : \|z\|_2 = \max\{u^T z : \|u\|_2 \leq 1\}$, we can express Eq.(3.28) in its dual form:

$$\tau_* := \min_{w \neq 0} \max_{u,v} \ \left\{ \lambda u^T \Sigma_x^{1/2} w + \kappa(\beta_0) v^T \Sigma_y^{1/2} w + \tau(1 - w^T(\overline{x} - \overline{y})) \right\}$$

$$\text{s.t.} \ \ \|u\|_2 \leq 1, \|v\|_2 \leq 1 \ .$$

We change the order of the min and max operators and consider the min:

$$\min_{w \neq 0} \ \{ \lambda u^T \Sigma_x^{1/2} w + \kappa(\beta_0) v^T \Sigma_y^{1/2} w + \tau(1 - w^T(\overline{x} - \overline{y})) \}$$

$$= \begin{cases} \tau, & \text{if } \tau\overline{x} - \lambda\Sigma_x^{1/2}u = \tau\overline{y} + \kappa(\beta_0)\Sigma_y^{1/2}v; \\ -\infty, & \text{otherwise.} \end{cases}$$

Thus, the dual problem can be further changed to:

$$\max_{\tau,u,v} \ \tau : \|u\|_2 \leq 1, \|v\|_2 \leq 1, \tau\overline{x} - \lambda\Sigma_x^{1/2}u = \tau\overline{y} + \kappa(\beta_0)\Sigma_y^{1/2}v. \quad (3.30)$$

By defining $\ell := 1/\tau$ we rewrite the dual problem as:

$$\min_{\ell,u,v} \ \ell : \overline{x} - \lambda\Sigma_x^{1/2}u = \overline{y} + \kappa(\beta_0)\Sigma_y^{1/2}v, \|u\|_2 \leq \ell, \|v\|_2 \leq \ell \ . \quad (3.31)$$

When the optimum is attained, we have

$$\tau_* = \lambda\|\Sigma_x^{1/2}w_*\|_2 + \kappa(\beta_0)\|\Sigma_y^{1/2}w_*\|_2 = 1/\ell_* \ . \quad (3.32)$$

We consider each side of Eq.(3.31) as an ellipsoid centered at the means $\overline{x}$ and $\overline{y}$ and shaped by the weighted covariance matrices $\lambda\Sigma_x$ and $\kappa(\beta_0)\Sigma_y$ respectively:

$$H_x(\ell) = \{x = \overline{x} + \lambda\Sigma_x^{1/2}u : \|u\|_2 \leq \ell\}, \quad (3.33)$$

$$H_y(\ell) = \{y = \overline{y} + \kappa(\beta_0)\Sigma_y^{1/2}v : \|v\|_2 \leq \ell\}. \quad (3.34)$$

The above optimization involves finding a minimum ℓ for which two ellipsoids intersect. For the optimum ℓ, these two ellipsoids would be tangent to each other. We further note that, according to Lemma 3.4, at the optimum, λ_*, which is maximized via a series of the above procedures, would satisfy

$$1 = \lambda_*\|\Sigma_x^{1/2}w_*\|_2 + \kappa(\beta_0)\|\Sigma_y^{1/2}w_*\|_2 = \tau_* = 1/\ell_* \ , \quad (3.35)$$

$$\Rightarrow \ell_* = 1 \ . \quad (3.36)$$

This means that the ellipsoid for the class y finally changes to the one centered at $\overline{y}$, whose Mahalanobis distance to $\overline{y}$ is exactly equal to $\kappa(\beta_0)$. Moreover, the ellipsoid for the class x would be the one centered at $\overline{x}$ and tangent to the ellipsoid for the class y. In comparison, for MPM, two ellipsoids grow with the same speed (with the same $\kappa(\alpha)$ and $\kappa(\beta)$). On the other hand, since MEMPM corresponds to solving a sequence of BMPMs, it similarly leads to a hyperplane tangent to two ellipsoids, which achieves to minimize the maximum of the worst-case Bayes error. Moreover, it is not necessarily attained in a balanced way as in MPM, i.e. two ellipsoids do not necessarily grow with the same speed and hence probably contain the unequal Mahalanobis distance from their corresponding centers. This is illustrated in Fig. 3.3.

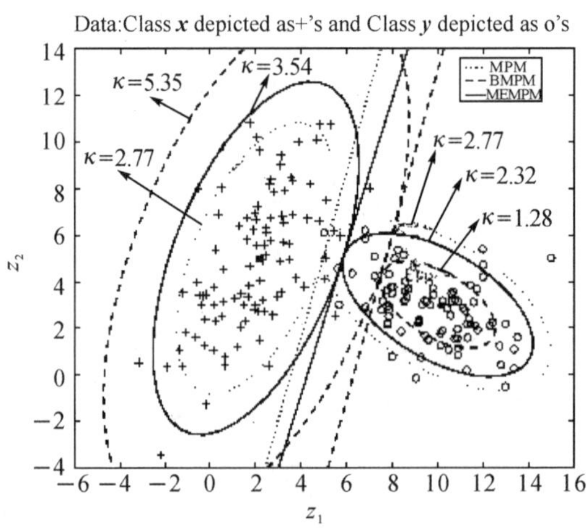

Fig. 3.3. The Geometrical interpretation of MEMPM and BMPM. Finding the optimal BMPM hyperplane corresponds to finding the decision plane (the black dashed line) tangent to an ellipsoid (the inner dashed ellipsoid on the y side) , which is centered at $\overline{y}$, shaped by the covariance Σ_y and whose Mahalanobis distance to $\overline{y}$ is exactly equal to $\kappa(\beta_0)$ ($\kappa(\beta_0) = 1.28$ in this example). The worst-case accuracy α for x is determined by the Mahalanobis distance κ ($\kappa = 5.35$ in this example), at which an ellipsoid (centered at $\overline{x}$ and shaped by Σ_x) is tangent to that $\kappa(\beta_0)$ ellipsoid, i.e. the outer dahsed ellipsoid on the x side. In comparison, MPM tries to find out the minimum equality-constrained κ, at which two ellipsoids for x and y intersect (both dotted ellipsoids with $\kappa = 2.77$). For MEMPM, it achieves a tangent hyperplane in a non-balanced fashion, i.e. two ellipsoids may not attain the same κ but are globally optimal in the worst-case setting (see the solid ellipsoids)

3.3 Robust Version

In the above, the estimates of means and covariance matrices are assumed reliable. We now consider how the probabilistic framework in Eq.(3.2) changes against the variation of the means and covariance matrices:

$$\max_{\alpha,\beta,\boldsymbol{w}\neq\boldsymbol{0},b} \{\theta\alpha + (1-\theta)\beta\} ,\tag{3.37}$$

$$\text{s.t.} \quad \inf_{\boldsymbol{x}\sim(\bar{\boldsymbol{x}},\boldsymbol{\Sigma}_{\boldsymbol{x}})} Pr\{\boldsymbol{w}^{\mathrm{T}}\boldsymbol{x} \geq b\} \geq \alpha, \forall(\bar{\boldsymbol{x}},\boldsymbol{\Sigma}_{\boldsymbol{x}}) \in X ,\tag{3.38}$$

$$\inf_{\boldsymbol{y}\sim(\bar{\boldsymbol{y}},\boldsymbol{\Sigma}_{\boldsymbol{y}})} Pr\{\boldsymbol{w}^{\mathrm{T}}\boldsymbol{y} \leq b\} \geq \beta, \forall(\bar{\boldsymbol{y}},\boldsymbol{\Sigma}_{\boldsymbol{y}}) \in Y ,\tag{3.39}$$

where X and Y are the sets of means and covariance matrices and are the subsets of $\mathbb{R}\times P_n^+$, where P_n^+ is the set of $n\times n$ symmetric positive semidefinite matrices.

Motivated by the tractability of the problem and from the statistical view, a specific setting of X and Y is proposed in [16]. However, they consider the same variations of the means for two classes, which is easy to handle but less general. Now, considering the unequal treatment of each class, we propose the following setting which is in a more general and complete form:

$$X = \left\{(\bar{\boldsymbol{x}},\boldsymbol{\Sigma}_{\boldsymbol{x}})\,|\,(\bar{\boldsymbol{x}} - \bar{\boldsymbol{x}}^0)\boldsymbol{\Sigma}_{\boldsymbol{x}}^{-1}(\bar{\boldsymbol{x}} - \bar{\boldsymbol{x}}^0) \leq \nu_{\boldsymbol{x}}^2, \boldsymbol{\Sigma}_{\boldsymbol{x}} \in \|\boldsymbol{\Sigma}_{\boldsymbol{x}} - \boldsymbol{\Sigma}_{\boldsymbol{x}}^0\|_{\mathrm{F}} \leq \rho_{\boldsymbol{x}}\right\} ,$$

$$Y = \left\{(\bar{\boldsymbol{y}},\boldsymbol{\Sigma}_{\boldsymbol{y}})\,|\,(\bar{\boldsymbol{y}} - \bar{\boldsymbol{y}}^0)\boldsymbol{\Sigma}_{\boldsymbol{y}}^{-1}(\bar{\boldsymbol{y}} - \bar{\boldsymbol{y}}^0) \leq \nu_{\boldsymbol{y}}^2, \boldsymbol{\Sigma}_{\boldsymbol{y}} \in \|\boldsymbol{\Sigma}_{\boldsymbol{y}} - \boldsymbol{\Sigma}_{\boldsymbol{y}}^0\|_{\mathrm{F}} \leq \rho_{\boldsymbol{y}}\right\} ,$$

where $\bar{\boldsymbol{x}}^0$, $\boldsymbol{\Sigma}_{\boldsymbol{x}}^0$ are the "nominal" means and covariance matrices obtained through estimating. Parameters $\nu_{\boldsymbol{x}}$, $\nu_{\boldsymbol{y}}$, $\rho_{\boldsymbol{x}}$, and $\rho_{\boldsymbol{y}}$ are positive constants. The matrix norm is defined as the Frobenius norm: $\|\boldsymbol{M}\|_{\mathcal{F}}^2 = \mathrm{Tr}(\boldsymbol{M}^{\mathrm{T}}\boldsymbol{M})$.

With the assumption that variations of the means for two classes are the same, the parameters $\nu_{\boldsymbol{x}}$ and $\nu_{\boldsymbol{y}}$ are required equal in [16]. This may enable the direct usage of the MPM optimization into its robust version. However, the assumption may not be true in real cases. Moreover, in MEMPM, this requirement is also not necessary and inappropriate. This will be later demonstrated in the experiment.

By applying the results from [16], we obtain the robust MEMPM as:

$$\max_{\alpha,\beta,\boldsymbol{w}\neq\boldsymbol{0},b} \{\theta\alpha + (1-\theta)\beta\} ,$$

$$\text{s.t.} \quad -b + \boldsymbol{w}^{\mathrm{T}}\bar{\boldsymbol{x}}^0 \geq (\kappa(\alpha) + \nu_{\boldsymbol{x}})\sqrt{\boldsymbol{w}^{\mathrm{T}}(\boldsymbol{\Sigma}_{\boldsymbol{x}}^0 + \rho_{\boldsymbol{x}}\boldsymbol{I}_n)\boldsymbol{w}},$$

$$b - \boldsymbol{w}^{\mathrm{T}}\bar{\boldsymbol{y}}^0 \geq (\kappa(\beta) + \nu_{\boldsymbol{y}})\sqrt{\boldsymbol{w}^{\mathrm{T}}(\boldsymbol{\Sigma}_{\boldsymbol{y}}^0 + \rho_{\boldsymbol{y}}\boldsymbol{I}_n)\boldsymbol{w}}.$$

Analogously, we transform the above optimization problem as:

$$\max_{\alpha,\beta,\boldsymbol{w}\neq\boldsymbol{0}} \theta\frac{\kappa_r^2(\alpha)}{1 + \kappa_r^2(\alpha)} + (1-\theta)\beta ,\tag{3.40}$$

$$\text{s.t.} \quad \boldsymbol{w}^{\mathrm{T}}(\bar{\boldsymbol{x}}^0 - \bar{\boldsymbol{y}}^0) = 1,\tag{3.41}$$

where $\kappa_r(\alpha) = \max\left(\dfrac{1-(\kappa(\beta)+\nu_y)\sqrt{\boldsymbol{w}^{\mathrm{T}}(\boldsymbol{\Sigma_y}^0+\rho_y\boldsymbol{I}_n)\boldsymbol{w}}}{\sqrt{\boldsymbol{w}^{\mathrm{T}}y(\boldsymbol{\Sigma_x}^0+\rho_x\boldsymbol{I}_n)\boldsymbol{w}}} - \nu_x, 0\right)$, and thus can be solved by the SBMPM method. The optimal b is therefore calculated by:

$$b_* = \boldsymbol{w}_*{}^{\mathrm{T}}\bar{\boldsymbol{x}}^0 - (\kappa(\alpha_*)+\nu_x)\sqrt{\boldsymbol{w}_*{}^{\mathrm{T}}(\boldsymbol{\Sigma_x}^0+\rho_x\boldsymbol{I}_n)\boldsymbol{w}_*}$$

$$= \boldsymbol{w}_*{}^{\mathrm{T}}\bar{\boldsymbol{y}}^0 + (\kappa(\beta_*)+\nu_y)\sqrt{\boldsymbol{w}_*{}^{\mathrm{T}}(\boldsymbol{\Sigma_y}^0+\rho_y\boldsymbol{I}_n)\boldsymbol{w}_*}\,.$$

Remarks. Interestingly, if MPM is treated with unequal robust parameters ν_x and ν_y, it leads to solving an optimization similar to MEMPM, since $\kappa(\alpha)+\nu_x$ will not be equal to $\kappa(\alpha)+\nu_y$. In addition, similar to the robust MPM, when applied in practice, the specific values of ν_x, ν_y, ρ_x and ρ_y can be provided based on the Central Limit Theorem.

3.4 Kernelization

We note that, in the above, the classifier derived from MEMPM is given in a linear configuration. In order to handle nonlinear classification problems, in this section, we seek to use the kernelization trick [22] to map the n-dimensional data points into a high-dimensional feature space $\mathbb{R}^f$, where a linear classifier corresponds to a nonlinear hyperplane in the original space.

Since the optimization of MEMPM corresponds to a sequence of BMPM optimization problems, this model naturally inherits the kernelization ability of BMPM. We thus in the following mainly address the kernelization of BMPM.

Assuming training data points are represented by $\{\boldsymbol{x}_i\}_{i=1}^{N_x}$ and $\{\boldsymbol{y}_j\}_{j=1}^{N_y}$ for the class $\boldsymbol{x}$ and $\boldsymbol{y}$, respectively, the kernel mapping can be formulated as:

$$\boldsymbol{x} \to \varphi(\boldsymbol{x}) \sim (\overline{\varphi(\boldsymbol{x})}, \boldsymbol{\Sigma}_{\varphi(\boldsymbol{x})})\,,$$

$$\boldsymbol{y} \to \varphi(\boldsymbol{y}) \sim (\overline{\varphi(\boldsymbol{y})}, \boldsymbol{\Sigma}_{\varphi(\boldsymbol{y})})\,,$$

where $\varphi : \mathbb{R}^n \to \mathbb{R}^f$ is a mapping function. The corresponding linear classifier in $\mathbb{R}^f$ is $\boldsymbol{w}^{\mathrm{T}}\varphi(\boldsymbol{z}) = b$, where $\boldsymbol{w}, \varphi(\boldsymbol{z}) \in \mathbb{R}^f$, and $b \in \mathbb{R}$. Similarly, the transformed FP optimization in BMPM can be written as:

$$\max_{\boldsymbol{w}\neq 0} \frac{1-\kappa(\beta_0)\sqrt{\boldsymbol{w}^{\mathrm{T}}\boldsymbol{\Sigma}_{\varphi(\boldsymbol{y})}\boldsymbol{w}}}{\sqrt{\boldsymbol{w}^{\mathrm{T}}\boldsymbol{\Sigma}_{\varphi(\boldsymbol{x})}\boldsymbol{w}}}, \quad \text{s.t.} \quad \boldsymbol{w}^{\mathrm{T}}(\overline{\varphi(\boldsymbol{x})} - \overline{\varphi(\boldsymbol{y})}) = 1. \qquad (3.42)$$

However, to make the kernel work, we need to represent the final decision hyperplane and the optimization in a kernel form, $K(\boldsymbol{z}_1, \boldsymbol{z}_2) = \varphi(\boldsymbol{z}_1)^{\mathrm{T}}\varphi(\boldsymbol{z}_2)$, namely an inner product form of the mapping data points.

3.4.1 Kernelization Theory for BMPM

In the following, we demonstrate that although BMPM possesses a significantly different optimization form from MPM, the kernelization theory proposed in [16] is still viable, provided that suitable estimates for means and covariance matrices are applied therein.

We first state a theory similar to Corollary 5 of [16] and prove its validity in BMPM.

Corollary 3.8. *If the estimates of means and covariance matrices are given in BMPM as:*

$$\overline{\varphi(\boldsymbol{x})} = \sum_{i=1}^{N_{\boldsymbol{x}}} \lambda_i \varphi(\boldsymbol{x}_i) \,, \quad \overline{\varphi(\boldsymbol{y})} = \sum_{j=1}^{N_{\boldsymbol{y}}} \omega_j \varphi(\boldsymbol{y}_j) \,,$$

$$\boldsymbol{\Sigma}_\varphi(\boldsymbol{x}) = \rho_{\boldsymbol{x}} \boldsymbol{I}_n + \sum_{i=1}^{N_{\boldsymbol{x}}} \Lambda_i (\varphi(\boldsymbol{x}_i) - \overline{\varphi(\boldsymbol{x})})(\varphi(\boldsymbol{x}_i) - \overline{\varphi(\boldsymbol{x})})^{\mathrm{T}} \,,$$

$$\boldsymbol{\Sigma}_\varphi(\boldsymbol{y}) = \rho_{\boldsymbol{y}} \boldsymbol{I}_n + \sum_{j=1}^{N_{\boldsymbol{y}}} \Omega_j (\varphi(\boldsymbol{y}_j) - \overline{\varphi(\boldsymbol{y})})(\varphi(\boldsymbol{y}_j) - \overline{\varphi(\boldsymbol{y})})^{\mathrm{T}} \,,$$

where $\boldsymbol{I}_n$ is the identity matrix of dimension n, then the optimal $\boldsymbol{w}$ in problem Eq.(3.42) lies in the space spanned by the training points.

Proof. Similar to Corollary 5 of [16], we write $\boldsymbol{w} = \boldsymbol{w}_p + \boldsymbol{w}_d$, where $\boldsymbol{w}_p$ is the projection of $\boldsymbol{w}$ in the vector space spanned by all the training data points and $\boldsymbol{w}_d$ is the orthogonal component to this span space. It can be easily verified that Eq.(3.42) changes to maximize the following:

$$\frac{1-\kappa(\beta_0)\sqrt{\boldsymbol{w}_p^{\mathrm{T}} \sum_{i=1}^{N_{\boldsymbol{x}}} \Lambda_i(\varphi(\boldsymbol{x}_i)-\overline{\varphi(\boldsymbol{x})})(\varphi(\boldsymbol{x}_i)-\overline{\varphi(\boldsymbol{x})})^{\mathrm{T}}\boldsymbol{w}_p + \rho_{\boldsymbol{x}}(\boldsymbol{w}_p^{\mathrm{T}}\boldsymbol{w}_p + \boldsymbol{w}_d^{\mathrm{T}}\boldsymbol{w}_d)}}{\sqrt{\boldsymbol{w}_p^{\mathrm{T}} \sum_{j=1}^{N_{\boldsymbol{y}}} \Omega_j(\varphi(\boldsymbol{y}_j)-\overline{\varphi(\boldsymbol{y})})(\varphi(\boldsymbol{y}_j)-\overline{\varphi(\boldsymbol{y})})^{\mathrm{T}}\boldsymbol{w}_p + \rho_{\boldsymbol{y}}(\boldsymbol{w}_p^{\mathrm{T}}\boldsymbol{w}_p + \boldsymbol{w}_d^{\mathrm{T}}\boldsymbol{w}_d)}} \,,$$

subject to the constraints of $\boldsymbol{w}_p^{\mathrm{T}}(\overline{\varphi(\boldsymbol{x})} - \overline{\varphi(\boldsymbol{y})}) = 1$. Since we intend to maximize the fractional form and both the denominator and the numerator are positive, the denominator needs to be as small as possible and the numerator needs to be as large as possible. This would finally lead to $\boldsymbol{w}_d = 0$. In other words, the optimal $\boldsymbol{w}$ lies in the vector space spanned by all the training data points. Note that the introduction of $\rho_{\boldsymbol{x}}$ and $\rho_{\boldsymbol{y}}$ actually enables a direct application of the robust estimates in the kernelization.

According to Corollary 3.8, if appropriate estimates of means and covariance matrices are applied, the optimal $\boldsymbol{w}$ can be written as the linear combination of training points. In particular, if we obtain the means and covariance matrices as the plug-in estimates, i.e.

$$\overline{\varphi(\boldsymbol{x})} = \frac{1}{N_{\boldsymbol{x}}} \sum_{i=1}^{N_{\boldsymbol{x}}} \varphi(\boldsymbol{x}_i) , \quad \overline{\varphi(\boldsymbol{y})} = \frac{1}{N_{\boldsymbol{y}}} \sum_{j=1}^{N_{\boldsymbol{y}}} \varphi(\boldsymbol{y}_j) ,$$

$$\boldsymbol{\Sigma}_{\varphi(\boldsymbol{x})} = \frac{1}{N_{\boldsymbol{x}}} \sum_{i=1}^{N_{\boldsymbol{x}}} (\varphi(\boldsymbol{x}_i) - \overline{\varphi(\boldsymbol{x})})(\varphi(\boldsymbol{x}_i) - \overline{\varphi(\boldsymbol{x})})^{\mathrm{T}} ,$$

$$\boldsymbol{\Sigma}_{\varphi(\boldsymbol{y})} = \frac{1}{N_{\boldsymbol{y}}} \sum_{j=1}^{N_{\boldsymbol{y}}} (\varphi(\boldsymbol{y}_j) - \overline{\varphi(\boldsymbol{y})})(\varphi(\boldsymbol{y}_j) - \overline{\varphi(\boldsymbol{y})})^{\mathrm{T}} ,$$

we can write $\boldsymbol{w}$ as:

$$\boldsymbol{w} = \sum_{i=1}^{N_{\boldsymbol{x}}} \mu_i \varphi(\boldsymbol{x}_i) + \sum_{j=1}^{N_{\boldsymbol{y}}} \upsilon_j \varphi(\boldsymbol{y}_j), \tag{3.43}$$

where the coefficients μ_i, $\upsilon_j \in \mathbb{R}$ for $i = 1, \ldots, N_{\boldsymbol{x}}$ and $j = 1, \ldots, N_{\boldsymbol{y}}$.

By simply substituting Eq.(3.43) and four plug-in estimates into Eq.(3.42), we can obtain the Kernelization Theorem of BMPM.

3.4.2 Notations in Kernelization Theorem of BMPM

Before we present the main kernelization result, we first introduce the notations. Let $\{\boldsymbol{z}\}_{i=1}^{N}$ denote all $N = N_{\boldsymbol{x}} + N_{\boldsymbol{y}}$ data points in the training set where

$$\begin{aligned}
\boldsymbol{z}_i &= \boldsymbol{x}_i, & i &= 1, 2, \ldots, N_{\boldsymbol{x}} , \\
\boldsymbol{z}_i &= \boldsymbol{y}_{i-N_{\boldsymbol{x}}}, & i &= N_{\boldsymbol{x}} + 1, N_{\boldsymbol{x}} + 2, \ldots, N.
\end{aligned}$$

The element of the Gram matrix $\boldsymbol{K}$ in the position of (i, j) is defined as $\boldsymbol{K}_{i,j} = \varphi(\boldsymbol{z}_i)^{\mathrm{T}} \varphi(\boldsymbol{z}_j)$ for $i, j = 1, 2, \ldots, N$. We further define $\boldsymbol{K}_{\boldsymbol{x}}$ and $\boldsymbol{K}_{\boldsymbol{y}}$ as the matrices formed by the first $N_{\boldsymbol{x}}$ rows and the last $N_{\boldsymbol{y}}$ rows of $\boldsymbol{K}$, respectively, namely,

$$\boldsymbol{K} := \begin{pmatrix} \boldsymbol{K}_{\boldsymbol{x}} \\ \boldsymbol{K}_{\boldsymbol{y}} \end{pmatrix}.$$

By setting the row average of the $\boldsymbol{K}_{\boldsymbol{x}}$ block and the $\boldsymbol{K}_{\boldsymbol{x}}$ block to zero, the block-row-averaged Gram matrix $\tilde{\boldsymbol{K}}$ is thus obtained:

$$\boldsymbol{K} := \begin{pmatrix} \tilde{\boldsymbol{K}}_{\boldsymbol{x}} \\ \tilde{\boldsymbol{K}}_{\boldsymbol{y}} \end{pmatrix} = \begin{pmatrix} \boldsymbol{K}_{\boldsymbol{x}} - \mathbf{1}_{N_{\boldsymbol{x}}} \tilde{\boldsymbol{k}}_{\boldsymbol{x}}^{\mathrm{T}} \\ \boldsymbol{K}_{\boldsymbol{y}} - \mathbf{1}_{N_{\boldsymbol{y}}} \tilde{\boldsymbol{k}}_{\boldsymbol{y}}^{\mathrm{T}} \end{pmatrix} ,$$

where $\tilde{\boldsymbol{k}}_{\boldsymbol{x}}, \tilde{\boldsymbol{k}}_{\boldsymbol{y}} \in \mathbb{R}^{N_{\boldsymbol{x}} + N_{\boldsymbol{y}}}$ are defined as:

$$[\tilde{k}_x]_i := \frac{1}{N_x}\sum_{j=1}^{N_x} K(x_j, z_i) \; , \quad [\tilde{k}_y]_i := \frac{1}{N_y}\sum_{j=1}^{N_y} K(y_j, z_i) \; .$$

In the above, $\mathbf{1}_{N_x} \in \mathbb{R}^{N_x}$ and $\mathbf{1}_{N_y} \in \mathbb{R}^{N_y}$, are defined as:

$$\mathbf{1}_i = 1, \quad i = 1, 2, \ldots, N_x \; ,$$
$$\mathbf{1}_j = 1, \quad j = 1, 2, \ldots, N_y \; .$$

Finally, we define vector formed by the coefficients of γ as:

$$w = [\mu_1, \mu_2, \ldots, \mu_{N_x}, v_1, v_2, \ldots, v_{N_y}]^{\mathrm{T}}. \tag{3.44}$$

3.4.3 Kernelization Results

Theorem 3.9. [Kernelization Theorem of BMPM] *The optimal decision hyperplane of the problem Eq.(3.42) involves solving the Fractional Programming problem:*

$$\kappa(\alpha_*) = \max_{w \neq 0} \frac{1 - \kappa(\beta_0)\sqrt{\frac{1}{N_y} w^{\mathrm{T}} \tilde{K}_y^{\mathrm{T}} \tilde{K}_y w}}{\sqrt{\frac{1}{N_x} w^{\mathrm{T}} \tilde{K}_x^{\mathrm{T}} \tilde{K}_x w}} \; ,$$

$$s.t. \quad w^{\mathrm{T}}(\tilde{k}_x - \tilde{k}_y) = 1 \; .$$

The intercept b is calculated as:

$$b_* = w_*^{\mathrm{T}}\tilde{k}_x - \kappa(\alpha_*)\sqrt{\frac{1}{N_x} w_*^{\mathrm{T}} \tilde{K}_x^{\mathrm{T}} \tilde{K}_x w_*} = w_*^{\mathrm{T}}\tilde{k}_y + \kappa(\beta_0)\sqrt{\frac{1}{N_y} w_*^{\mathrm{T}} \tilde{K}_y^{\mathrm{T}} \tilde{K}_y w_*} \; ,$$

where $\kappa(\alpha_*)$ is obtained when the above equation attains its optimum (w_*, b_*). For the robust version of BMPM, we can incorporate the variations of the means and covariances by conducting the following replacements:

$$\frac{1}{N_x} w_*^{\mathrm{T}} \tilde{K}_x^{\mathrm{T}} \tilde{K}_x w_* \to w_*^{\mathrm{T}}(\frac{1}{N_x}\tilde{K}_x^{\mathrm{T}}\tilde{K}_x + \rho_x K)w_* \; ,$$
$$\frac{1}{N_y} w_*^{\mathrm{T}} \tilde{K}_y^{\mathrm{T}} \tilde{K}_y w_* \to w_*^{\mathrm{T}}(\frac{1}{N_y}\tilde{K}_y^{\mathrm{T}}\tilde{K}_y + \rho_y K)w_* \; ,$$
$$\kappa(\beta_0) \to \kappa(\beta_0) + \mu_y \; ,$$
$$\kappa(\alpha_*) \to \kappa(\alpha_*) + \mu_x \; .$$

The optimal decision hyperplane can be represented as a linear form in the kernel space

$$f(z) = \sum_{i=1}^{N_x} w_{*i} K(z, x_i) + \sum_{i=1}^{N_y} w_{*N_x+i} K(z, y_i) - b_* \; .$$

3.5 Experiments

In this section, we first evaluate our model on a synthetic dataset. Then we compare the performance of MEMPM with that of MPM, on six real-world benchmark datasets (since MPM is reported comparable to SVM, we do not perform comparisons with SVM). To demonstrate that BMPM is ideal for imposing a specified bias in classification, we also implement it on the Heart-disease dataset. The means and covariance matrices for two classes are obtained directly from the training datasets by plug-in estimations. The prior probability θ is given by the proportion of x data in the training dataset.

3.5.1 Model Illustration on a Synthetic Dataset

To verify that the MEMPM model achieves the minimum Bayes error rate in the Gaussian distribution, we synthetically generate two classes of two-dimensional Gaussian data. As plotted in Fig. 3.4(a), data associated with the class x are generated with the mean $\overline{x}$ as $[3,0]^{\mathrm{T}}$ and the covariance matrix Σ_x as $[4, 0; 0, 1]$, while data associated with the class y are generated with the mean $\overline{y}$ as $[-1,0]^{\mathrm{T}}$ and the covariance matrix Σ_y as $[1, 0; 0, 5]$. The solved decision hyperplane $z_1 = 0.333$ given by MPM is plotted as the solid line and the solved decision hyperplane $z_1 = 0.660$ given by MEMPM is plotted as the dashed line. From the geometrical interpretation, both hyperplanes should be perpendicular to the z_1 axis.

As shown in Fig. 3.4(b), the MEMPM hyperplane exactly represents the optimal thresholding under the distributions of the first dimension for two classes of data, i.e. the intersection point of two density functions. On the other hand, we find that the MPM hyperplane exactly corresponds to the thresholding point with the same error rate for two classes of data, since the cumulative distribution $P_x(z_1 < 0.333)$ and $P_y(z_1 > 0.333)$ are exactly the same.

3.5.2 Evaluations on Benchmark Datasets

We next evaluate our algorithm on six benchmark datasets. Data for the Twonorm problem were generated according to [4]. The rest five datasets including the Breast, Ionosphere, Pima, Heart-disease, and Vote data were obtained from UCI machine learning repository [3]. Since handling the missing attribute values is out of the scope of this chapter, we simply remove instances with missing attribute values in these datasets.

We randomly partition data into 90% training and 10% test sets. The final results are averaged over 50 random partitions of data. We compare the performance of MEMPM and MPM in both the linear setting and Gaussian kernel setting. The width parameter (σ) for the Gaussian kernel is obtained

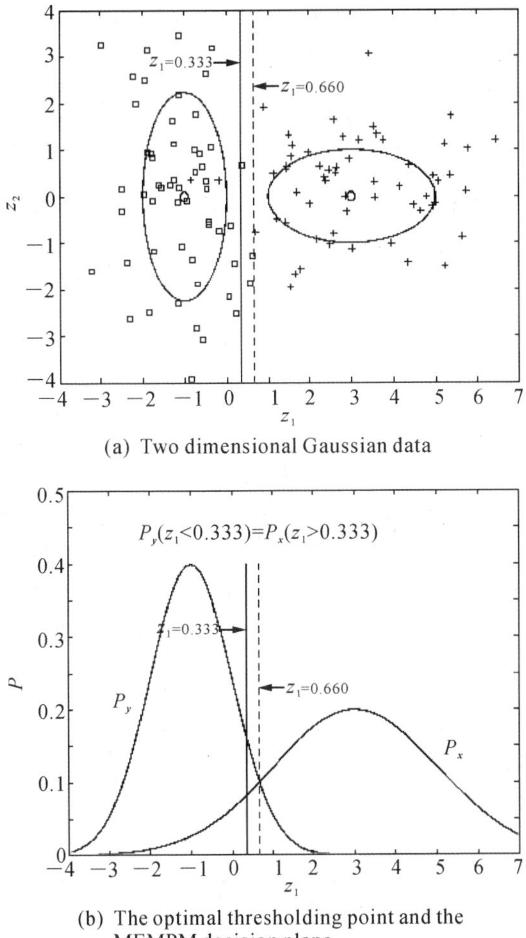

(a) Two dimensional Gaussian data

(b) The optimal thresholding point and the
MEMPM decision plane

Fig. 3.4. An evaluation of MEMPM and MPM on a synthetic dataset. The decision hyperplane derived from MEMPM (the dashed line) exactly corresponds to the optimal threshholding point, i.e. the intersection point, while the decision hyperplane given by MPM (the solid line) corresponds to the point on which two error rates for two classes of data are equal

via cross validations over 50 random partitions of the training set. The experimental results are summarized in Tables 3.1 and 3.2 for the linear kernel and Guassian kernel respectively.

From the results we can see that our MEMPM demonstrates better performance than MPM in both the linear and Gaussian kernel setting. Moreover, as observed in these benchmark datasets, the MEMPM hyperplanes are ob-

Table 3.1. Lower bound α, β, and test accuracy compared to MPM in the linear setting

Dataset	Performance of MEMPM(%)				Performance of MPM(%)	
	α	β	$\theta\alpha + (1 - \theta)\beta$	Accuracy	α	Accuracy
Twonorm	80.3 ± 0.2	79.9 ± 0.1	80.1 ± 0.1	97.9 ± 0.1	80.1 ± 0.1	97.9 ± 0.1
Breast	77.8 ± 0.8	91.4 ± 0.5	86.7 ± 0.5	96.9 ± 0.3	84.4 ± 0.5	97.0 ± 0.2
Ionosphere	95.9 ± 1.2	36.5 ± 2.6	74.5 ± 0.8	88.5 ± 1.0	63.4 ± 1.1	84.8 ± 0.8
Pima	0.9 ± 0.0	62.9 ± 1.1	41.3 ± 0.8	76.8 ± 0.6	32.0 ± 0.8	76.1 ± 0.6
Heart-disease	43.6 ± 2.5	66.5 ± 1.5	56.3 ± 1.4	84.2 ± 0.7	54.9 ± 1.4	83.2 ± 0.8
Vote	82.6 ± 1.3	84.6 ± 0.7	83.9 ± 0.9	94.9 ± 0.4	83.8 ± 0.9	94.8 ± 0.4

Table 3.2. Lower bound α, β, and test accuracy compared to MPM in the Gaussian kernel

Dataset	Performance of MEMPM(%)				Performance of MPM(%)	
	α	β	$\theta\alpha + (1 - \theta)\beta$	Accuracy	α	Accuracy
Twonorm	91.7 ± 0.2	91.7 ± 0.2	91.7 ± 0.2	97.9 ± 0.1	91.7 ± 0.2	97.9 ± 0.1
Breast	88.4 ± 0.6	90.7 ± 0.4	89.9 ± 0.4	96.9 ± 0.2	89.9 ± 0.4	96.9 ± 0.3
Ionosphere	94.2 ± 0.8	80.9 ± 3.0	89.4 ± 0.8	93.8 ± 0.4	89.0 ± 0.8	92.2 ± 0.4
Pima	2.6 ± 0.1	62.3 ± 1.6	41.4 ± 1.1	77.0 ± 0.7	32.1 ± 1.0	76.2 ± 0.6
Heart-disease	47.1 ± 2.2	66.6 ± 1.4	58.0 ± 1.5	83.9 ± 0.9	57.4 ± 1.6	83.1 ± 1.0
Vote	85.1 ± 1.3	84.3 ± 0.7	84.7 ± 0.8	94.7 ± 0.5	84.4 ± 0.8	94.6 ± 0.4

tained with significantly unequal α and β except in the Twonorm set. This further confirms the validity of our proposition, i.e. the optimal minimax machine is not certain to achieve the same worst-case accuracies for two classes. For the Twonorm, it is also not an exception. The two classes of data in this set are generated under the multivariate normal distributions with the same covariance matrices. In this special case, the intersection point of two density functions will exactly represent the optimal thresholding point and the one with the same error rate for each class as well. Another important finding is that the accuracy bounds, namely $\theta\alpha + (1 - \theta)\beta$ in MEMPM and α in MPM are all increased in the Gaussian kernel setting when compared with those in the linear setting. This shows the advantage of the kernelized probability machine over the linear probability machine.

In addition, to clearly see the relationship between the bounds and the test set accuracies (TSA), we plot them in Fig. 3.5. As observed, the test set accuracies including TSA_x (for the class x), TSA_y (for the class y), and the overall accuracies TSA are all greater than their corresponding accuracy bounds both in MPM and MEMPM. This demonstrates how the accuracy bound can serve as the performance indicator on future data.

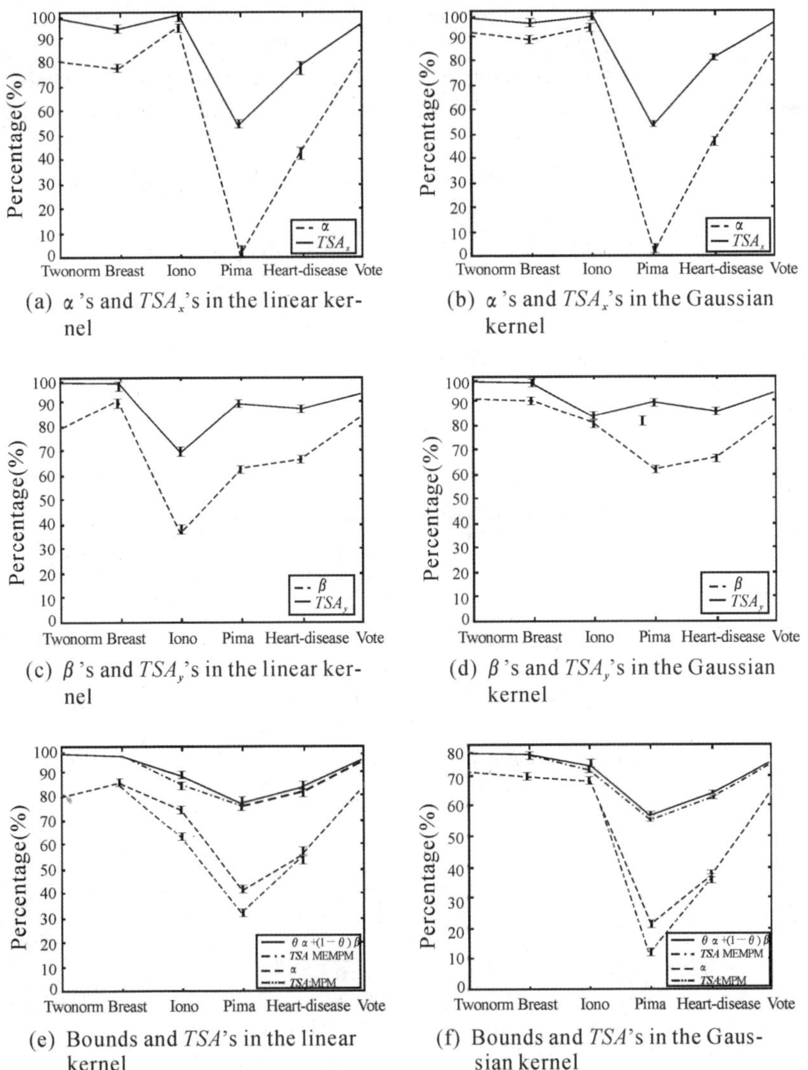

(a) α's and TSA_x's in the linear kernel

(b) α's and TSA_x's in the Gaussian
kernel

(c) β's and TSA_y's in the linear kernel

(d) β's and TSA_y's in the Gaussian
kernel

(e) Bounds and TSA's in the linear
kernel

(f) Bounds and TSA's in the Gaussian kernel

Fig. 3.5. Empirical evaluations on bounds and test set accuracies of MEMPM. The test accuracies including TSA_x (for the class x), TSA_y (for the class y), and the overall accuracies TSA are all greater than their corresponding accuracy bounds both in MPM and MEMPM. This demonstrates how the accuracy bound can serve as the performance indicator on future data

It is also observed that the overall worst-case accuracies $\theta\alpha + (1-\theta)\beta$ in MEMPM are greater than α in MPM both in the linear and Gaussian settings. This again demonstrates the advantages of MEMPM over MPM.

Since the lower bounds keep well with the test accuracies in the above experimental results, we do not perform the robust version of both models for the real-world datasets. To see how the robust version works we generate two classes of Gaussian data. As illustrated in Fig. 3.6, the x data are sampled

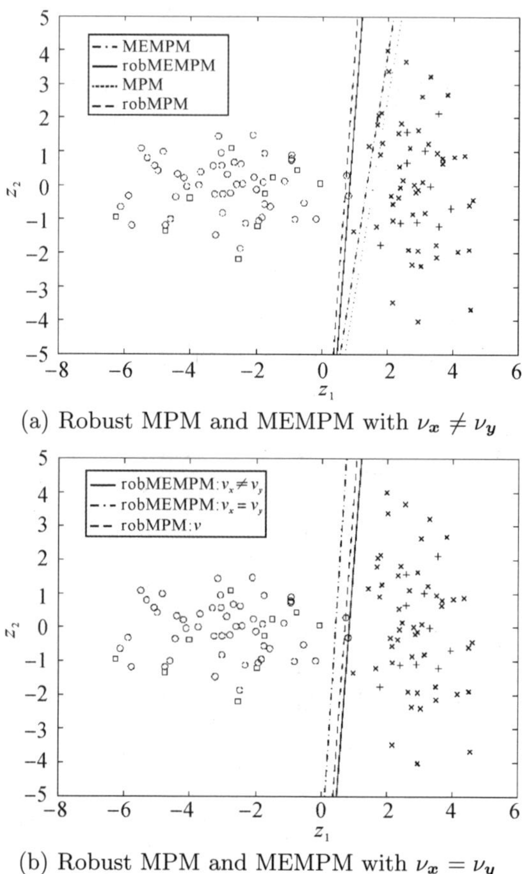

(a) Robust MPM and MEMPM with $\nu_x \neq \nu_y$

(b) Robust MPM and MEMPM with $\nu_x = \nu_y$

Fig. 3.6. An example in $\mathbb{R}^2$ demonstrates the results of robust versions of MEMPM and MPM. Training points are indicated with black $+$'s for the class x and magenta $\square$'s for class y. Test points are represented by blue $\times$'s for class x and by green o's for the class y. In (a), the robust MEMPM outperforms both MEMPM and the robust MPM. In (b), the robust MEMPM with $\nu_x \neq \nu_y$ outperforms the robust MEMPM with $\nu_x = \nu_y$.

from the Gaussian distribution with the mean as $[3, 0]^{\mathrm{T}}$ and the covariance as $[1\ 0; 0\ 3]$, while the y data are sampled from another Gaussian distribution with the mean as $[-3, 0]^{\mathrm{T}}$ and the covariance as $[3\ 0; 0\ 1]$. We randomly select

10 points of each class for training and leave the rest points for test from the above synthetic dataset. We present the result in the following.

First, we calculate the corresponding means $\bar{x}^0$ and $\bar{y}^0$, covariance matrices $\Sigma_x^{\ 0}$ and $\Sigma_y^{\ 0}$ and plug them into the linear MPM and the linear MEMPM. We obtain the MPM decision line (dotted line) with a lower bound (assuming the Gaussian distribution) being 99.1% and the MEMPM decision line (dash-dot line) with a lower bound as 99.7% respectively. However, for the test set we only obtain the accuracies 93.0% for MPM and 97.0% for MEMPM (see Fig. 3.6(a)). This obviously violates the lower bound.

Based on our knowledge of the real means and covariance matrices in this example, we set the parameters as

$$\nu_x = \sqrt{(\bar{x} - \bar{x}^0)^{\mathrm{T}} \Sigma_x^{-1} (\bar{x} - \bar{x}^0)} = 0.046 \ ,$$

$$\nu_y = \sqrt{(\bar{y} - \bar{y}^0)^{\mathrm{T}} \Sigma_y^{-1} (\bar{y} - \bar{y}^0)} = 0.496 \ ,$$

$$\rho_x = \| \Sigma_x - \Sigma_x^{\ 0} \|_{\mathrm{F}} = 1.561 \ ,$$

$$\rho_y = \| \Sigma_y - \Sigma_y^{\ 0} \|_{\mathrm{F}} = 0.972 \ ,$$

$$\nu = \max(\nu_x, \nu_y) \ .$$

We then train the robust linear MPM and the robust linear MEMPM by these parameters and obtain the robust MPM decision line (dashed line), the robust MEMPM decision line (solid line), as seen in Fig. 3.6(a). The lower bounds decrease to 87.3% for MPM and 93.2% for MEMPM respectively, but the test accuracies increase to 98.0% for MPM and 100.0% for MEMPM. Obviously, the lower bounds accord with the test accuracies.

Note that in the above, the robust MEMPM also achieves a better performance than the robust MPM. Moreover, ν_x and ν_y are not necessarily the same. To see the result of MEMPM when ν_x and ν_y are forced to be the same, we train the robust MEMPM again by setting the parameters as $\nu_x = \nu_y = \nu$ as used in MPM. We obtain the corresponding decision line (dash-dot line) as seen in Fig. 3.6(b). The lower bound decreases to 91.0% and the test accuracy decreases to 98.0%. The above example indicates how the robust MEMPM clearly improves over the standard MEMPM when a bias is incorporated by the inaccurate plug-in estimates and also validates that ν_x need not be equal to ν_y.

3.5.3 Evaluations of BMPM on Heart-disease Dataset

To demonstrate the advantages of the BMPM model in dealing with biased classifications, we implement BMPM on the Heart-disease dataset, where different treatments for different classes are necessary. The x class is associated with data with heart diseases, whereas the y class corresponds to data without heart diseases. Obviously, a bias should be considered for x, since misclassification of an x case into the opposite class would delay the therapy

and is more risky than the other way round. Similarly, we randomly partition data into 90% training and 10% test sets. Also, the width parameter
(σ) for the Gaussian kernel is obtained via cross validations over 50 random
partitions of the training set. We repeat the above procedures 50 times and
report the average results.

By intentionally varying β_0 from 0 to 1, we obtain a series of test accu-
racies, including the $\boldsymbol{x}$ accuracy $TSA_{\boldsymbol{x}}$, the $\boldsymbol{y}$ accuracy $TSA_{\boldsymbol{y}}$ for both the
linear and Gaussian kernels. For simplicity, we denote the $\boldsymbol{x}$ accuracy in the
linear setting as $TSA_{\boldsymbol{x}}(\text{L})$, while others are similarly defined.

The results are summarized in Fig. 3.5. Four observations are worth high-
lighting. First, in both linear and Gaussian kernel settings, the smaller β_0,
the higher the test accuracy for $\boldsymbol{x}$. This indicates a bias can be indeed embed-
ded in the classification boundary for the important class $\boldsymbol{x}$ by specifying a
relatively smaller β_0. In comparison, MPM forces an equal treatment on each
class and thus is not suitable for biased classification. Second, the test accura-
cies for $\boldsymbol{y}$ and $\boldsymbol{x}$ are strictly lower bounded by β_0 and α. This shows how a bias
can be quantitatively, directly and rigorously imposed towards the important
class $\boldsymbol{x}$. Note that again, for other weight-adapting-based biased classifiers,
the weights themselves lack accurate interpretations and thus cannot rigorously impose a specified bias, i.e. they would try for different weights for a
specified bias. Third, when given a prescribed β_0, the test accuracy for $\boldsymbol{x}$ and
its worst-case accuracy α in the Gaussian kernel setting are both increased
compared to the corresponding accuracies in the linear setting. Once again,
this demonstrates the power of the kernelization. Fourth, we note that β_0
actually contains an upper bound which is around 90% for the linear BMPM
in this dataset. This is reasonable. Observed from Eq.(3.11), the maximum
β_0 denoted as β_{0max} is decided by setting $\alpha = 0$, i.e.

$$\kappa(\beta_{0\max}) = \max_{\boldsymbol{w}\neq\boldsymbol{0}} \ \frac{1}{\sqrt{\boldsymbol{w}^{\mathrm{T}}\boldsymbol{\Sigma}_{\boldsymbol{y}}\boldsymbol{w}}}, \quad \text{s.t.} \quad \boldsymbol{w}^{\mathrm{T}}(\overline{\boldsymbol{x}} - \overline{\boldsymbol{y}}) = 1 \ . \tag{3.45}$$

It is interesting noting that when β_0 is set to zero, the test accuracies for
$\boldsymbol{y}$ in the linear and Gaussian settings are both around 50% (see Fig. 3.7(b)).
This seeming "irrationality" is actually reasonable. We will discuss this in
the next section.

3.6 How Tight Is the Bound?

A natural question for MEMPM is how tight is the worst-case bound. In this
section, we present a theoretical analysis in addressing this problem.

In Marshall and Olkin Theory, if we define $S = \{\boldsymbol{w}^{\mathrm{T}}\boldsymbol{y} \geq b\}$, the theorem
is changed to:

$$\sup_{\boldsymbol{y}\sim\{\overline{\boldsymbol{y}},\boldsymbol{\Sigma}_{\boldsymbol{y}}\}} Pr\{\boldsymbol{w}^{\mathrm{T}}\boldsymbol{y} \geq b\} = \frac{1}{1+d^2}, \quad \text{with} \quad d^2 = \inf_{\boldsymbol{w}^{\mathrm{T}}\boldsymbol{y}\geq b} (\boldsymbol{y} - \overline{\boldsymbol{y}})^{\mathrm{T}}\boldsymbol{\Sigma}_{\boldsymbol{y}}^{-1}(\boldsymbol{y} - \overline{\boldsymbol{y}}) \ .$$

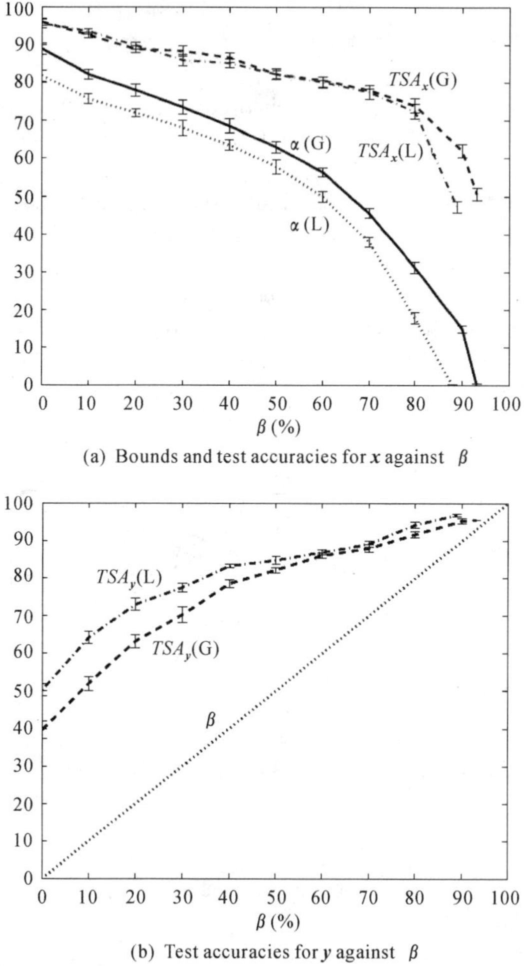

(a) Bounds and test accuracies for x against β

(b) Test accuracies for y against β

Fig. 3.7. Bounds and real accuracies for BMPM in Heart-disease dataset. With β_0 varying from 0 to 1, the real accuracies are lower bounded by the worst-case accuracies. In addition, $\alpha(G)$ is above $\alpha(L)$, which shows the power of the kernelization

Looking into the above equation and Eq.(3.4), for a given hyperplane $\{\boldsymbol{w}, b\}$ we can easily obtain:

$$\beta = \frac{d^2}{1 + d^2} \; . \tag{3.46}$$

Moreover, in [16], a simple closed-form expression for the minimum distance d is derived:

$$d^2 = \inf_{\boldsymbol{w}^{\mathrm{T}}\boldsymbol{y} \geq b}(\boldsymbol{y} - \overline{\boldsymbol{y}})^{\mathrm{T}}\boldsymbol{\Sigma_y}^{-1}(\boldsymbol{y} - \overline{\boldsymbol{y}}) = \frac{\max((b - \boldsymbol{w}^{\mathrm{T}}\overline{\boldsymbol{y}}), 0)}{\boldsymbol{w}^{\mathrm{T}}\boldsymbol{\Sigma_y}\boldsymbol{w}} . \tag{3.47}$$

It is easy to see that when the decision hyperplane $(\boldsymbol{w}, b)$ passes the center $\overline{\boldsymbol{y}}$, d would be equal to 0 and the worst-case accuracy β would be 0 according to Eq.(3.46).

However, if we consider the Gaussian data (which we assume as $\boldsymbol{y}$ data) in Fig. 3.8, a vertical line approximating $\overline{\boldsymbol{y}}$ would achieve about 50% test accuracy. The large gap between the worst-case accuracy and the real test accuracy seems strange. In the following, we construct an example of one-dimensional data to show the inner rationality of this observation. We attempt to provide the worst-case distribution containing the given mean and covariance, while a hyperplane passing its mean achieves a real test accuracy of zero.

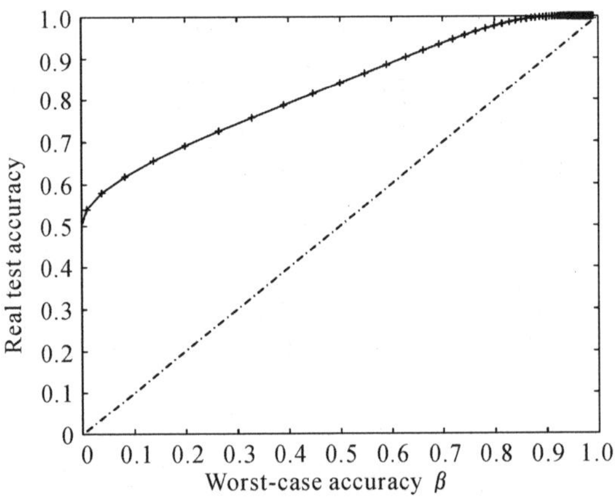

Fig. 3.8. Theoretical comparison between the worst-case accuracy and the real test accuracy for the Gaussian data in Fig. 3.10(a)

Consider the one-dimensional data $\boldsymbol{y}$ consisting of $N-1$ observations with values as m and one single observation with the value as $\sigma\sqrt{N} + m$. If we calculate the mean and the covariance, we obtain:

$$\overline{y} = m + \frac{\sigma}{\sqrt{N}} ,$$

$$\Sigma_y = \frac{N-1}{N}\sigma^2 .$$

When N goes to infinity, the above one-dimensional data have the mean as m and the covariance as σ. In this extreme case, a hyperplane passing the mean will achieve a zero test accuracy which is exactly the worst-case accuracy given the fixed mean and covariance as m and σ respectively. This example demonstrates the inner rationality of the minimax probability machines.

To further examine the tightness of the worst-case bound in Fig. 3.9(a), we vary β from 0 to 1 and plot against β the real test accuracy that a vertical

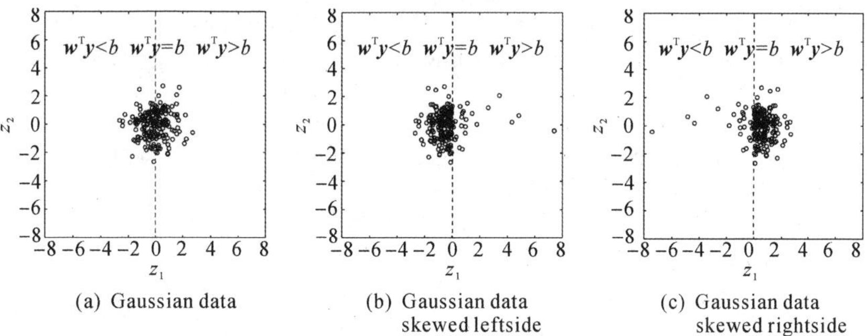

(a) Gaussian data

(b) Gaussian data skewed leftside

(c) Gaussian data skewed rightside

Fig. 3.9. Three two-dimensional data with the same means and covariances but with different skewness. The worst-case accuracy bound of (a) is tighter than that of (b) and looser than that of (c)

line classifies the y data by using Eq.(3.46). Note that the real accuracy can be calculated as $\Phi(z \leq d)$. This curve is plotted in Fig. 3.10.

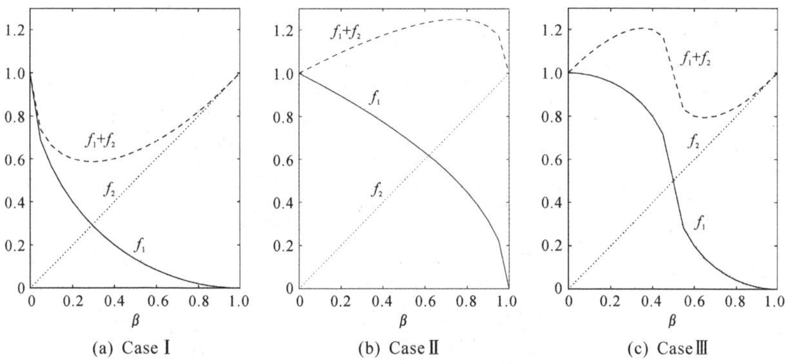

(a) Case I

(b) Case II

(c) Case III

Fig. 3.10. Three two-dimensional data with the same means and covariances but with different skewness. The worst-case accuracy bound of (a) is tighter than that of (b) and looser than that of (c)

Observed from Fig. 3.9, the smaller the worst-case accuracy, the looser it is. On the other hand, if we skew the y data towards the left side, while simultaneously maintaining the mean and covariance unchanged (see Fig. 3.9(b)), even a bigger gap will be generated when β is small; analogically, if we skew the data towards the right side (see Fig. 3.9(c)), a tighter accuracy bound will be expected. This finding would mean that only adopting up to the second order moments may not achieve a satisfactory bound. In other words, for a tighter bound, higher order moments such as skewness need to be considered. This problem of estimating a probability bound based on moments is presented as the (n, k, Ω)-bound problem, which means "finding the tightest bound for n-dimensional variable in the set Ω based on up to the k-th moments." Unfortunately, as proved in [24], it is NP-hard for $(n, k, \mathbb{R}^n)$-bound problems with $k \geq 3$. Thus tightening the bound by simply scaling up the moment order may be intractable in this sense. We may have to exploit other statistical techniques to achieve this goal. Certainly, this deserves a closer examination in the future.

3.7 On the Concavity of MEMPM

We address the issue of the concavity on the MEMPM model in this section. We will demonstrate that although MEMPM cannot generally guarantee its concavity, there is strong empirical evidence showing that many real-world problems demonstrate reasonable concavity in MEMPM. Hence, the MEMPM model can be solved successfully by standard optimization methods, e.g. the linear search method proposed in this chapter.

We first present a lemma on BMPM.

Lemma 3.10. *The optimal solution for BMPM is a strictly and monotonically decreasing function with respect to β_0.*

Proof. Let the corresponding optimal worst-case accuracies on $\boldsymbol{x}$ be α_1 and α_2 respectively, when β_{01} and β_{02} are set as the acceptable accuracy levels for $\boldsymbol{y}$ in BMPM. We will prove that if $\beta_{01} > \beta_{02}$, then $\alpha_1 < \alpha_2$.

This can be proved by considering the contrary case, i.e. we assume $\alpha_1 \geq \alpha_2$. From the problem definition of BMPM, we have:

$$\alpha_1 \geq \alpha_2 \implies \kappa(\alpha_1) \geq \kappa(\alpha_2)$$

$$\implies \frac{1 - \kappa(\beta_{01})\sqrt{\boldsymbol{w}_1^{\mathrm{T}}\boldsymbol{\Sigma}_y\boldsymbol{w}_1}}{\sqrt{\boldsymbol{w}_1^{\mathrm{T}}\boldsymbol{\Sigma}_x\boldsymbol{w}_1}} \geq \frac{1 - \kappa(\beta_{02})\sqrt{\boldsymbol{w}_2^{\mathrm{T}}\boldsymbol{\Sigma}_y\boldsymbol{w}_2}}{\sqrt{\boldsymbol{w}_2^{\mathrm{T}}\boldsymbol{\Sigma}_x\boldsymbol{w}_2}} , \quad (3.48)$$

where, $\boldsymbol{w}_1$ and $\boldsymbol{w}_2$ are the corresponding optimal solutions which maximize $\kappa(\alpha_1)$ and $\kappa(\alpha_2)$ respectively, when β_{01} and β_{02} are specified.

From $\beta_{01} > \beta_{02}$ and Eq.(3.48), we have

$$\frac{1 - \kappa(\beta_{02})\sqrt{\boldsymbol{w}_1^{\mathrm{T}}\boldsymbol{\Sigma}_y\boldsymbol{w}_1}}{\sqrt{\boldsymbol{w}_1^{\mathrm{T}}\boldsymbol{\Sigma}_x\boldsymbol{w}_1}} > \frac{1 - \kappa(\beta_{01})\sqrt{\boldsymbol{w}_1^{\mathrm{T}}\boldsymbol{\Sigma}_y\boldsymbol{w}_1}}{\sqrt{\boldsymbol{w}_1^{\mathrm{T}}\boldsymbol{\Sigma}_x\boldsymbol{w}_1}} \quad (3.49)$$

$$\geq \frac{1 - \kappa(\beta_{02})\sqrt{\boldsymbol{w}_2^{\mathrm{T}}\boldsymbol{\Sigma}_y\boldsymbol{w}_2}}{\sqrt{\boldsymbol{w}_2^{\mathrm{T}}\boldsymbol{\Sigma}_x\boldsymbol{w}_2}} . \quad (3.50)$$

On the other hand, since w_2 is the optimal solution of

$$\max_{w\neq 0}\frac{1-\kappa(\beta_{02})\sqrt{w^{\mathrm{T}}\Sigma_y w}}{\sqrt{w^{\mathrm{T}}\Sigma_x w}},$$

we have

$$\frac{1-\kappa(\beta_{02})\sqrt{w_2^{\mathrm{T}}\Sigma_y w_2}}{\sqrt{w_2^{\mathrm{T}}\Sigma_x w_2}}\geq\frac{1-\kappa(\beta_{02})\sqrt{w_1^{\mathrm{T}}\Sigma_y w_1}}{\sqrt{w_1^{\mathrm{T}}\Sigma_x w_1}}.$$

This is obviously contradictory to Eq.(3.50).

From the sequential solving method of MEMPM, we know that MEMPM actually corresponds to a one-dimensional line search problem. More specifically, it further corresponds to maximizing the sum of two functions, namely, $f_1(\beta)+f_2(\beta)$[6], where $f_1(\beta)$ is determined by the BMPM optimization and $f_2(\beta)=\beta$. According to Lemma 3.10, $f_1(\beta)$ strictly decreases as β increases. Thus it is strictly pseudo-concave. However, generally speaking, the sum of a pseudo-concave function and a linear function is not necessarily a pseudo-concave function and thus cannot assure that every local optimum is the global optimum. This can be clearly observed in Fig. 3.10. In this figure, f_1 is pseudo-concave in three sub-figures; however, the sum f_1+f_2 does not necessarily lead to a pseudo-concave function.

Nevertheless, there is strong empirical evidence showing that for many "well-behaved" real world classification problems, f_1 is overall concave, which results in the concavity of f_1+f_2. This is first verified by the datasets used in this chapter. We shift β from 0 to the corresponding upper bound and plot out α against β in Fig. 3.11. It is clearly observed that in all six datasets including both kernel and linear cases, the curves of α against β are overall concave. This motivates us to look further into the concavity of MEMPM. As shown in the following, when two classes of data are "well-separated," f_1 would be concave in the main "interest" region.

We analyze the concavity of $f_1(\beta)$ by imagining that β changes from 0 to 1. In this process, the decision hyperplane moves slowly from $\overline{y}$ to $\overline{x}$ according to Eq.(3.46) and Eq.(3.47). At the same time, $\alpha=f_1(\beta)$ should decrease accordingly. More precisely, if we denote d_x and d_y respectively as the Mahalanobis distances that $\overline{x}$ and $\overline{y}$ are from the associated decision hyperplane with a specified β, we can formulate the changing of α and β as:

$$\alpha\rightarrow\alpha-k_1(d_x)\Delta d_x,$$
$$\beta\rightarrow\beta+k_2(d_y)\Delta d_y,$$

where $k_1(d_x)$ and $k_2(d_y)$ can be considered as the changing rate of α and β when the hyperplane lies d_x distance far away from $\overline{x}$ and d_y distance far

---

[6]For simplicity, we assume θ as 0.5. Since a constant does not influence the concavity analysis, the factor of 0.5 is simply dropped.

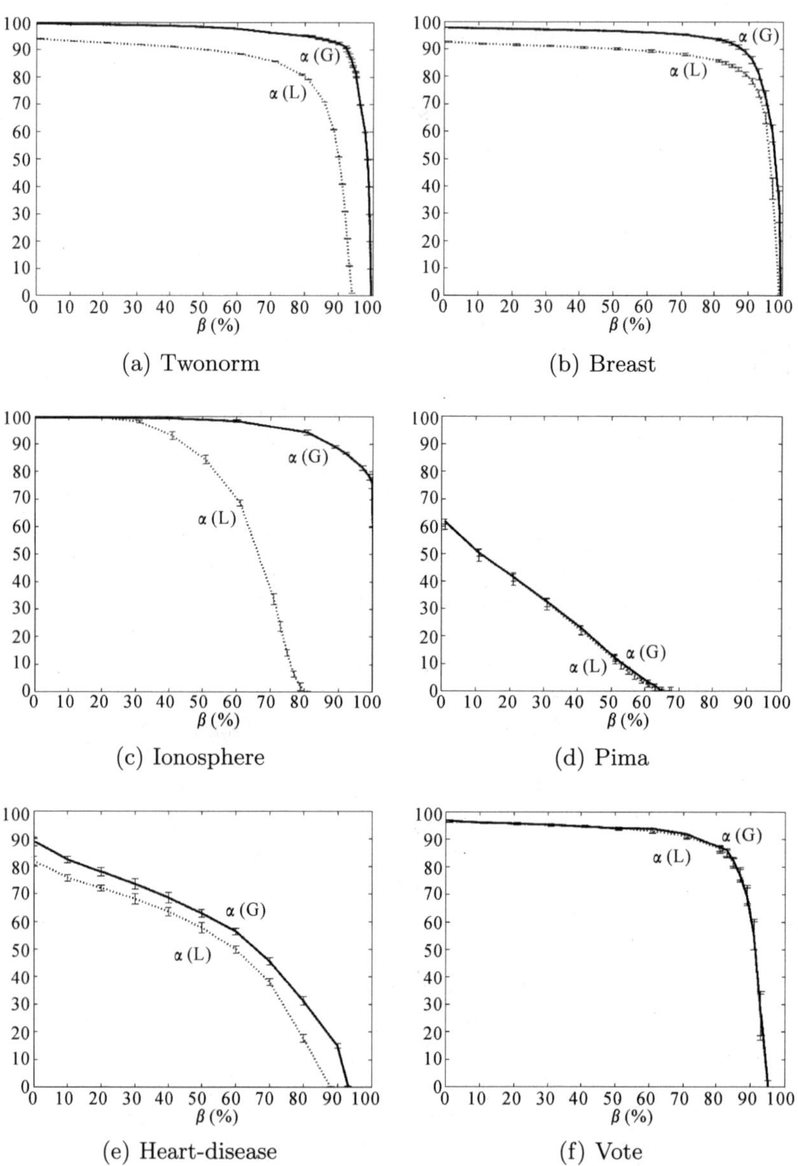

Fig. 3.11. The curves of α against β (f_1) are all concave-like in the datasets used in this chapter

away from $\overline{y}$ respectively. We consider the changing of α against β, namely, f_1':

$$f_1' = \frac{-k_1(d_{\boldsymbol{x}})\Delta d_{\boldsymbol{x}}}{k_2(d_{\boldsymbol{y}})\Delta d_{\boldsymbol{y}}} \ .$$

If we consider that $d_{\boldsymbol{x}}$ and $\Delta d_{\boldsymbol{y}}$ insensitively change against each other or change with a proportional rate, i.e. $\Delta d_{\boldsymbol{x}} \approx c\Delta d_{\boldsymbol{y}}$ (c is a positive constant) as the decision hyperplane moves, the above equation can be further written as

$$f_1' = c\frac{-k_1(d_{\boldsymbol{x}})}{k_2(d_{\boldsymbol{y}})} \ .$$

Lemma 3.11. *(1) If $d_{\boldsymbol{y}} \geq 1/\sqrt{3}$ or the corresponding $\beta \geq 0.25$, $k_2(d_{\boldsymbol{y}})$ decreases as $d_{\boldsymbol{y}}$ increases. (2) If $d_{\boldsymbol{x}} \geq 1/\sqrt{3}$ or the corresponding $\alpha \geq 0.25$, $k_1(d_{\boldsymbol{x}})$ decreases as $d_{\boldsymbol{x}}$ increases.*

Proof. Since (1) and (2) are actually very similar statements, we only prove (1). $k_2(d)$ is actually the first order derivative of $d^2/(1+d^2)$ according to Eq.(3.46). We consider the first order derivative of $k_2(d)$ or the second order derivative of $d^2/(1+d^2)$. It is easily verified that $(d^2/(1+d^2))'' \leq 0$ when $d \geq 1/\sqrt{3}$. This is also illustrated in Fig. 3.12. According to the definition of the second derivative, we immediately obtain the lemma. Note that $d \geq 1/\sqrt{3}$ corresponds to $\beta \geq 0.25$. Thus the condition can be also replaced by $\beta \geq 0.25$.

In the above procedure, $d_{\boldsymbol{y}}$, β increase and $d_{\boldsymbol{x}}$, α decrease as the hyperplane moves towards $\overline{x}$. Therefore, according to Lemma 3.11, $k_1(d_{\boldsymbol{x}})$ increases while $k_2(d_{\boldsymbol{y}})$ decreases when $\alpha, \beta \in [0.25, 1)$. This shows that f_1' is getting smaller as the hyperplane moves towards $\overline{x}$. In other words, f_1'' would be less than 0 and thus is concave when $\alpha, \beta \in [0.25, 1)$. It should be noted that in many well-separated real world datasets, the optimal α and β will be greater than 0.25 with a high possibility, since to achieve good performance, the worst-case accuracies are naturally required to be greater than a smaller amount, e.g. 0.25. This is observed in the datasets used in the chapter. All the datasets except Pima attain their optimums satisfying this constraint. For Pima, the overall accuracy is relatively lower, which implies that two classes of data in this dataset appear to largely overlap each other[7].

An illustration can be also seen in Fig. 3.13. We generate two classes of Gaussian data with $\overline{x} = [0, \ 0]^{\mathrm{T}}$, $\overline{y} = [L, \ 0]^{\mathrm{T}}$, and $\boldsymbol{\Sigma}_{\boldsymbol{x}} = \boldsymbol{\Sigma}_{\boldsymbol{y}} = [1, \ 0; 0, \ 1]$. The prior probability for each data is set as an equal value 0.5. We plot the curves of $f_1(\beta)$ and $f_1(\beta) + \beta$ when L is set as different values. It is

---

[7]It is observed, even for Pima, the proposed solving algorithm is still successful, since α is approximately linear as shown in Fig. 3.11. Moreover, due to the fact that the slope of α is slightly greater than -1, the final optimum naturally leads β to achieve its maximum.

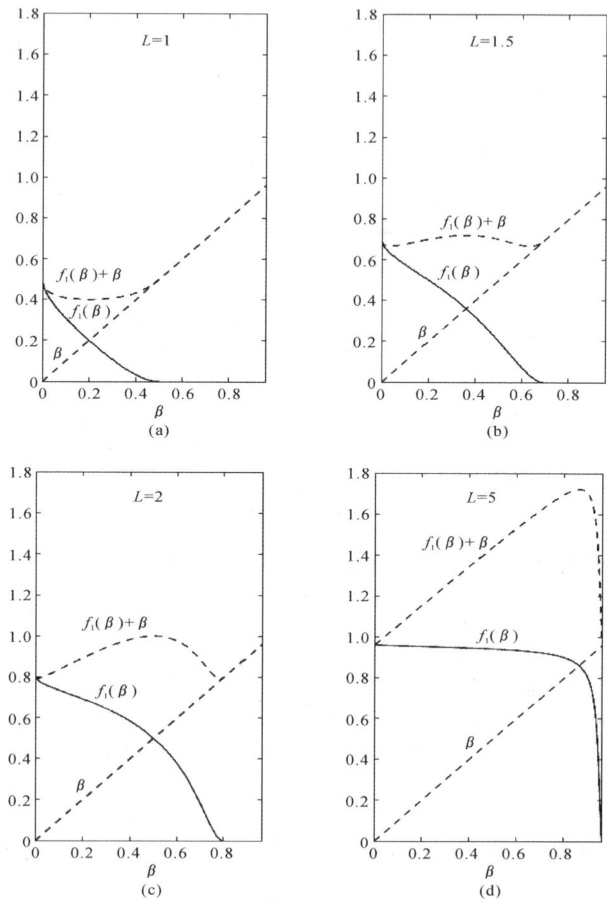

Fig. 3.12. An illustration of the concavity of MEMPM. Subfigure (a) shows that when two classes of data overlap largely each other, the optimal solution of MEMPM lies in the small-value range of α and β which is usually not concave. (b), (c), and (d) show that when two classes of data are well-separated, the optimal solutions lie in the region with $\alpha, \beta \in [0.25, 1)$ which is often concave

observed that when two classes of data largely overlap each other, for example in Fig. 3.12(a) with $L = 1$, the optimal solution of MEMPM lies in the small-value range of α and β, which is usually not concave. On the other hand, Fig. 3.12(b), (c), and (d) show that when two classes of data are well-separated, the optimal solutions lie in the region with $\alpha, \beta \in [0.25, 1)$, which is often concave.

Note that, in the above, we make an assumption that as the decision hyperplane moves, d_x and d_y change at an approximately fixed proportional

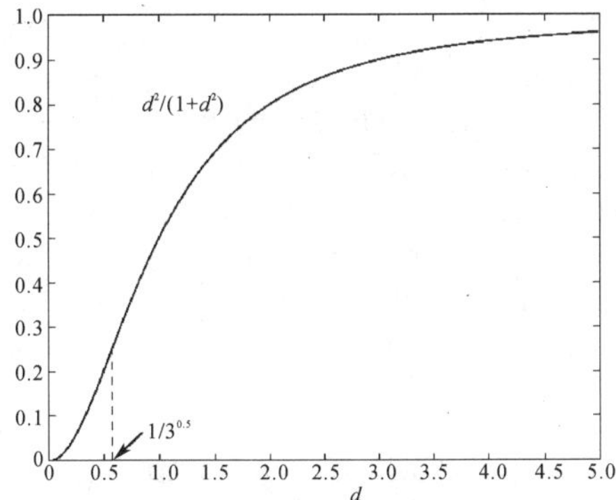

Fig. 3.13. The curve of $d^2/(1+d^2)$. This function is concave when
$d \geq 1/\sqrt{3}$

rate. From the definition of d_x and d_y, this assumption implies that w, the direction of the optimal decision hyperplane, is insensitive to β. This assumption does not hold in all cases; however, observed from the geometrical interpretation of MEMPM, for those data with isotropic or not significantly anisotropic Σ_x and Σ_y, w would be indeed insensitive to β.

We summarize the above analysis into the following proposition.

Proposition 3.12. *Assuming (1) two classes of data are well-separated and (2) d_x and d_y change at an approximately fixed proportional rate as the optimal decision hyperplane (associated with a specified β) moves, the one-dimensional line search problem of MEMPM is often concave in the range of $\alpha, \beta \in [0.25, 1)$ and will often attain its optimum in this range. Therefore the proposed solving method leads to a satisfactory solution.*

Remarks. As demonstrated in the above, although MEMPM is often overall concave in real world tasks, there exist cases that MEMPM optimization problem is not concave. This may lead to the case that the solved local optimum, based on the SBMPM method, is not the global optimum. In these instances, we may need carefully choose the initial starting point. In addition, the physical interpretation of β as the worst-case accuracy, may make it relatively easy to choose a suitable initial value. For example, we can set the initial value by using the information obtained from prior domain knowledge.

3.8 Limitations and Future Work

In this section, we present the limitations and future work.

First, although MEMPM achieves better performance than MPM, its sequential optimization of Biased Minimax Probability Machine may cost more training time than MPM. In our experiments, MEMPM needs to solve $5-15$ BMPM optimizations on the average. Supposing that BMPM is solved based on Conjugate Gradient Methods (with a worst-case time complexity in the same order as MPM), MEMPM would be $5-15$ times as expensive as MPM. Although in pattern recognition tasks, especially in off-line classifications, effectiveness is often more important than efficiency, expensive time-cost presents one of the main limitations of the MEMPM model, in particular for large scale datasets with millions of samples. To solve this problem, one possible direction is to reduce those redundant points which actually make less contributions to the classification. In this way, the problem dimension (in the kernelization) would be greatly decreased and therefore may help in reducing the computational time required. Another possible direction is to exploit some techniques to decompose the Gram matrix (as is done in SVM) and to develop some specialized optimization procedures for MEMPM. Undoubtedly, speeding up the algorithm will be a highly worthy topic in the future.

Second, as a generalized model, MEMPM actually incorporates some other variations. For example, when the prior probability (θ) cannot be estimated reliably (e.g. in sparse data), maximizing $\alpha + \beta$, namely the sum of the accuracies or the difference between true positive and false positive, would be considered. This type of approaches is widely used in pattern recognition field, e.g. in medical diagnosis [10] and in graph detection, especially line detection and arc detection, where it is called Vector Recovery Index [9, 17]. Moreover, when there are domain experts at hand, a variation of MEMPM, namely, the maximization of $C_{\boldsymbol{x}}\alpha + C_{\boldsymbol{y}}\beta$ may be used, where $C_{\boldsymbol{x}}$ $(C_{\boldsymbol{y}})$ is the cost of a misclassification of $\boldsymbol{x}$ $(\boldsymbol{y})$ obtained from experts. Exploring these variations in some specific domains is thus a valuable direction in the future (we actually will discuss these variations as criteria for biased or imbalanced learning in Chapter 5).

Third, [16] has built up a connection between MPM and SVM from the perspective of the margin definition, i.e. MPM corresponds to finding the hyperplane with the maximal margin from the class center. Nevertheless, some deeper connections need to be investigated, e.g. how is the bound of MEMPM related to the generation bound of SVM? More recently, [11] and also the next chapter have disclosed the relationship between them from either a local or global viewpoint of data. It is particularly useful to look into these links and explore their further connections in the future.

3.9 Summary

In this chapter, we have proposed a novel global learning model named Minimum Error Minimax Probability Machine. By minimizing the upper bound of the Bayes error of future data points, our model derives the distribution-free Bayes optimal hyperplane in the worst-case setting. This thus distinguishes itself from the traditional global learning approaches, or more particularly from traditional Bayes optimal classsifers. More importantly, we have shown that the worst-case Bayes optimal hyperplane derived by MEMPM becomes the true Bayes optimal hyperplane, when some conditions are satisfied, e.g. when a Gaussian distribution is assumed on data. We have shown that how to exploit Mercer kernels in this setting to derive a nonlinear classification boundary. We also have demonstrated that how a robust framework can be introduced to make solid the foundation of the proposed model. Moreover, we have demonstrated that this novel model permits an explicit accuracy bound on future data theoretically and validate this proposition empirically as well. We have evaluated our algorithms on both synthetic datasets and real-world benchmark datasets. The performance of MEMPM is demonstrated to outperform MPM, a comparable model with SVM.

References

1. Bazaraa MS (1993) Nonlinear Programming: Theory and Algorithms. New York, NY: John Wiley & Sons, 2nd edition
2. Bertsekas DP (1999) Nonlinear Programming. Athena Scientific, Belmont, Massachusetts, 2nd edition
3. Blake CL, Merz CJ(1998) Repository of machine learning databases, University of California, Irvine, http://www.ics.uci.edu/~mlearn/MLRepository.html
4. Breiman L(1997) Arcing Classifiers. Technical Report 460, Statistics Department, University of California
5. Chow YS, Teicher H(1997) Probability Theory: Independence, Interchangeability, Martingales. New York, NY: Springer-Verlag, 3rd edition
6. Craven BD (1978) Mathematical Programming and Control Theory. London, UK: Chapman & Hall
7. Craven BD (1988) Fractional Programming, Sigma Series in Applied Mathematics 4. Berlin: Heldermann Verlag
8. Deco G, Obradovic D (1996) An Information-theoretic Approach to Neural Computing. Heidelberg; New York: Springer-Verlag
9. Dori D, Liu W (1999) Sparse pixel vectorization: An algorithm and its performance evaluation. IEEE Trans. Pattern Analysis and Machine Intelligence 21:202–215
10. Grzymala-Busse JW, Goodwin LK, Zhang X (2003) Increasing sensitivity of preterm birth by changing rule strengths. Pattern Recognition Letters 24:903–910
11. Huang K, Yang H, King I, Lyu MR (2004) Learning large margin classifiers locally and globally. In The 21st International Conference on Machine Learning (ICML-2004)
12. Huang K, Yang H, King I, Lyu MR, Chan L (2003) Biased minimax probability machine for medical diagnosis. In the Eighth International Symposium on Artificial Intelligence and Mathematics
13. Ibaraki T (1981). Solving mathematical programming problems with fractional objective functions In S. Schaible and W. T. Ziemba., editors, Generalized

Concavity in Optimization and Economics. New York, NY: Academic Press 441–472

14. Keysers D, Och FJ, Ney H(2002) Maximum entropy and Gaussian models for image object recognition. In Proceedings of the 24th DAGM Symposium, Lecture Notes in Computer Science. Heidelberg: Springer-Verlag, LNCS 2449: 498–506

15. Lanckriet GRG, Ghaoui LE, Bhattacharyya C, Jordan MI (2001) Minimax probability machine. In Advances in Neural Information Processing Systems (NIPS)

16. Lanckriet GRG, Ghaoui LE, Bhattacharyya C, Jordan MI (2002) A robust minimax approach to classification. Journal of Machine Learning Research 3:555–582

17. Liu W, Dori D (1997) A protocol for performance evaluation of line detection algorithms. Machine Vision and Application 9:240–250

18. Maloof MA, Langley P, Binford TO, Nevatia R, Sage S (2003) Improved rooftop detection in aerial images with machine learning. Machine Learning 53:157–191

19. Mangasarian Olvi L (1994) Nonlinear Programming. Philadelphia: Society for Industrial and Applied Mathematics

20. Marshall AW, Olkin I (1960) Multivariate Chebyshev inequalities. Annals of Mathematical Statistics 31(4):1001–1014

21. Moulin Hervé (1995) Cooperative Microeconomics: a game-theoretic introduction. Princeton, NJ: Princeton University Press

22. Müller KR, Mika S, Rätsch G, Tsuda K, Schölkopf B (2001) An introduction to Kernel-based Learning Algorithms. IEEE Transactions on Neural Networks 12:181–201

23. Osuna E, Freund R, Girosi F (1997) Support Vector Machines: Training and Applications. Technical Report AIM-1602, Cambridge, MA: The MIT Press

24. Popescu I, Bertsimas D (2001) Optimal inequalities in probability theory: A convex optimization approach. Technical Report TM62, INSEAD

25. Schaible S (1977) Fractional programming. Zeitschrift für Operational Research, Serie A 27(1):39–54

26. Schaible S (1995) Fractional programming. In R. Horst and P. M. Pardalos, editors, Handbook of Global Optimization, Nonconvex Optimization and its Applications. Dordrecht,Boston,London: Kluwer Academic Publishers 495–608

27. Schölkopf B, Smola A(2002) Learning with Kernels. Cambridge, MA: The MIT Press

4

Learning Locally and Globally: Maxi-Min Margin Machine

The proposed MEMPM model obtains the decision hyperplane by using only global information, e.g. the mean and covariance matrices. However, although these moments can be more reliably obtained than estimating the distribution, they may still be inaccurate in many cases, e.g. when the data are very sparse.

Recently, local learning methods, especially large margin classifiers [19] have attracted much interest in the community of machine learning and pattern recognition. Support Vector Machine (SVM) [25], the most famous one of them, represents a state-of-the-art classifier. The essential point of SVM is to find a linear separating hyperplane, which achieves the maximal margin among different classes of data. Furthermore, one can extend SVM to build nonlinear separating decision hyperplanes by exploiting kernelization techniques.

These methods do not try to summarize any global information beforehand, but to focus on obtaining the decision hyperplane in a "local" way. For example, in SVM the decision boundary is exclusively determined by some critical points which are called support vectors, whereas all other points are totally irrelevant to this hyperplane. Although this scheme is both theoretically and empirically demonstrated to be powerful, it actually discards the global information of data.

An illustration example can be seen in Fig. 4.1. In this figure, the classification boundary is intuitively observed to be mainly determined by the dotted axis, i.e. the long axis of the y data (represented by $\square$'s) or the short axis of the x data (represented by o's). Moreover, along this axis, the y data are more possible to scatter than the x data, since y contains a relatively larger variance in this direction. Noting this "global" fact, a good decision hyperplane seems reasonable to lie closer to the x side (see the dash-dot line). However, SVM ignores this kind of "global" information, i.e. the statistical trend of data occurrence: the derived SVM decision hyperplane (the solid line) lies unbiasedly right in the middle of two "local" points (the support vectors)[1].

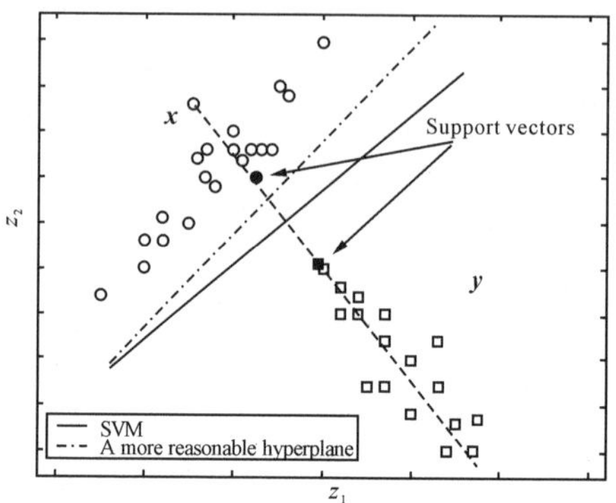

Fig. 4.1. A decision hyperplane with considerations of both local and global information

Aiming to construct classifiers both locally and globally, we propose the Maxi-Min Margin Machine (M^4) in this chapter. We will attempt to combine the local learning into the global information, i.e. the covariance information, which can represent the data trend. Moreover, as this model also contains the properties of local learning, it will naturally neutralize the impact when the global information is inaccurate.

As we show later, one critical contribution of this novel model is that M^4 actually presents a unified model of SVM and another recently-proposed promising model Minimax Probability Machine (MPM) [11]. Moreover, based on our proposed local and global view of data, another popular model, Fisher Discriminant Analysis (FDA) [4] can also be interpreted as its special case.

Another good feature of the M^4 model is that it can be cast as a sequential Conic Programming problem [17], or more specifically, a sequential Second Order Cone Programming (SOCP) problem [12, 15, 10], which thus can be practically solved in polynomial time. In addition, with incorporating the global information, a reduction method is proposed for decreasing the computation time of this new model.

The third important feature of our proposed model is that the kernelization methodology is also applicable for this formulation. This thus generalizes the linear M^4 to a more powerful classification approach which can derive nonlinear decision boundaries.

The rest of this chapter is organized as follows. In the next section, we introduce the M^4 model in detail, including its model definition, the geometri-

---

[1]This figure has appeared earlier in Chapter 2. However, for the purpose of self-containing for each chapter, we still present it here.

cal interpretation, connections with other models, and the associated solving methods. In Section 4.2, we derive a generation bound for the M^4 model. In Section 4.3, we develop a reduction method to remove redundant points for decreasing the computational time. In Section 4.4, we exploit the kernelization trick to extend M^4 to nonlinear classification tasks. In Section 4.5, we evaluate this novel model on both synthetic datasets and real world benchmark datasets. In Section 4.6, we make discussions on the M^4 model and also present future work. Finally, we conclude this chapter in Section 4.7. This work can be also seen in [5] [7] for a short version.

4.1 Maxi-Min Margin Machine

In the following, we first, for the purpose of clarity, divide M^4 into separable and nonseparable categories, and then introduce the corresponding hard-margin M^4 and soft-margin M^4 sequently. In this section, we will also establish the connections of the M^4 model with other large margin classifiers including SVM, MPM, FDA and Mininum Error Minimax Probability Machine (MEMPM) [6].

4.1.1 Separable Case

Assuming the classification samples are separable, we first introduce the model definition and the geometrical interpretation. We then transform the model optimization problem into a sequential SOCP problem and discuss the detailed optimization method.

4.1.1.1 Problem Definition

Only two-category classification tasks are considered in this chapter. Let a training dataset contain two classes of samples represented by $\boldsymbol{x}_i \in \mathbb{R}^n$ and $\boldsymbol{y}_j \in \mathbb{R}^n$ respectively, where $i = 1, 2, \ldots, N_{\boldsymbol{x}}$, $j = 1, 2, \ldots, N_{\boldsymbol{y}}$. The basic task here can be informally described to find a suitable hyperplane $f(\boldsymbol{z}) = \boldsymbol{w}^{\mathrm{T}}\boldsymbol{z} + b$ separating two classes of data as robustly as possible ($\boldsymbol{w} \in \mathbb{R}^n \backslash \{\boldsymbol{0}\}$, $b \in \mathbb{R}$, and $\boldsymbol{w}^{\mathrm{T}}$ is the transpose of $\boldsymbol{w}$). Future data points $\boldsymbol{z}$ for which $f(\boldsymbol{z}) \geq 0$ are then classified as the class $\boldsymbol{x}$; otherwise, they are classified as the class $\boldsymbol{y}$.

The formulation for M^4 can be written as:

$$\max_{\rho, \boldsymbol{w} \neq \boldsymbol{0}, b} \quad \rho \, , \tag{4.1}$$

$$\text{s.t.} \quad \frac{(\boldsymbol{w}^{\mathrm{T}}\boldsymbol{x}_i + b)}{\sqrt{\boldsymbol{w}^{\mathrm{T}}\boldsymbol{\Sigma}_{\boldsymbol{x}}\boldsymbol{w}}} \geq \rho \, , \quad i = 1, 2, \ldots, N_{\boldsymbol{x}} \, , \tag{4.2}$$

$$\frac{-(\boldsymbol{w}^{\mathrm{T}}\boldsymbol{y}_j + b)}{\sqrt{\boldsymbol{w}^{\mathrm{T}}\boldsymbol{\Sigma}_{\boldsymbol{y}}\boldsymbol{w}}} \geq \rho \, , \quad j = 1, 2, \ldots, N_{\boldsymbol{y}} \, , \tag{4.3}$$

where Σ_x and Σ_y refer to the covariance matrices of the x and the y data, respectively.

This model tries to *maximize* the margin defined as the *minimum* Mahalanobis distance for all training samples,while simultaneously classifying all the data correctly. Compared to SVM, M^4 incorporates the data information in a global way; namely, the covariance information of data or the statistical trend of data occurrence is considered, while SVMs, including l_1-SVM [27] and l_2-SVM [24] (l_p-SVM means the "p-norm" distance-based SVM) [19], simply discard this information or consider the same covariance for each class.

4.1.1.2 Geometrical Interpretation

A geometrical interpretation of M^4 can be seen in Fig. 4.2. In this figure, the

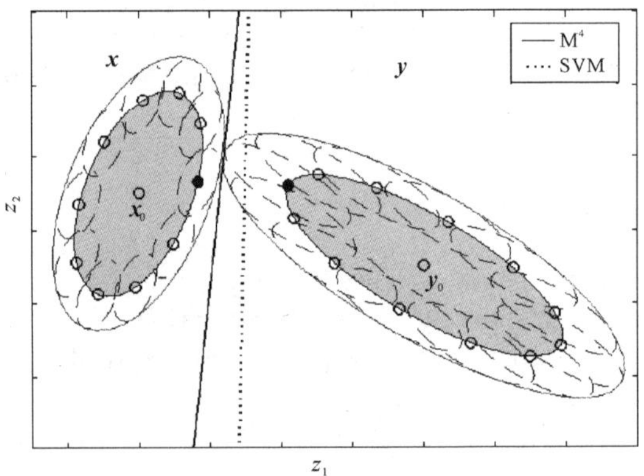

Fig. 4.2. A geometric interpretation of M^4. The M^4 hyperplane corresponds to the tangent line (the solid line) of two small dashed ellipsoids centered at the support vectors (the local information) and shaped by the corresponding covariances (the global information). It is thus more reasonable than SVM (the dotted line)

x data are represented by the inner ellipsoid on the left side with its center as x_0, while the y data are represented by the inner ellipsoid on the right side with its center as y_0. It is observed that these two ellipsoids contain unequal covariances or risks of data occurrence. However, SVM does not consider this global information: its decision hyperplane (the dotted line) is located unbiasedly in the middle of two support vectors (filled points). In comparison, M^4 defines the margin as a Maxi-Min Mahalanobis distance, which thus constructs a decision plane (the solid line) with considerations of both the local and global information: the M^4 hyperplane corresponds to the tangent line of two dashed ellipsoids centered at the support vectors (the local information) and shaped by the corresponding covariances (the global information).

4.1.1.3 Optimization Method

In the following, we propose the optimization method for the M^4 model. We will demonstrate that the above problem can be cast as a sequential Conic Programming problem, or more specifically, a sequential SOCP problem.

Our strategy is based on the "Divide and Conquer" technique. One may note that in the optimization problem of M^4, if ρ is fixed to a constant ρ_n, the problem is exactly changed to "conquer" the problem of checking whether the constraints of Eqs.(4.2) and (4.3) can be satisfied. Moreover, as will be demonstrated shortly, this "checking" procedure can be stated as an SOCP problem. Thus the problem now becomes that how ρ is set, which we can use "divide" to handle: if the constraints are satisfied, we can increase ρ_n accordingly; otherwise, we decrease ρ_n.

We detail this solving technique in the following two steps:

(1) Divide: Set $\rho_n = (\rho_0 + \rho_m)/2$, where ρ_0 is a feasible ρ, ρ_m is an infeasible ρ, and $\rho_0 \leq \rho_m$.
(2) Conquer: Call the Modified Second Order Cone Programming (MSOCP) procedure elaborated in the following to check whether ρ_n is a feasible ρ. If yes, set $\rho_0 = \rho_n$; otherwise, set $\rho_m = \rho_n$.

In the above, if a ρ satisfies the constraints of Eqs.(4.2) and (4.3), we call it a feasible ρ; otherwise, we call it an infeasible ρ. These two steps are iterated until $|\rho_0 - \rho_m|$ is less than a small positive value.

We propose the following Theorem 4.1 showing that the MSOCP procedure, namely, the checking problem with ρ fixed to a constant ρ_n, is solvable by casting it as an SOCP problem.

Theorem 4.1. *The problem of checking whether there exist a w and a b satisfying the following two sets of constraints Eqs.(4.4) and (4.5) can be transformed as an SOCP problem which can be solved in polynomial time,*

$$(w^{\mathrm{T}} x_i + b) \geq \rho_n \sqrt{w^{\mathrm{T}} \Sigma_x w}, \ i = 1, \ldots, N_x \,, \tag{4.4}$$

$$-(w^{\mathrm{T}} y_j + b) \geq \rho_n \sqrt{w^{\mathrm{T}} \Sigma_y w}, \ j = 1, \ldots, N_y \,. \tag{4.5}$$

Proof. Introducing dummy variables τ, we rewrite the above checking problem as an equivalent optimization problem:

$$\max_{w \neq 0, b, \tau} \ \left\{ \min_{k=1}^{N_x + N_y} \ \tau_k \right\}$$

$$\text{s.t.} \ (w^{\mathrm{T}} x_i + b) \geq \rho_n \sqrt{w^{\mathrm{T}} \Sigma_x w} - \tau_i \,,$$

$$-(w^{\mathrm{T}} y_j + b) \geq \rho_n \sqrt{w^{\mathrm{T}} \Sigma_y w} - \tau_{j+N_x} \,,$$

where $i = 1, \ldots, N_x$ and $j = 1, \ldots, N_y$.

By checking whether the minimum τ_k at the optimum point is positive, we can know whether the constraints of Eqs.(4.2) and (4.3) can be satisfied. If we go further, we can introduce another dummy variable and transform the above problem into an SOCP problem:

$$\max_{\boldsymbol{w} \neq \boldsymbol{0}, b, \boldsymbol{\tau}, \eta} \quad \eta$$

$$\text{s.t.} \ \ (\boldsymbol{w}^{\mathrm{T}} \boldsymbol{x}_i + b) \geq \rho_n \sqrt{\boldsymbol{w}^{\mathrm{T}} \boldsymbol{\Sigma}_x \boldsymbol{w}} - \tau_i \ ,$$

$$-(\boldsymbol{w}^{\mathrm{T}} \boldsymbol{y}_j + b) \geq \rho_n \sqrt{\boldsymbol{w}^{\mathrm{T}} \boldsymbol{\Sigma}_y \boldsymbol{w}} - \tau_{j+N_x} \ ,$$

$$\eta \leq \tau_k \ ,$$

where $i = 1, \ldots, N_x$, $j = 1, \ldots, N_y$, and $k = 1, \ldots, N_x + N_y$. By checking whether the optimal η is greater than 0, we can immediately know whether there exist a $\boldsymbol{w}$ and a b satisfying the constraints of Eqs.(4.2) and (4.3). Moreover, the above optimization is easily verified to be the standard SOCP form, since the optimization function is a linear form and the constraints are either linear or the typical second order conic constraints.

Remarks. In practice, many SOCP programs, e.g. Sedumi [20], provide schemes to directly handle the above checking procedure. It thus need not introduce dummy variables as what we have done in the proof.

We now analyze the time complexity of M^4. As indicated in [12], if the SOCP is solved based on interior-point methods, it contains a worst-case complexity of $O(n^3)$. If we denote the range of feasible ρ's as $L = \rho_{\max} - \rho_{\min}$ and the required precision as ε, then the number of iterations for M^4 is $\log(L/\varepsilon)$ in the worst case. Adding the cost of forming the system matrix (constraint matrix) which is $O(Nn^3)$ (N represents the number of training points), the total complexity would be $O(\log(L/\varepsilon)n^3 + Nn^3) \approx O(Nn^3)$ which is relatively large but can still be solved in polynomial time[2].

4.1.2 Connections with Other Models

In this section, we establish connections between M^4 and other models. We show that SVM and MPM are actually special cases of our model. Moreover, FDA can be interpreted and extended according to our local and global views of data.

4.1.2.1 Connection with Minimax Probability Machine

If one expands the constraints of Eq.(4.2) and adds all of them together, one can immediately obtain the following equation:

---

[2]Note that the system matrix needs to be formed only once.

$$w^{\mathrm{T}} \sum_{i=1}^{N_x} x_i + N_x b \geq N_x \rho \sqrt{w^{\mathrm{T}} \Sigma_x w} \;\Rightarrow\; w^{\mathrm{T}} \overline{x} + b \geq \rho \sqrt{w^{\mathrm{T}} \Sigma_x w} \,, \quad (4.6)$$

where $\overline{x}$ denotes the mean of the x training data.

Similarly, from Eq.(4.3) one can obtain:

$$-\left(w^{\mathrm{T}} \sum_{j=1}^{N_y} y_j + N_y b\right) \geq N_y \rho \sqrt{w^{\mathrm{T}} \Sigma_y w}$$

$$\Rightarrow -(w^{\mathrm{T}} \overline{y} + b) \geq \rho \sqrt{w^{\mathrm{T}} \Sigma_y w} \,, \quad (4.7)$$

where $\overline{y}$ denotes the mean of the y training data.

Adding Eqs.(4.6) and (4.7), one can obtain:

$$\max_{\rho, w \neq 0} \quad \rho$$

$$\text{s.t.} \quad w^{\mathrm{T}}(\overline{x} - \overline{y}) \geq \rho\left(\sqrt{w^{\mathrm{T}} \Sigma_x w} + \sqrt{w^{\mathrm{T}} \Sigma_y w}\right). \quad (4.8)$$

The above optimization is exactly the MPM optimization [11]. Note, however, that the above procedure cannot be reversed. This means that MPM is a special case of M^4.

Remarks. In MPM, since the decision is completely determined by the global information, namely, the mean and covariance matrices [11][3], to assure an accurate performance the estimates of mean and covariance matrices need to be reliable. However, it cannot always be the case in real world tasks. On the other hand, M^4 seems to solve this problem in a natural way, because the impact caused by inaccurately estimated mean and covariance matrices can be neutralized by utilizing the local information, namely by satisfying those constraints of Eqs.(4.2) and (4.3) for each local data point. This is also demonstrated in the later experiment.

4.1.2.2 Connection with Support Vector Machine

If one assumes $\Sigma_x = \Sigma_y = \Sigma$, the optimization of M^4 can be changed as:

$$\max_{\rho, w \neq 0, b} \quad \rho,$$

$$\text{s.t.} \quad (w^{\mathrm{T}} x_i + b) \geq \rho \sqrt{w^{\mathrm{T}} \Sigma w} \,,$$

$$-(w^{\mathrm{T}} y_j + b) \geq \rho \sqrt{w^{\mathrm{T}} \Sigma w} \,,$$

where $i = 1, \ldots, N_x$ and $j = 1, \ldots, N_y$.

Observing that the magnitude of w will not influence the optimization, without loss of generality, one can further assume $\rho \sqrt{w^{\mathrm{T}} \Sigma w} = 1$. Therefore the optimization can be changed as:

---

[3]This can be directly observed from Eq.(4.8).

$$\min_{\boldsymbol{w} \neq \boldsymbol{0}, b} \quad \boldsymbol{w}^{\mathrm{T}} \boldsymbol{\Sigma} \boldsymbol{w}, \tag{4.9}$$

$$\text{s.t.} \ \ (\boldsymbol{w}^{\mathrm{T}} \boldsymbol{x}_i + b) \geq 1 \,, \tag{4.10}$$

$$-(\boldsymbol{w}^{\mathrm{T}} \boldsymbol{y}_j + b) \geq 1 \,, \tag{4.11}$$

where $i = 1, \ldots, N_x$ and $j = 1, \ldots, N_y$.

A special case of the above with $\boldsymbol{\Sigma} = \boldsymbol{I}$ is precisely the optimization of SVM, where $\boldsymbol{I}$ is the identity matrix.

Remarks. In the above, two assumptions are implicitly made by SVM: One is the assumption on data "orientation" or data shape, i.e. $\boldsymbol{\Sigma}_x = \boldsymbol{\Sigma}_y = \boldsymbol{\Sigma}$, and the other is the assumption on data "scattering magnitude" or data compactness, i.e. $\boldsymbol{\Sigma} = \boldsymbol{I}$. However, these two assumptions are inappropriate. We demonstrate this in Figs. 4.3 and 4.4. We assume the orientation and the magnitude of each ellipsoid represent the data shape and compactness, respectively, in these figures.

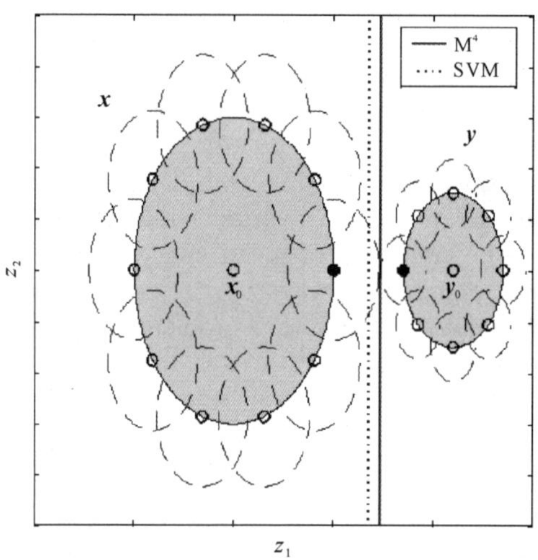

Fig. 4.3. An illustration on that SVM omits the data compactness information

Fig. 4.3 plots two types of data with the same data orientations but different data scattering magnitudes. It is obvious that by ignoring data scattering SVM is improper to locate itself unbiasedly in the middle of the support vectors (filled points), since $\boldsymbol{x}$ is more possible to scatter on the horizontal axis. Instead, M^4 is more reasonable (see the solid line in this figure). Furthermore, Fig. 4.4 plots the case with the same data scattering magnitudes but different data orientations. Similarly, SVM does not capture the orientation information. In comparison, M^4 grasps this information and demonstrates a more

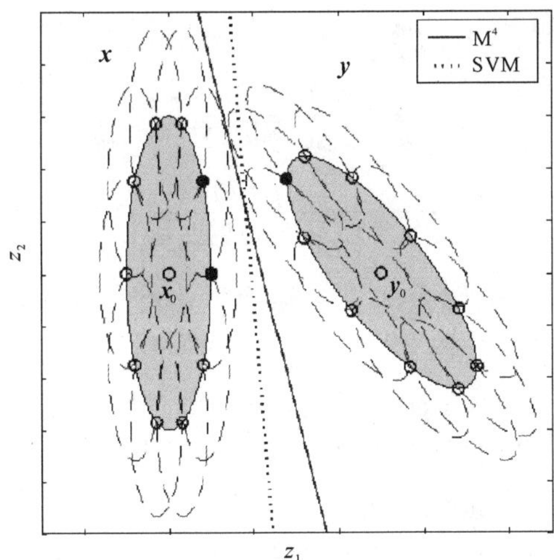

Fig. 4.4. An illustration on that SVM discards the data orientation information

suitable decision plane: M^4 represents the tangent line between two small dashed ellipsoids centered at the support vectors (filled points). Note that SVM and M^4 do not need to achieve the same support vectors. In Fig. 4.4, M^4 contains the above two filled points as support vectors, whereas SVM has all the three filled points as support vectors.

4.1.2.3 Link with Fisher Discriminant Analysis

FDA, an important and popular method, is used widely in constructing decision hyperplanes and reducing the feature dimensionality. In the following discussion, we mainly consider its application as a classifier. FDA involves solving the following optimization problem:

$$\max_{w \neq 0} \frac{|w^{\mathrm{T}}(\overline{x} - \overline{y})|}{\sqrt{w^{\mathrm{T}}\Sigma_x w + w^{\mathrm{T}}\Sigma_y w}} \, .$$

Similar to MPM, FDA also focuses on using the global information rather than considering data both locally and globally. We now show that FDA can be modified to consider data both locally and globally.

If one changes the denominators in Eqs.(4.2) and (4.3) as $\sqrt{w^{\mathrm{T}}\Sigma_x w + w^{\mathrm{T}}\Sigma_y w}$, the optimization can be changed as:

$$\max_{\rho,\, \boldsymbol{w}\neq\boldsymbol{0},b} \rho, \tag{4.12}$$

$$\text{s.t.}\quad \frac{(\boldsymbol{w}^{\mathrm{T}}\boldsymbol{x}_i + b)}{\sqrt{\boldsymbol{w}^{\mathrm{T}}\boldsymbol{\Sigma}_x\boldsymbol{w} + \boldsymbol{w}^{\mathrm{T}}\boldsymbol{\Sigma}_y\boldsymbol{w}}} \geq \rho, \tag{4.13}$$

$$\frac{-(\boldsymbol{w}^{\mathrm{T}}\boldsymbol{y}_j + b)}{\sqrt{\boldsymbol{w}^{\mathrm{T}}\boldsymbol{\Sigma}_x\boldsymbol{w} + \boldsymbol{w}^{\mathrm{T}}\boldsymbol{\Sigma}_y\boldsymbol{w}}} \geq \rho, \tag{4.14}$$

where $i = 1,\ldots,N_x$ and $j = 1,\ldots,N_y$. The above optimization is actually a generalized case of FDA, which considers data locally and globally. This is verified as follows.

If one performs the procedure similar to that of Section 4.1.2.1, the above optimization problem is easily verified to be the following optimization:

$$\max_{\rho,\, \boldsymbol{w}\neq\boldsymbol{0},b} \rho, \tag{4.15}$$

$$\text{s.t.}\quad \boldsymbol{w}^{\mathrm{T}}(\overline{\boldsymbol{x}} - \overline{\boldsymbol{y}}) \geq \rho\sqrt{\boldsymbol{w}^{\mathrm{T}}\boldsymbol{\Sigma}_x\boldsymbol{w} + \boldsymbol{w}^{\mathrm{T}}\boldsymbol{\Sigma}_y\boldsymbol{w}}\,.$$

One can change Eq.(4.15) as: $\rho \leq \dfrac{|\boldsymbol{w}^{\mathrm{T}}(\overline{\boldsymbol{x}}-\overline{\boldsymbol{y}})|}{\sqrt{\boldsymbol{w}^{\mathrm{T}}\boldsymbol{\Sigma}_x\boldsymbol{w}+\boldsymbol{w}^{\mathrm{T}}\boldsymbol{\Sigma}_y\boldsymbol{w}}}$, which is exactly the optimization of the FDA ($\boldsymbol{w}^{\mathrm{T}}(\overline{\boldsymbol{x}} - \overline{\boldsymbol{y}})$ is implicitly implied as a positive value from Eqs.(4.13) and (4.14)).

Remarks. The extended FDA optimization actually focuses on considering the data orientation, while omitting the data scattering magnitude information. Using the analysis similar to that of Section 4.1.2.2, we can know that the extended FDA lacks the consideration on the data scattering magnitude. Its decision hyperplane in the example of Fig. 4.3 coincides with that of SVM. With respect to the data orientation, it actually uses the average of covariances for two types of data. As illustrated in Fig. 4.5, the extended FDA corresponds to the line lying exactly in the middle of the long axes of the $\boldsymbol{x}$ and $\boldsymbol{y}$ data. This shows that the extended FDA considers the data orientation partially yet incompletely.

4.1.3 Nonseparable Case

In this section, we modify the M^4 model to handle the nonseparable case. We need to introduce slack variables in this case. The optimization of M^4 is changed as:

$$\max_{\rho,\, \boldsymbol{w}\neq\boldsymbol{0},b,\boldsymbol{\xi}} \left\{ \rho - C \sum_{k=1}^{N_x+N_y} \xi_k \right\}, \tag{4.16}$$

$$\text{s.t.}\quad (\boldsymbol{w}^{\mathrm{T}}\boldsymbol{x}_i + b) \geq \rho\sqrt{\boldsymbol{w}^{\mathrm{T}}\boldsymbol{\Sigma}_x\boldsymbol{w}} - \xi_i, \tag{4.17}$$

$$-(\boldsymbol{w}^{\mathrm{T}}\boldsymbol{y}_j + b) \geq \rho\sqrt{\boldsymbol{w}^{\mathrm{T}}\boldsymbol{\Sigma}_y\boldsymbol{w}} - \xi_{j+N_x}, \tag{4.18}$$

$$\xi_k \geq 0,$$

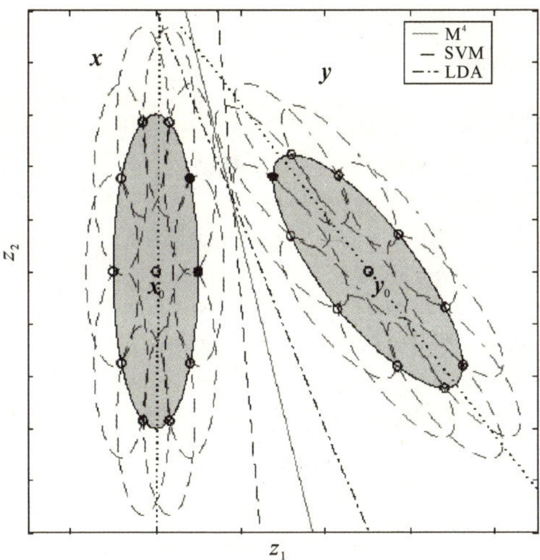

Fig. 4.5. An illustration on that FDA partly yet incompletely considers the data orientation

where $i = 1, \ldots, N_x$, $j = 1, \ldots, N_y$, and $k = 1, \ldots, N_x + N_y$. C is the positive penalty parameter and ξ_k is the slack variable which can be considered as the extent how the training point z_k disobeys the ρ margin ($z_k = x_k$ when $1 \leq k \leq N_x$; $z_k = y_{k-N_y}$ when $N_x + 1 \leq k \leq N_x + N_y$). Thus $\sum_{k=1}^{N_x+N_y} \xi_k$ can be conceptually regarded as the training error or the empirical error. In other words, the above optimization achieves maximizing the minimum margin while minimizing the total training error.

4.1.3.1 Solving Method

As clearly observed, when ρ is fixed, the optimization is equivalent to minimizing $\sum_{k=1}^{N_x+N_y} \xi_k$ under the same constraints. This is once again an SOCP problem and thus can be solved in polynomial time. We can then update ρ according to some rules and repeat the whole process until an optimal ρ is found. This is once again the so-called line search problem. We still adopt Quadratic Interpolation method to solve this problem, which converges superlinearly to the global optimum if suitable starting points are assigned [1]. Since we have introduced this linear search method in Chapter 3, we simply omit it here.

In summary, we iterate the following two steps to solve the modified optimization.

Step 1. Generate a new ρ_n from three previous ρ_1, ρ_2, ρ_3 by using the Quadratic Interpolation method.

Step 2. Fix $\rho = \rho_n$, perform the optimization based on SOCP algorithms. Update ρ_1, ρ_2, ρ_3.

4.1.4 Further Connection with Minimum Error Minimax Probability Machine

In this section, we show how the M^4 can be connected with Minimum Error Minimax Probability Machine [6], which is a worst-case Bayes optimal classifier and a superset of MPM as well.

If one looks into carefully the optimization of nonseparable M^4, a more precise form is the one replacing ξ_k with $\xi_k\sqrt{w^T\Sigma_x w}$ in Eq.(4.17) and $\xi_k\sqrt{w^T\Sigma_y w}$ in Eq.(4.18). However, this optimization may prove to be a difficult problem. Nevertheless, we can start from this precise form and derive the connection of M^4 with MEMPM.

We reformulate the optimization of Eqs.(4.17) and (4.18) as their precise forms as follows:

$$\max_{\rho,w\neq 0,b,\boldsymbol{\xi}} \left\{ \rho - C \sum_{k=1}^{N_x+N_y} \xi_k \right\}, \tag{4.19}$$

$$\text{s.t.} \quad \frac{w^T x_i + b}{\sqrt{w^T\Sigma_x w}} \geq \rho - \xi_i , \tag{4.20}$$

$$-\frac{w^T y_j + b}{\sqrt{w^T\Sigma_y w}} \geq \rho - \xi_{j+N_x} , \tag{4.21}$$

$$\xi_k \geq 0 , \tag{4.22}$$

where $i = 1,\ldots,N_x$, $j = 1,\ldots,N_y$, and $k = 1,\ldots,N_x + N_y$.

Maximizing Eq.(4.20) contains a similar meaning as minimizing $B\sum_{k=1}^{N_x+N_y}\xi_k + 1/\rho^2$ (B is a positive parameter) in a sense that they both attempt to maximize the margin ρ and minimize the error rate. If we consider $\sum_{k=1}^{N_x+N_y}\xi_k$ as the residue and regard $1/\rho^2$ as the regularization term, the optimization can be cast into the framework of solving ill-posed problems. [4]

According to [24, 26], the above optimization pointed as the Tikhonov's Variation Method [22] is equivalent to the optimization below refereed to Ivannov's Quasi-Solution Method [8],in the sense that if one of the methods for a given value of the parameter (say C) produces a solution $\{w,b\}$, then the other method can derive the same solution by adapting its corresponding parameter (say A).

---

[4] A trick can be made by assuming $1/\rho^2$ as a new variable and thus the condition that the regularization is convex can be satisfied.

$$\min_{\rho, \boldsymbol{w} \neq \boldsymbol{0}, b, \boldsymbol{\xi}} \sum_{k=1}^{N_x + N_y} \xi_k, \tag{4.23}$$

$$\text{s.t.} \quad \frac{\boldsymbol{w}^{\mathrm{T}} \boldsymbol{x}_i + b}{\sqrt{\boldsymbol{w}^{\mathrm{T}} \boldsymbol{\Sigma}_x \boldsymbol{w}}} \geq \rho - \xi_i, \tag{4.24}$$

$$-\frac{\boldsymbol{w}^{\mathrm{T}} \boldsymbol{y}_j + b}{\sqrt{\boldsymbol{w}^{\mathrm{T}} \boldsymbol{\Sigma}_y \boldsymbol{w}}} \geq \rho - \xi_{j+N_x}, \tag{4.25}$$

$$\rho \geq A, \xi_k \geq 0, \tag{4.26}$$

where A is a positive constant parameter.

Now if we expand Eq.(4.24) for each i and add them all together, we can obtain:

$$N_x \frac{\boldsymbol{w}^{\mathrm{T}} \overline{\boldsymbol{x}} + b}{\sqrt{\boldsymbol{w}^{\mathrm{T}} \boldsymbol{\Sigma}_x \boldsymbol{w}}} \geq N_x \rho - \sum_{i=1}^{N_x} \xi_i. \tag{4.27}$$

This equation can easily be changed as:

$$\sum_{i=1}^{N_x} \xi_i \geq N_x \rho - N_x \frac{\boldsymbol{w}^{\mathrm{T}} \overline{\boldsymbol{x}} + b}{\sqrt{\boldsymbol{w}^{\mathrm{T}} \boldsymbol{\Sigma}_x \boldsymbol{w}}}. \tag{4.28}$$

Similarly, if we expand Eq.(4.25) for each j and add them all together, we obtain:

$$\sum_{j=1}^{N_y} \xi_{j+N_x} \geq N_y \rho + N_y \frac{\boldsymbol{w}^{\mathrm{T}} \overline{\boldsymbol{y}} + b}{\sqrt{\boldsymbol{w}^{\mathrm{T}} \boldsymbol{\Sigma}_y \boldsymbol{w}}}. \tag{4.29}$$

By adding Eq.(4.28) and Eq.(4.29), we obtain:

$$\sum_{k=1}^{N} \xi_k \geq N\rho - \left(N_x \frac{\boldsymbol{w}^{\mathrm{T}} \overline{\boldsymbol{x}} + b}{\sqrt{\boldsymbol{w}^{\mathrm{T}} \boldsymbol{\Sigma}_x \boldsymbol{w}}} - N_y \frac{\boldsymbol{w}^{\mathrm{T}} \overline{\boldsymbol{y}} + b}{\sqrt{\boldsymbol{w}^{\mathrm{T}} \boldsymbol{\Sigma}_y \boldsymbol{w}}} \right). \tag{4.30}$$

To achieve minimum training error, namely, $\min_{\rho, \boldsymbol{w} \neq \boldsymbol{0}, b, \boldsymbol{\xi}} \sum_{k=1}^{N_x+N_y} \xi_k$, we may consider to minimize its lower bound as specified by the right hand side of Eq.(4.30). Hence in this case ρ should attain its lower bound A, while the second part should be as large as possible, i.e.

$$\max_{\boldsymbol{w} \neq \boldsymbol{0}, b} \left\{ \theta \frac{\boldsymbol{w}^{\mathrm{T}} \overline{\boldsymbol{x}} + b}{\sqrt{\boldsymbol{w}^{\mathrm{T}} \boldsymbol{\Sigma}_x \boldsymbol{w}}} - (1 - \theta) \frac{\boldsymbol{w}^{\mathrm{T}} \overline{\boldsymbol{y}} + b}{\sqrt{\boldsymbol{w}^{\mathrm{T}} \boldsymbol{\Sigma}_y \boldsymbol{w}}} \right\}, \tag{4.31}$$

where θ is defined as N_x/N and thus $1 - \theta$ denotes N_y/N. If one further transforms the above to:

$$\max_{\boldsymbol{w}\neq\boldsymbol{0},b}\ \{\theta t + (1-\theta)s\}, \tag{4.32}$$

$$\text{s.t.}\ \ \frac{\boldsymbol{w}^{\mathrm{T}}\overline{\boldsymbol{x}}+b}{\sqrt{\boldsymbol{w}^{\mathrm{T}}\boldsymbol{\Sigma}_x\boldsymbol{w}}} \geq t\,, \tag{4.33}$$

$$-\frac{\boldsymbol{w}^{\mathrm{T}}\overline{\boldsymbol{y}}+b}{\sqrt{\boldsymbol{w}^{\mathrm{T}}\boldsymbol{\Sigma}_y\boldsymbol{w}}} \geq s\,, \tag{4.34}$$

one can see that the above optimizes a very similar form as the MEMPM model except that Eq.(4.33) changes to [6]

$$\min_{\boldsymbol{w}\neq\boldsymbol{0},b}\{\theta\frac{t^2}{1+t^2} + (1-\theta)\frac{s^2}{1+s^2}\}.$$

In MEMPM, $t^2 s^2/(1+t^2)(1+s^2)$ (denoted as α (β)) represents the worst-case accuracy for the classification of future $\boldsymbol{x}$ ($\boldsymbol{y}$) data. Thus MEMPM maximizes the weighted accuracy on the future data. In M^4, s and t represent the corresponding margin which is defined as the distance from the hyperplane to the class center. Therefore, it represents the weighted maximum margin machine in this sense. Moreover, since the function of $g(u) = u^2/(1+u^2)$ increases monotonically with u, maximizing the above formulae contains a physical meaning similar to the optimization of MEMPM in some sense.

Remarks. Implicit constraints are contained for the optimization of the above derived special case of M^4. Empirically, Eq.(4.27) cannot achieve the equality in the normal case, since Eqs.(4.24) and (4.25) can only achieve equalities for support vectors. Moreover, the slack variables are usually far smaller than ρ. This implies we can consider

$$\frac{\boldsymbol{w}^{\mathrm{T}}\overline{\boldsymbol{x}}+b}{\sqrt{\boldsymbol{w}^{\mathrm{T}}\boldsymbol{\Sigma}_x\boldsymbol{w}}} > \rho = A.$$

Analogously, for $\boldsymbol{y}$, a similar statement can be obtained. The presence of these two constraints is essential, since with the constraints the parameter ρ is involved in the optimization. Moreover, these two constraints also prevent the circumstance that the decision hyperplane is extremely far away from one class center, while being very close to the other class center.

4.2 Bound on the Error Rate

In this section, we provide theoretical results on the bound of the error rate of M^4. We first borrow the leave-one-out theorem from [13] and [25].

Lemma 4.2. *The leave-one-out estimator is almost unbiased.*

We then present the generation bound of M^4 as the following theorem:

Theorem 4.3. *If (1) the training set containing N samples is separated by the decision hyperplane derived by M^4 and (2) the mean and covariance matrices are reliably estimated, then the expectation of the probability of the test error is bounded by the expectation of the minimum of two values: the ratio*

$$m/N \text{ and } \theta \frac{1}{1+d_x^2} + (1-\theta)\frac{1}{1+d_y^2},$$

where m is the number of support vectors, d_x and d_y are the corresponding Mahalanobis distances from the class centers $\overline{x}$ and $\overline{y}$ to the decision hyperplane, and θ is prior probability of the x data. Namely,

$$E[P_{\mathrm{error}}] \leq E\left\{\min\left[\frac{m}{N}, \theta\frac{1}{1+d_x^2} + (1-\theta)\frac{1}{1+d_y^2}\right]\right\} . \qquad (4.35)$$

Proof. According to Lemma 4.2, to prove $E[P_{\mathrm{error}}] \leq E[\frac{m}{N}]$, we only need to show that the number of errors by the leave-one-out method does not exceed the number of support vectors. Actually, this is the case. If we leave a non-support vector out and then we perform training on the remaining data, the decision hyperplane will not change, since the decision hyperplane is just decided by support vectors and the covariance matrices (statistically, one point will not influence the covariance of data). Therefore, this non-support vector will be recognized correctly. Thus the leave-one-out method classifies correctly all the samples that are not support vectors, i.e. the number of the leave-one-out errors does not exceed the number of the support vectors.

We next prove $E[P_{\mathrm{error}}] \leq E\left\{\min\left[\frac{m}{N}, \theta\frac{1}{1+d_x^2} + (1-\theta)\frac{1}{1+d_y^2}\right]\right\}$. According to [11, 6, 14], if the means and covariances are reliably estimated, $d_x^2/(1+d_x^2)$ and $d_y^2/(1+d_y^2)$ represent the worst-case rates in recognizing correctly the x data and y data respectively. Therefore,

$$\theta\frac{1}{1+d_x^2} + (1-\theta)\frac{1}{1+d_y^2}$$

represents the expected maximum error rate, i.e.

$$E[P_{\mathrm{error}}] \leq E\left\{\min\left[\frac{m}{N}, \theta\frac{1}{1+d_x^2} + (1-\theta)\frac{1}{1+d_y^2}\right]\right\} .$$

Remarks. Note that the above two items actually represent two meanings of the M^4 model, i.e. minimizing the leave-one-out error presents the contribution by considering the local information from data; on the other hand, the second item describes the effect by considering the global information from data. Moreover, if we further examine the second item, d_x (d_y) is actually determined by two parts: the Mahalanobis distance from the support vectors to the corresponding class center x (y) and the margin ρ. This can be observed in Fig. 4.2. Intuitively, the larger the margin ρ is, the larger d_x and d_y are, which leads to a smaller expected test error in the future. This motivates the margin maximization in the large margin machines.

4.3 Reduction

The variables in previous sections are $[w, b, \xi_1, \ldots, \xi_{N_x}, \ldots, \xi_{N_x+N_y}]$, whose dimension is $n + 1 + N_x + N_y$. The number of the second order conic constraints is easily verified to be $N_x + N_y$. This size of the generated constraint matrix will be a big number and may thus encounter problems in solving large scale classification tasks. Therefore, we should reduce both the number of constraints and the number of variables.

Since this problem is caused by the number of the data points, we consider removing some redundant points to reduce both the space and time complexity. The reduction rule is introduced as follows.

Reduction Rule: Set a threshold $\nu \in [0, 1)$. In each class, calculate the Manhalanobis distance d_i of each point to its corresponding class center. if $d_i^2/(1 + d_i^2)$ denoted as ν_i is greater than ν, namely, $\nu_i \geq \nu$, keep this point; otherwise, remove this point.

The intuition under this rule is that, in general the more discriminant information the point contains, the further it is from its center (unless it is a noise point). The inner justification under this rule is from [11]: $d^2/(1+d^2)$ is the worst-case classification accuracy for future data, where d is the minimax Manhalanobis distance from the class center to the decision hyperplane. Thus removing those points with small ν's, namely, $d_i^2/(1 + d_i^2)$ will not affect the worst-case classification accuracy and will not greatly reduce the overall performance.

Nevertheless, to cancel the negative impact caused by removing those points, we add the following global constraint:

$$w^{\mathrm{T}}(\overline{x} - \overline{y}) \geq \rho(\sqrt{w^{\mathrm{T}}\Sigma_x w} + \sqrt{w^{\mathrm{T}}\Sigma_y w}) \, . \tag{4.36}$$

Integrating the above, we formulate the modified model as follows:

$$\max_{\rho, w \neq 0, b, \xi} \left\{ \rho - C \left(\sum_{k=1}^{r_x+r_y} \xi_k + (N_x + N_y - r_x - r_y)\xi_m \right) \right\}$$

$$\text{s.t.} \ \ (w^{\mathrm{T}}x_i + b) \geq \rho(\sqrt{w^{\mathrm{T}}\Sigma_x w}) - \xi_i, \ i = 1, \ldots, r_x \, ,$$

$$-(w^{\mathrm{T}}y_j + b) \geq \rho(\sqrt{w^{\mathrm{T}}\Sigma_y w}) - \xi_{j+r_x}, \ j = 1, \ldots, r_y \, ,$$

$$w^{\mathrm{T}}(\overline{x} - \overline{y}) \geq \rho(\sqrt{w^{\mathrm{T}}\Sigma_x w} + \sqrt{w^{\mathrm{T}}\Sigma_y w}) - \xi_m \, ,$$

$$\xi_m \geq 0, \ \ \xi_k \geq 0, \ k = 1, \ldots, r_x + r_y \, ,$$

where, ξ_m is the slack variable for the global constraint Eq.(4.36), ξ_k are modified slack variables for the remaining data points, r_x is the number of the remaining points for x, and r_y is the number of the remaining points for y.

Remarks. An interesting observation from the above is that when we set the reduction threshold ν to a larger value, or simply to the maximum value 1, the M^4 optimization degrades to the standard MPM optimization. This would imply that the above modified M^4 model contains a worst-case performance of MPM, if the incorporated local information is useful.

4.4 Kernelization

One may note that in the above, the classifier derived from M^4 is provided in a linear configuration. In order to handle nonlinear classification problems, in this section, we seek to use the kernelization trick [18] to map the n-dimensional data points into a high-dimensional feature space $\mathbb{R}^f$, where a linear classifier corresponds to a nonlinear hyperplane in the original space.

The kernel mapping can be formulated as: $x_i \rightarrow \varphi(x_i)$, $y_j \rightarrow \varphi(y_j)$, where $i = 1, \ldots, N_x$, $j = 1, \ldots, N_y$, and $\varphi : \mathbb{R}^n \rightarrow \mathbb{R}^f$ is a mapping function. The corresponding linear classifier in $\mathbb{R}^f$ is $\gamma^T \varphi(z) = b$, where $\gamma, \varphi(z) \in \mathbb{R}^f$, and $b \in \mathbb{R}$.

The optimization of M^4 in the feature space can be written as:

$$\max_{\rho, \gamma \neq \mathbf{0}, b} \rho \, , \tag{4.37}$$

$$\text{s.t.} \quad \frac{(\gamma^T \varphi(x_i) + b)}{\sqrt{\gamma^T \Sigma_{\varphi(x)} \gamma}} \geq \rho, \quad i = 1, 2, \ldots, N_x \, , \tag{4.38}$$

$$\frac{-(\gamma^T \varphi(y_j) + b)}{\sqrt{\gamma^T \Sigma_{\varphi(y)} \gamma}} \geq \rho, \quad j = 1, 2, \ldots, N_y \, . \tag{4.39}$$

However, to make the kernel work we need to represent the optimization and the final decision hyperplane in a kernel form, $K(z_1, z_2) = \varphi(z_1)^T \varphi(z_2)$, namely, an inner product form of the mapping data points.

4.4.1 Foundation of Kernelization for M^4

In the following, we demonstrate that the kernelization trick indeed works in M^4, provided suitable estimates of means and covariance matrices are applied therein.

Corollary 4.4. *If the estimates of means and covariance matrices are given in M^4 as the following estimates:*

$$\overline{\varphi(\boldsymbol{x})} = \sum_{i=1}^{N_{\boldsymbol{x}}} \lambda_i \varphi(\boldsymbol{x}_i), \quad \overline{\varphi(\boldsymbol{y})} = \sum_{j=1}^{N_{\boldsymbol{y}}} \omega_j \varphi(\boldsymbol{y}_j) \,,$$

$$\boldsymbol{\Sigma}_{\varphi}(\boldsymbol{x}) = \rho_{\boldsymbol{x}} \boldsymbol{I}_n + \sum_{i=1}^{N_{\boldsymbol{x}}} \Lambda_i \left(\varphi(\boldsymbol{x}_i) - \overline{\varphi(\boldsymbol{x})} \right) \left(\varphi(\boldsymbol{x}_i) - \overline{\varphi(\boldsymbol{x})} \right)^{\mathrm{T}} \,,$$

$$\boldsymbol{\Sigma}_{\varphi}(\boldsymbol{y}) = \rho_{\boldsymbol{y}} \boldsymbol{I}_n + \sum_{j=1}^{N_{\boldsymbol{y}}} \Omega_j \left(\varphi(\boldsymbol{y}_j) - \overline{\varphi(\boldsymbol{y})} \right) \left(\varphi(\boldsymbol{y}_j) - \overline{\varphi(\boldsymbol{y})} \right)^{\mathrm{T}} \,,$$

where $\boldsymbol{I}_n$ is the identity matrix of dimension n, then the optimal $\boldsymbol{\gamma}$ in Eqs.(4.37)–(4.39) lies in the space spanned by the training points.

Proof. We write $\boldsymbol{\gamma} = \boldsymbol{\gamma}_p + \boldsymbol{\gamma}_d$, where $\boldsymbol{\gamma}_p$ is the projection of $\boldsymbol{\gamma}$ in the vector space spanned by all the training data points and $\boldsymbol{\gamma}_d$ is the orthogonal component to this span space. By using $\boldsymbol{\gamma}_d^{\mathrm{T}} \varphi(\boldsymbol{x}_i) = 0$ and $\boldsymbol{\gamma}_d^{\mathrm{T}} \varphi(\boldsymbol{y}_j) = 0$, one can easily verify that the optimization Eqs.(4.37)-(4.39) change to:

$$\max_{\rho, \{\boldsymbol{\gamma}_p, \boldsymbol{\gamma}_d\} \neq \boldsymbol{0}, b} \rho,$$

$$\text{s.t.} \quad \frac{-(\boldsymbol{\gamma}_p^{\mathrm{T}} \varphi(\boldsymbol{x}_i) + b)}{\sqrt{\boldsymbol{\gamma}_p^{\mathrm{T}} \sum_{i=1}^{N_{\boldsymbol{x}}} \Lambda_i (\varphi(\boldsymbol{x}_j) - \overline{\varphi(\boldsymbol{x})})(\varphi(\boldsymbol{x}_i) - \overline{\varphi(\boldsymbol{x})})^{\mathrm{T}} \boldsymbol{\gamma}_p + \rho_{\boldsymbol{x}} (\boldsymbol{\gamma}_p^{\mathrm{T}} \boldsymbol{\gamma}_p + \boldsymbol{\gamma}_d^{\mathrm{T}} \boldsymbol{\gamma}_d)}} \geq \rho,$$

$$\frac{-(\boldsymbol{\gamma}_p^{\mathrm{T}} \varphi(\boldsymbol{y}_j) + b)}{\sqrt{\boldsymbol{\gamma}_p^{\mathrm{T}} \sum_{j=1}^{N_{\boldsymbol{y}}} \Omega_j (\varphi(\boldsymbol{y}_j) - \overline{\varphi(\boldsymbol{y})})(\varphi(\boldsymbol{y}_j) - \overline{\varphi(\boldsymbol{y})})^{\mathrm{T}} \boldsymbol{\gamma}_p + \rho_{\boldsymbol{y}} (\boldsymbol{\gamma}_p^{\mathrm{T}} \boldsymbol{\gamma}_p + \boldsymbol{\gamma}_d^{\mathrm{T}} \boldsymbol{\gamma}_d)}} \geq \rho,$$

where $i = 1, \ldots, N_{\boldsymbol{x}}$, $j = 1, \ldots, N_{\boldsymbol{y}}$. Since we intend to maximize the margin ρ, the denominators in the above two constraints need to be as small as possible. This would lead to $\boldsymbol{\gamma}_d = 0$. In other words, the optimal $\boldsymbol{\gamma}$ lies in the vector space spanned by all the training data points. Note that the above discussion is assumed in the feature space.

According to Corollary 4.4, if we use the plug-in estimates to approximate the means and covariance matrices, we can write $\boldsymbol{\gamma}$ as a linear combination form of training data points:

$$\boldsymbol{\gamma} = \sum_{i=1}^{N_{\boldsymbol{x}}} \mu_i \varphi(\boldsymbol{x}_i) + \sum_{j=1}^{N_{\boldsymbol{y}}} \upsilon_j \varphi(\boldsymbol{y}_j) \,, \tag{4.40}$$

where the coefficients $\mu_i, \upsilon_j \in \mathbb{R}, i = 1, \ldots, N_{\boldsymbol{x}}, j = 1, \ldots, N_{\boldsymbol{y}}$.

4.4.2 Kernelization Result

We present the kernelization result as the following theorem.

Theorem 4.5. [Kernelization Theorem of M^4] *The optimal decision hyperplane for M^4 involves solving the following optimization problem:*

$$\max_{\rho,\boldsymbol{\eta}\neq\mathbf{0},b} \rho,$$

$$s.t. \quad \frac{(\boldsymbol{\eta}^{\mathrm{T}}\boldsymbol{K}_i + b)}{\sqrt{\frac{1}{N_x}\boldsymbol{\eta}^{\mathrm{T}}\tilde{\boldsymbol{K}}_x^{\mathrm{T}}\tilde{\boldsymbol{K}}_x\boldsymbol{\eta}}} \geq \rho, \quad i = 1,2,\ldots,N_x\,,$$

$$\frac{-(\boldsymbol{\eta}^{\mathrm{T}}\boldsymbol{K}_{j+N_x} + b)}{\sqrt{\frac{1}{N_y}\boldsymbol{\eta}^{\mathrm{T}}\tilde{\boldsymbol{K}}_y^{\mathrm{T}}\tilde{\boldsymbol{K}}_y\boldsymbol{\eta}}} \geq \rho, \quad j = 1,2,\ldots,N_y\,.$$

Proof. The theorem can easily be proved by simply substituting the plug-in estimations of means and covariances matrices and Eq.(4.40) into Eqs.(4.38)–(4.39).

The optimal decision hyperplane can be represented as a linear form in the kernel space:

$$f(\boldsymbol{z}) = \sum_{i=1}^{N_x}\boldsymbol{\eta}_{*i}\boldsymbol{K}(\boldsymbol{z},\boldsymbol{x}_i) + \sum_{i=1}^{N_y}\boldsymbol{\eta}_{*N_x+i}\boldsymbol{K}(\boldsymbol{z},\boldsymbol{y}_i) + b_*\,,$$

where $\boldsymbol{\eta}_*$ and b_* are the optimal parameters obtained by the optimization procedure. The notations in the above are defined similar to Chapter 3. However, for an easy reference, we also summarize them in Table 4.1.

Table 4.1. Notations used in Kernelization

Notation	
$\boldsymbol{z} \in \mathbb{R}^{N_x+N_y}$	$\boldsymbol{z}_i := \boldsymbol{x}_i \quad i = 1,2,\ldots,N_x$ $\boldsymbol{z}_i := \boldsymbol{y}_{i-N_x} \quad i = N_x+1, N_x+2, \ldots, N_x+N_y$
$\boldsymbol{\eta} \in \mathbb{R}^{N_x+N_y}$	$\boldsymbol{\eta} := [\mu_1,\ldots,\mu_{N_x},\upsilon_1,\ldots,\upsilon_{N_y}]^{\mathrm{T}}$
$\boldsymbol{K}$ is Gram matrix	$\boldsymbol{K}_{i,j} := \varphi(\boldsymbol{z}_i)^{\mathrm{T}}\varphi(\boldsymbol{z}_j)$
	$\boldsymbol{K}_x := \begin{pmatrix} \boldsymbol{K}_{1,1} & \boldsymbol{K}_{1,2} & \cdots & \boldsymbol{K}_{1,N_x+N_y} \\ \boldsymbol{K}_{2,1} & \boldsymbol{K}_{2,2} & \cdots & \boldsymbol{K}_{2,N_x+N_y} \\ \vdots & \vdots & \vdots & \vdots \\ \boldsymbol{K}_{N_x,1} & \boldsymbol{K}_{N_x,2} & \cdots & \boldsymbol{K}_{N_x,N_x+N_y} \end{pmatrix}$
	$\boldsymbol{K}_y := \begin{pmatrix} \boldsymbol{K}_{N_x+1,1} & \boldsymbol{K}_{N_x+1,2} & \cdots & \boldsymbol{K}_{N_x+1,N_x+N_y} \\ \boldsymbol{K}_{N_x+2,1} & \boldsymbol{K}_{N_x+2,2} & \cdots & \boldsymbol{K}_{N_x+2,N_x+N_y} \\ \vdots & \vdots & \vdots & \vdots \\ \boldsymbol{K}_{N_x+N_y,1} & \boldsymbol{K}_{N_x+N_y,2} & \cdots & \boldsymbol{K}_{N_x+N_y,N_x+N_y} \end{pmatrix}$
$\tilde{\boldsymbol{k}}_x, \tilde{\boldsymbol{k}}_y \in \mathbb{R}^{N_x+N_y}$	$[\tilde{\boldsymbol{k}}_x]_i := \frac{1}{N_x}\sum_{j=1}^{N_x}\boldsymbol{K}(\boldsymbol{x}_j,\boldsymbol{z}_i)\,.$ $[\tilde{\boldsymbol{k}}_y]_i := \frac{1}{N_y}\sum_{j=1}^{N_y}\boldsymbol{K}(\boldsymbol{y}_j,\boldsymbol{z}_i)$
$\mathbf{1}_{N_x} \in \mathbb{R}^{N_x}$ $\mathbf{1}_{N_y} \in \mathbb{R}^{N_y}$	$\mathbf{1}_i := 1, \quad i = 1,2,\ldots N_x$ $\mathbf{1}_i := 1, \quad i = 1,2,\ldots N_y$
$\tilde{\boldsymbol{K}} :=$	$\begin{pmatrix} \tilde{\boldsymbol{K}}_x \\ \tilde{\boldsymbol{K}}_y \end{pmatrix} := \begin{pmatrix} \boldsymbol{K}_x - \mathbf{1}_{N_x}\tilde{\boldsymbol{k}}_x^{\mathrm{T}} \\ \boldsymbol{K}_y - \mathbf{1}_{N_y}\tilde{\boldsymbol{k}}_y^{\mathrm{T}} \end{pmatrix}$

4.5 Experiments

In this section, we present the evaluation results of M^4 in comparison with SVM and MPM on both synthetic toy datasets and real world benchmark datasets. SOCP problems are solved based on the general software named Sedumi [20, 21]. The covariance matrices are given by the plug-in estimates.

4.5.1 Evaluations on Three Synthetic Toy Datasets

We demonstrate the advantages of our approach in comparison with SVM and MPM in the following synthetic toy datasets first.

As illustrated in Fig. 4.6, we generate two types of data with the same data orientations but different data magnitudes in Fig. 4.6 (a), while we generate two types of data with the same data magnitudes but different data orientations in Fig. 4.6 (b). In (a), the x data are randomly sampled from the Gaussian distribution with the mean as $[-3.5, \ 0]^{\mathrm{T}}$ and the covariance as $[3, \ 0; 0, \ 4.5]$, while the y data are randomly sampled from another Gaussian distribution with the mean and the covariance as $[3.5, \ 0]^{\mathrm{T}}$ and $[1, \ 0; 0, \ 1.5]$ respectively. In (b), the x data are randomly sampled from the Gaussian distribution with the mean as $[-4, \ 0]^{\mathrm{T}}$ and the covariance as $[1, \ 0; 0, \ 5]$, while the y data are randomly sampled from another distribution with the mean and the covariance as $[4, \ 0]^{\mathrm{T}}$ and $[1, \ 0; 0, \ 5]$ respectively. Moreover, to generate different data orientation, in Fig. 4.6 the y data are rotated anti-clockwise at the angle of $-\frac{7}{8}\pi$. In both (a) and (b), training (test) data consisting of 120 (250) data points for each class are presented as o's (+'s) and ×'s (□'s) for x and y respectively. Observed from Fig. 4.6, M^4 demonstrates its advantages over SVM. More specifically, in Fig. 4.6 (a), SVM discards the information of the data magnitudes, whose decision hyperplane lies basically in the middle of boundary points of two types of data, while M^4 successfully utilizes this information, i.e. its decision hyperplane lies closer to the compact class (y data), which is more reasonable. Similarly, in Fig. 4.6 (b), M^4 takes advantage of the information of the data orientation, while SVM simply overlooks this information, which results in a lot of points incorrectly classified.

In comparison of MPM with M^4, since in the above two datasets the global information, i.e. the mean and the covariance can be reliably estimated from data, they achieve similar performance. To see the difference between M^4 and MPM, we generate another dataset as illustrated in Fig. 4.7, where we intentionally generate a very small number of training data, i.e. only 20 training points. Similarly, the data are generated under two Gaussian distributions: the x data are randomly sampled from the Gaussian distribution with the mean as $[-3, \ 0]^{\mathrm{T}}$ and the covariance as $[0.5, \ 0; 0, \ 8]$, while the y data are randomly sampled from another distribution with the mean and the covariance as $[4, \ 0]^{\mathrm{T}}$ and $[6, \ 0; 0, \ 1]$ respectively. Training data and test data are represented using similar symbols to Fig. 4.6. From Fig. 4.7, once again M^4 achieves ideal decision boundary which considers data both locally and

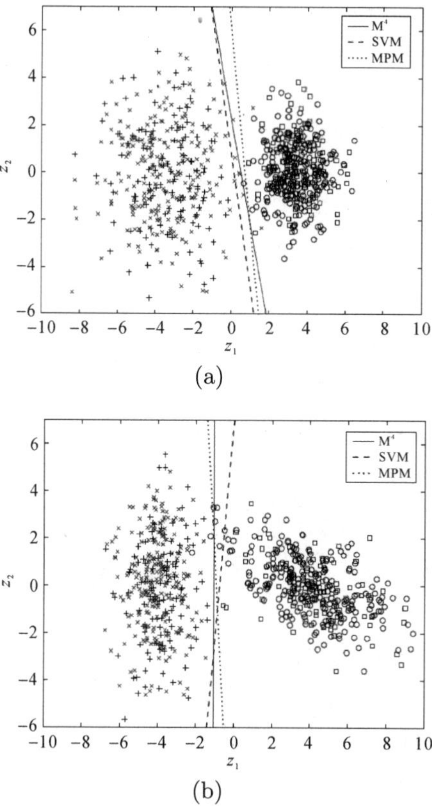

Fig. 4.6. The first two synthetic toy examples to illustrate M^4. Training (test) data consisting of 120 (250) data points for each class are presented as o's (+'s) and ×'s ($\square$'s) for x and y respectively. Subfigure (a) demonstrates that SVM omits the data compactness information and (b) demonstrates that SVM discards the data orientation information, while M^4 achieves ideal decision boundary which considers data both locally and globally

globally; whereas SVM obtains local boundary just in the middle of the support vectors, which discards the global information, namely the statistical "trend" of data occurrence. For MPM, its decision hyperplane is exclusively dependent on the mean and covariance matrices. Thus we can see that this hyperplane coincides with the data shape, i.e. the long axis of training data of x is nearly in the same direction as the MPM decision hyperplane. However, the estimated mean and covariance are inaccurate due to the small number of data points. This results in a relatively lower test accuracy as illustrated in Fig. 4.7(b). In comparison, M^4 incorporates the information of the local points to neutralize the effect caused by inaccurate estimations. The test ac-

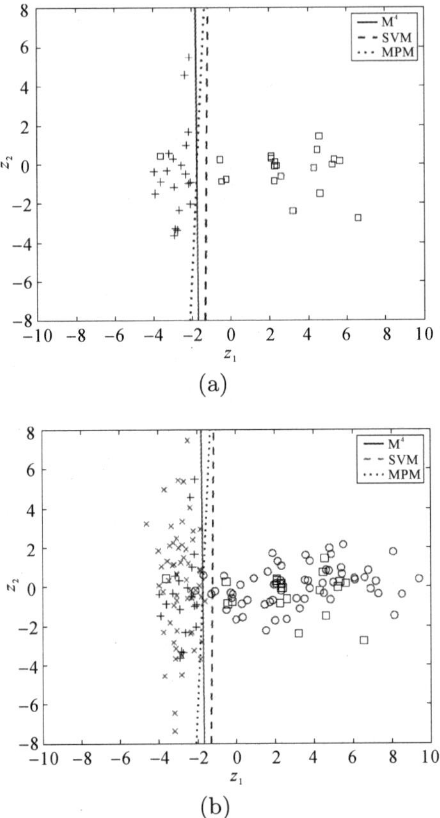

Fig. 4.7. The third synthetic toy example to illustrate M^4. Training (test) data, consisting of 20 (60) data points for each class are presented as o's (+'s) and ×'s ($\square$'s) for x and y respectively. Subfigure (a) demonstrates the decision boundaries derived from training data, while (b) illustrates the performance of these hyerplanes on the test set. The M^4 achieves ideal decision boundary which considers data both locally and globally

curacies for the above three toy datasets listed in Table 4.2 also demonstrate the advantages of M^4.

4.5.2 Evaluations on Benchmark Datasets

We perform evaluations on seven standard datasets. Data for Twonorm problem are synthetically generated according to [3]. The remaining six datasets are real world data obtained from the UCI machine learning repository [2]. We compared M^4 with SVM and MPM engaging with both the linear and Gaussian kernels. The parameter C for both M^4 and SVM was tuned via

Table 4.2. Comparisons of classification accuracies between M^4, SVM, and MPM on the toy datasets

Dataset	Classification accuracy (%)		
	M^4	SVM	MPM
I(%)	98.8	96.8	98.8
II(%)	98.8	97.2	98.8
III(%)	98.3	97.5	95.8

cross validations [9], so was the width parameter in the Gaussian kernel for all three models. The final performance results were obtained via the 10-fold cross validation. Table 4.3 summarizes the evaluation results.

Table 4.3. Comparisons of classification accuracies among M^4, SVM, and MPM

Dataset	Classification accuracy of linear kernel(%)			Classification accuracy of Gaussian kernel(%)		
	M^4	SVM	MPM	M^4	SVM	MPM
Twonorm	96.5 ± 0.6	95.1 ± 0.7	$\mathbf{97.6 \pm 0.5}$	96.5 ± 0.7	96.1 ± 0.4	$\mathbf{97.6 \pm 0.5}$
Breast	$\mathbf{97.5 \pm 0.7}$	96.6 ± 0.5	96.9 ± 0.8	$\mathbf{97.5 \pm 0.6}$	96.7 ± 0.4	96.9 ± 0.8
Ionosphere	$\mathbf{87.7 \pm 0.8}$	86.9 ± 0.6	84.8 ± 0.8	$\mathbf{94.5 \pm 0.4}$	94.2 ± 0.3	92.3 ± 0.6
Pima	77.7 ± 0.9	$\mathbf{77.9 \pm 0.7}$	76.1 ± 1.2	77.6 ± 0.8	$\mathbf{78.0 \pm 0.5}$	76.2 ± 1.2
Sonar	$\mathbf{77.6 \pm 1.2}$	76.2 ± 1.1	75.5 ± 1.1	84.9 ± 1.2	86.5 ± 1.1	$\mathbf{87.3 \pm 0.8}$
Vote	$\mathbf{96.1 \pm 0.5}$	95.1 ± 0.4	94.8 ± 0.4	$\mathbf{96.2 \pm 0.5}$	95.9 ± 0.6	94.6 ± 0.4
Heart-disease	$\mathbf{86.6 \pm 0.8}$	84.1 ± 0.7	83.2 ± 0.8	$\mathbf{86.2 \pm 0.8}$	83.8 ± 0.5	83.1 ± 1.0

From the results we observe that M^4 achieves the best overall performance. In comparison with SVM and MPM, M^4 wins five cases in the linear kernel and four in the Gaussian kernel. The evaluations on these standard bench-mark datasets demonstrate that it is worth considering data both locally and globally, which is emphasized in M^4. Inspecting the differences between M^4 and SVM, the kernelized M^4 appears marginally better than the kernelized SVM, while the linear M^4 demonstrates a distinctive advantage over the linear SVM. This phenomenon may be explained on two hands. On one hand, this can be explained from the fact that the data points are very sparse in the kernelized space or feature space (compared with the huge dimensionality in the Gaussian kernel). Thus the plug-in estimates of the covariance matrices may not accurately represent the data information in this case. On the other hand, it is well-known that the kernelization will not keep the structure information in the feature space. One direct consequence is that maximizing the margin in the feature space does not necessarily maximize the margin in the original space [23]. Therefore, without building some connections between the original space and the feature space, utilizing the structure information, e.g. covariance matrices in the feature space seems not to do much help in this sense. Inspecting these two points, one interesting topic in the future is to consider forcing constraints on the mapping function so as to maintain the data topology in the kernelization process.

In the above, we do not perform the reduction on these datasets. To illustrate how the reduction algorithm works for decreasing the computation time while maintaining the test accuracy, we implement it on the Heart-disease dataset. We perform the reduction in training sets and then keep test sets unchanged. We repeat this process for different thresholds ν. We then plot the curve of the cross validation accuracy against the threshold ν. Moreover, we also plot the curve of the computation time against the threshold. This can be seen in Fig. 4.8. From this figure, we can see that both that the computation time and the test accuracy change insensitively against ν when ν is set to some small values, e.g. $\nu \leq 0.7$. If looking into the Heart-disease dataset, we find that most data points are far away from their corresponding class center in terms of the Manhalanobis distance. Thus setting small values to ν does not actually reduce many data points. This generates both a relatively flat changing curve in the test accuracy and the computation time in this range. As ν is changing larger, the computation time decreases fast as more and more data points are removed, while the test accuracy goes down slowly. When the threshold is set to 1, the M^4 degrades to the MPM model, yielding the test accuracy of M^4 achieves the same value of MPM. This demonstrates how the proposed reduction algorithms can decrease the computation time while maintaining good performance. When used in practice, the threshold can be set according to the required response time.

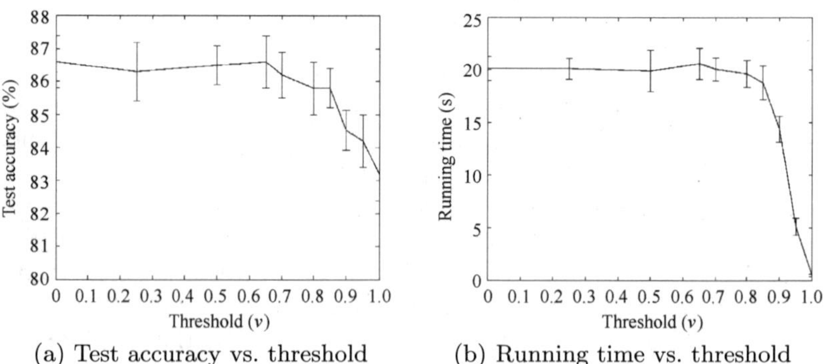

(a) Test accuracy vs. threshold   (b) Running time vs. threshold

Fig. 4.8. Reduction on the Heart-disease dataset

4.6 Discussions and Future Work

We will discuss several important issues in this section. First, although M^4 can be solved in polynomial time, the large computation time is still one of its biggest limitations. This may cause problems especially in its kernelization version. Note that the proposed reduction algorithm in this chapter does not completely solve this problem, since removing points will inevitably lose information. In this sense, it is crucial to develop some special algorithms for M^4. Due to the sparsity of M^4 (it also contains support vectors), it is therefore very interesting to investigate whether decomposable methods or an analogy to the Sequential Minimal Optimization [16] designed for SVM can also be applied in training M^4. We believe that there is much to obtain from such explorations. Certainly, this is a highly worthy research direction in the future.

Second, although we have derived an error bound for M^4, digging out the direct connection or performing empirical comparison of this bound with those of its special cases is still interesting, namely, SVM and MPM maintains an interesting problem. Especially, it is an open problem whether there exists a unified form of the bounds for M^4, SVM, and MPM. This interesting subject deserves future deep explorations.

Third, since in this chapter we mainly discuss M^4 for two-category classifications, how to extend its application to multi-way classifications is also an important topic in the future.

4.7 Summary

Local learning approaches, e.g. large margin machines have demonstrated their advantages in machine learning and pattern recognition. However, they derive the decision boundary only in a local way. For example, the most popular large margin classifier, Support Vector Machine obtains the decision hyperplane by focusing on considering some critical local points called support vectors, while discarding all other points; on the other hand, global learning models (e.g. Minimax Probability Machine) obtain the classifier only based on global information, i.e. the mean and covariance information in MPM, while ignoring all individual local points. Differently, our proposed model is constructed based on both domestic and global view of data. This new model is theoretically important in the sense that SVM and MPM can both be considered as its special cases. Furthermore, the optimization of M^4 can be cast as a sequential Conic Programming problem which can be solved in polynomial time.

We have provided a clear geometrical interpretation, and established detailed connections among our model and other models such as Support Vector Machine, Minimax Probability Machine, Fisher Discriminant Analysis, and Minimum Error Minimax Probability Machine. We have also shown to exploit

Mercer kernels to extend our model to build up nonlinear decision boundaries. In addition, we have also proposed a reduction method to decrease the computation time. Experimental results on both synthetic datasets and real world benchmark datasets have demonstrated the advantages of M^4 over Support Vector Machine and Minimax Probability Machine.

References

1. Bertsekas DP (1999) Nonlinear Programming. Belmont, MA: Athena Scientific 2nd edition
2. Blake CL, Merz CJ (1998) Repository of machine learning databases, University of California, Irvine, http://www.ics.uci.edu/~mlearn/MLRepository.html
3. Breiman L (1997) Arcing classifiers. Technical Report 460, Statistics Department, University of California
4. Fukunaga K(1990). Introduction to Statistical Pattern Recognition. San Diego, CA: Academic Press, 2nd edition
5. Huang K, Yang H, King I, Lyu MR (2004) Learning large margin classifiers locally and globally. In the 21st International Conference on Machine Learning (ICML-2004)
6. Huang K, Yang H, King I, Lyu MR, Chan L (2004) The minimum error minimax probability machine. Journal of Machine Learning Research 5:1253–1286
7. Huang K, Yang H, King I, Lyu MR, Chan L (2007). Maxi-Min Margin Machine: Learning large margin classifiers globally and locally. To appear in IEEE Trans. Neural Networks
8. Ivannov VV (1962) On linear problems which are not well-posed. Soviet Math. Docl. 3(4):981–983
9. Kohavi R (1995). A study of cross validation and bootstrap for accuracy estimation and model selection. In Proceedings of the Fourtheenth International Joint Conference on Artificial Intelligence (IJCAI-1995). San Francisco, CA:Morgan Kaufmann 338–345
10. Kruk S, Wolkowicz H (2000) General nonlinear programming. In H. Wolkowicz, R. Saigal, and L. Vandenberghe, editors, Handbook of Semidefinite Programming: Theory, Algorithms, and Applications. Boston, MA: Kluwer Academic Publishers 563–575
11. Lanckriet GRG, Ghaoui LE, Bhattacharyya C, Jordan MI (2002) A robust minimax approach to classification. Journal of Machine Learning Research 3:555–582
12. Lobo M, Vandenberghe L, Boyd S, Lebret H (1998) Applications of second order cone programming. Linear Algebra and its Applications 284:193–228
13. Luntz A, Brailovsky V(1969) On estimation of characters obtained in statistical procedure of recognition (in Russian). Technicheskaya Kibernetica 3(6)
14. Marshall AW, Olkin I (1960) Multivariate Chebyshev inequalities. Annals of Mathematical Statistics 31(4):1001–1014
15. Nesterov Y, Nemirovsky A (1994) Interior point polynomial methods in convex programming: Theory and applications. Philadelphia, PA: SIAM
16. Platt J(1998) Sequential minimal optimization: A fast algorithm for training support vector machines. Technical Report MSR-TR-98-14

17. Pruessner A(2003). Conic programming in GAMS. In Optimization Software—The State of the Art. INFORMS Atlanta, http://www.gamsworld.org/cone/links.htm

18. Schölkopf, Smola A(2002) Learning with Kernels. Cambridge, MA: The MIT Press

19. Smola AJ , Bartlett PL , Scholkopf B, Schuurmans D(2000) Advances in Large Margin Classifiers. Cambridge, MA: The MIT Press

20. Sturm JF (1999) Using sedumi 1.02, a matlab toolbox for optimization over symmetric cones. Optimization Methods and Software 11:625–653

21. Sturm JF (2000) Central region method. In J. B. G. Frenk, C. Roos, T. Terlaky, and S. Zhang, editors, High Performance Optimization. Boston, MA: Kluwer Academic Publishers 157–194

22. Tikhonov AN (1963) On solving ill-posed problem and method of regularization. Doklady Akademii Nauk USSR 153:501–504

23. Tong S, Koller D (2000) Restricted Bayes optimal classifiers. In Proceedings of the 17th National Conference on Artificial Intelligence (AAAI), Austin, Texas 658–664

24. Vapnik VN (1998) Statistical Learning Theory. New York, NY: John Wiley & Sons

25. Vapnik VN (1999) The Nature of Statistical Learning Theory. New York, NY: Springer Verlag, 2nd edition

26. Vasin VV (1970) Relationship of several variational methods for approximate solutions of ill-posed problems. Math. Notes 7:161–166

27. Zhu J, Rosset S, Hastie T, Tibshirani R(2003) 1-norm support vector machines. In Advances in Neural Information Processing Systems (NIPS 16)

5

Extension I: BMPM for Imbalanced Learning

In this chapter, we consider the imbalanced learning problem. This problem means the task of binary classification on imbalanced data, in which nearly all the instances are labeled as one class, while far fewer instances are labeled as the other class, usually the more important class. Traditional machine learning methods seeking accurate performance over a full range of instances are not suitable to deal with this problem, since they tend to classify all the data into the majority class, usually the less important class. Moreover, many current methods have tried to utilize some intermediate factors, e.g. the distribution of the training set, the decision thresholds or the cost matrix, to impose a bias towards the important class. However, it remains uncertain whether these roundabout methods can improve the performance in a systematic way. In this chapter, we apply Biased Minimax Probability Machine, one of the special cases of Minimum Error Minimax Probability Machine to deal with the imbalanced learning tasks. Different from previous methods, this model achieves in a worst-case scenario to derive the biased classifier by directly controlling the classification accuracy on each class. More precisely, BMPM builds up an explicit connection between the classification accuracy and the bias, which thus provides a rigorous treatment on imbalanced data. We examine different models and compare BMPM with three other competitive methods, i.e. the Naive Bayesian classifier, the k-Nearest Neighbor method, and the decision tree method C4.5. The experimental results demonstrate the superiority of this model.

This chapter is organized as follows. In the next section, we briefly present an introduction to the imbalanced learning. We then reiterate in a tight version the theoretical foundation of this chapter, namely the BMPM model. Following that in Section 5.3 we apply the BMPM model to deal with the imbalanced learning tasks. In Section 5.4, we evaluate the BMPM model based on a series of experiments, and in Section 5.5, we make discussions and present future work. Finally, we summarize this chapter in Section 5.6.

5.1 Introduction to Imbalanced Learning

Learning classifiers from imbalanced or skewed datasets is an important topic, arising very often in practice in classification problems. In such problems, almost all the instances are labeled as one class, while far fewer instances are labeled as the other class, usually the more important class. It is obvious that traditional classifiers seeking accurate performance over a full range of instances are not suitable to deal with imbalanced learning tasks, since they tend to classify all the data into the majority class, which is usually the less important class.

To cope with imbalanced datasets, there are types of methods such as the methods of sampling [4, 22, 15], the methods of moving the decision thresholds [26, 29], and the methods of adjusting the cost matrix [3, 26]. The first school of methods aims to reduce the data imbalance by "down-sampling" (removing) instances from the majority class or "up-sampling" (duplicating) the training instances from the minority class or both. The second school of methods tries to adapt the decision threshold to impose a bias on the minority class. Similarly, the third school of methods improves the prediction performance by adjusting the weight (cost) for each class.

A common problem for all the three families of methods is that they lack a rigorous and systematic treatment on imbalanced data. For the sampling method, either up- or down-sampling is unsuitable: up-sampling will introduce noise, while down-sampling the data will lose information. Moreover, to incorporate a good bias, it is usually difficult to know what a proportion should be sampled. For these reasons, Provost stated it as an open problem whether simply varying the skewness of the data distribution can improve prediction performance systematically [29]. For the method of adjusting the cost matrix or adapting weights, similar problems are also encountered, i.e. they are hard to build direct connections between the cost matrix or the weights and the biased classification quantitatively. To impose a suitable bias towards the important class, they have to adapt these factors by trials. Therefore, these methods cannot rigorously handle imbalanced data.

In this chapter, we apply Biased Minimax Probability Machine (BMPM) to handle the tasks of learning from imbalanced data. Different from the sampling methods, BMPM does not remove or duplicate data. When compared with the methods of changing the thresholds or weights, our model builds up an explicit connection between the classification accuracy and the bias. It thus offers an elegant way to incorporate the bias into classification by directly controlling the real accuracy.

5.2 Biased Minimax Probability Machine

Suppose two random n-dimensional vectors x and y represent two classes of data, where x belongs to the family of distributions with a given mean $\bar{x}$

and a covariance Σ_x, denoted as $x \sim (\bar{x}, \Sigma_x)$; similarly, y belongs to the family of distributions with a given mean $\bar{y}$ and a covariance Σ_y, denoted as $y \sim (\bar{y}, \Sigma_y)$. Here x, y, $\bar{x}$, $\bar{y} \in \mathbb{R}^n$, and Σ_x, $\Sigma_y \in \mathbb{R}^{n \times n}$. In this chapter, the class x also represents the important or minority class and the class y represents the corresponding less important or majority class.

The Biased Minimax Probability Machine can be described as follows[1]:

$$\max_{\alpha, \beta, b, w \neq 0} \quad \alpha \,,$$

$$\text{s.t.} \quad \inf_{x \sim (\bar{x}, \Sigma_x)} Pr\{w^{\mathrm{T}} x \geq b\} \geq \alpha \,, \tag{5.1}$$

$$\inf_{y \sim (\bar{y}, \Sigma_y)} Pr\{w^{\mathrm{T}} y \leq b\} \geq \beta \,, \tag{5.2}$$

$$\beta \geq \beta_0 \,. \tag{5.3}$$

Here α means the lower bound of the probability (accuracy) for the classification of future cases of the class x with respect to all distributions with the mean and covariance as (x, Σ_x); in other words, α is the worst-case accuracy for the class x. Similarly, β is the lower bound of the accuracy of the class y. This optimization achieves to maximize the accuracy (the probability α) for the biased class x while simultaneously maintaining the class y's accuracy at an acceptable level β_0 by setting a lower bound as Eq.(5.3). In comparison, the Minimax Probability Machine (MPM) in [16, 17] considers the balanced dataset; therefore, it makes α equal to β.

This optimization setting seems to be more useful in incorporating a bias into classifications for imbalanced learning problems. A typical example can be seen in the epidemic disease diagnosis problem which is usually an imbalanced classification problem as well. The "ill" cases are usually much fewer than the healthy cases. However, misclassification of the "ill" class results in more serious consequence than misclassification of the "healthy" case. Thus an unequal treatment on different classes is obviously necessary.

We summarize the advantages of our biased model in the following. First, this method provides a different treatment on different classes, i.e. the hyperplane $w^{*\mathrm{T}} z = b^*$ given by the solution of this optimization favors the classification of the important class x over the less important class y. Second, given reliable mean and covariance matrices, the derived decision hyperplane is directly associated with two real accuracy indicators, i.e. α and β, for each class. Thus, by varying the lower bound of β, i.e. β_0 and deriving the corresponding classifier, we can quantitatively incorporate a bias into the classification. Third, this model contains a distribution-free feature. With no distribution assumption on data, the derived hyperplane seems to be more general and valid than a large family of classifiers, namely the generative classifiers [10, 12] including the Naive Bayesian classifier [18], which has to make

---

[1]Note that, for easy explanations, the model description is in the slightly different but essentially the same form as the one introduced in Chapter 3.

specific distribution assumptions. Fourth, as shown shortly in Section 5.3, either we can simply modify this BMPM optimization to automatically search the best β_0 in terms of some standard criteria, or slightly different from the current setting, we can quantitatively generate the trade-off curve between the accuracies on different classes and leave the task of choosing the best β_0 to the users. Finally, although the BMPM contains the above advantages, it does not trade them for efficiency. It is shortly shown that the optimization of BMPM can be cast as a Fractional Programming (FP) problem and thus can be solved efficiently. In short, with these important features, BMPM appears to offer a more direct and rigorous scheme to handle biased classification tasks, especially the imbalanced classifications, where the importance or cost for each class is unequal.

5.3 Learning from Imbalanced Data by Using BMPM

In this section, we apply the novel BMPM model to the tasks of learning from imbalanced data. We first review four standard imbalanced learning criteria, then based on two of them, we apply BMPM to the imbalanced learning tasks.

5.3.1 Four Criteria to Evaluate Learning from Imbalanced Data

In general, four criteria are used to evaluate the imbalanced learning. They are (1) the criterion of Minimum Cost (MC), (2) the criterion of Maximum Geometry Mean (MGM) of the accuracies on the majority class and the minority class, (3) the criterion of the Maximum Sum (MS) of the accuracies on the majority class and the minority class, and (4) the criterion of Receiver Operating Characteristic (ROC) analysis. We review these criteria as follows.

Aiming to solve the problems caused by maximizing the accuracy over a full range of data, instead, Grzymala-Busse, et al. [9] maximized the sum of the accuracies on the minority class and the majority class (or maximized the difference between the true positive and false positive accuracy). This criterion is also widely used in other fields, e.g. graph detection, especially line detection and arc detection, where it is called Vector Recovery Index [6, 23]. Similarly, Kubat, et al. [14] proposed to use the geometric mean instead of the sum of the accuracies. However, compared to maximizing the sum, this criterion has a nonlinear form, which is not easy to be automatically optimized. On the other hand, when the cost of misclassification is known, a minimum cost measure defined as Eq.(5.4) should be used [2]:

$$Cost = F_{\mathrm{p}} \cdot C_{F_{\mathrm{p}}} + F_{\mathrm{n}} \cdot C_{F_{\mathrm{n}}} , \tag{5.4}$$

where F_{p} is the number of the false positive, $C_{F_{\mathrm{p}}}$ is the cost of a false positive, F_{n} is the number of the false negative, and $C_{F_{\mathrm{n}}}$ is the cost of a false negative. However, because the cost of misclassification is generally unknown in real cases, the usage of this measure is somewhat restricted. Considering this point, some researchers introduced the ROC analysis [25, 26, 34]. This criterion plots a so-called ROC curve to visualize the tradeoff between the false positive rate and the true positive rate and leaves the task of the selection of a specific tradeoff to the practitioners. Fig. 5.1 illustrates an artificially generated ROC curve. It has been suggested that the area beneath an ROC curve can be used as a measure of accuracy in many applications [30, 33]. Thus, a good classifier for imbalanced learning should have a larger area.

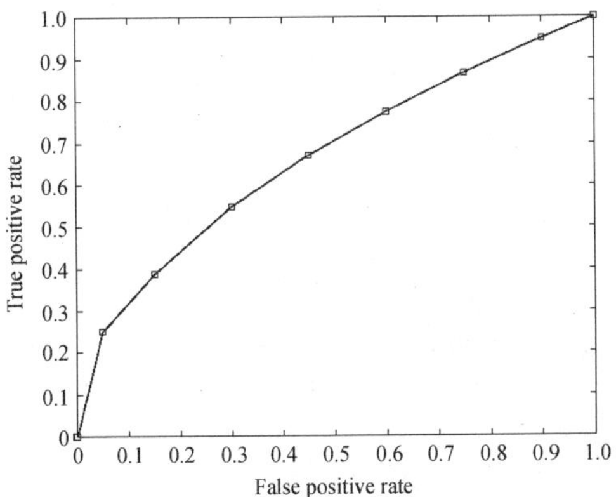

Fig. 5.1. An artificially generated Receiver Operating Characteristic (ROC) curve

Based on the above review, in this chapter we will focus on using the criterion of MS and the ROC curve analysis to evaluate the classifiers.

5.3.2 BMPM for Maximizing the Sum of the Accuracies

In the following, we first modify the formulation of BMPM to maximize the sum of the accuracies for two classes. Next, we make an analysis on the solvability of the modification version. Finally, we present the optimization method.

5.3.2.1 Model Modification

When using BMPM for the criterion of MS, we can modify the formulation of BMPM as follows:

$$\max_{\alpha,\beta,b,\boldsymbol{w}\neq\boldsymbol{0}} (\alpha + \beta) , \tag{5.5}$$

$$\text{s.t.} \quad \inf_{\boldsymbol{x}\sim\{\overline{\boldsymbol{x}},\boldsymbol{\Sigma}_{\boldsymbol{x}}\}} Pr\{\boldsymbol{w}^{\mathrm{T}}\boldsymbol{x} \geq b\} \geq \alpha , \tag{5.6}$$

$$\inf_{\boldsymbol{y}\sim\{\overline{\boldsymbol{y}},\boldsymbol{\Sigma}_{\boldsymbol{y}}\}} Pr\{\boldsymbol{w}^{\mathrm{T}}\boldsymbol{y} \leq b\} \geq \beta . \tag{5.7}$$

The above formulate directly maximize the sum of the lower bounds of the accuracies so as to maximize the sum of the accuracies. In comparison, to achieve the maximum sum of the accuracies, some other approaches, e.g. the methods of sampling or the methods of adapting the weights have to search the best sampling proportion or the best weights by trials, which are in general very time-consuming. Since the above optimization is in fact nearly the same as the Minimum Error Probability Machine, it can be similarly solved by the Sequential Biased Minimax Probability Machine optimization method as introduced in Chapter 3. We thus do not elaborate it here.

5.3.3 BMPM for ROC Analysis

It is straightforward to apply the BMPM model to plot the ROC curve, since the lower bounds α and β directly and quantitatively control the accuracies for two classes. We only need to adapt the acceptable level for β, namely β_0, from 0 to 1, to obtain a sequence of trade-offs between the accuracies of the important class and the negative class. We address that again, since β_0 represents the lower bound of the accuracy of the less important class, varying β_0 provides a direct and quantitative way to move the decision plane with different trade-offs. Directly associating accuracies with the moving of the hyperplane while assuming no distribution is one of advantages of BMPM over the other methods by adapting the weights or thresholds.

5.4 Experimental Results

In this section, we first illustrate the BMPM model with a toy example, and then evaluate the performance of BMPM on two real world imbalanced datasets, namely the recidivism dataset and the rooftop dataset in comparison with the Naive Bayesian (NB) classifier, the k-Nearest Neighbor (k-NN) method [1], and the decision tree classifier C4.5 [31].

5.4.1 A Toy Example

We present a toy example to illustrate the BMPM model in this section. Suppose 15 data points of the class x are generated from a 2D Gaussian distribution with the mean and covariance matrix as $\overline{x} = [0\ 1.5]^{\mathrm{T}}$ and $\Sigma_x = [0.5\ 0; 0\ 0.5]$ and 65 data points of the class y from another 2D Gaussian distribution with $\overline{y} = [0\ 0]^{\mathrm{T}}$ and $\Sigma_y = [0.5\ 0; 0\ 0.5]$.

By adapting the lower bound accuracy β_0 for the class y, with optimizing the corresponding BMPM, we obtain a series of decision boundaries for the toy example when using the Gaussian kernel $e^{-\|x-y\|^2/\sigma}$ with the parameter σ as 5. These boundaries are illustrated in Fig. 5.2. Gray regions are classified as the class x represented by $+$'s, whereas those outside gray regions are judged

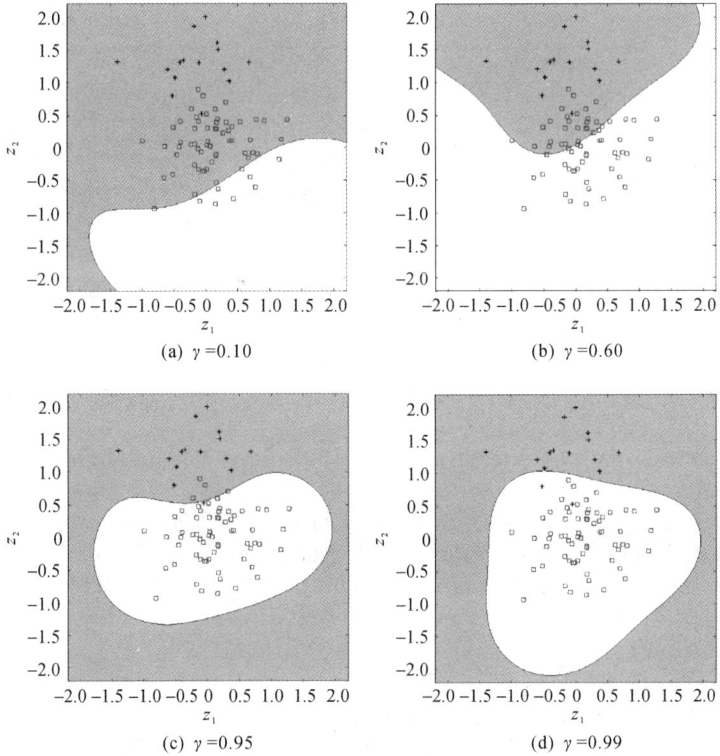

Fig. 5.2. A toy example to illustrate BMPM. Data of the class x is plotted as $+$'s, and data of class y as $\square$'s. The gray area represents the classification region of the class x, while the area outside the gray region is classified as the class y

as the class y plotted as $\square$'s. It is clear to observe that the lower bound β_0 directly controls the accuracy of the class y. More specifically, when β_0 is set to small values such as 10.00%, 60.00% and 95.00%, the boundary is biased towards the class x. When β_0 is set to larger values such as 99.00%, the classification is biased towards the class y. Moreover, Table 5.1 demonstrates that the lower bounds β_0 and α can serve as the accuracy indictors. It is observed that these lower bounds keep well, i.e. the corresponding accuracies are slightly higher than the lower bounders except in the case when $\beta_0 = 0.95$. The exception, i.e. that the value of α, 99.16% is greater than the real accuracy 93.33%, is understandable due to the relatively smaller number of training samples: one single misclassification will influence the classification results significantly. This toy example demonstrates that by changing β_0,

Table 5.1. Lower bounds of accuracies, α, β_0 and the real accuracies

$\beta_0(\%)$	True negative rate(%)	$\alpha(\%)$	True positive rate(%)
10.00	13.85	100.00	100.00
60.00	63.08	100.00	100.00
95.00	95.38	99.16	93.33
99.00	100.00	81.94	86.67

BMPM provides an elegant and direct way to incorporate the bias into the classification.

5.4.2 Evaluations on Real World Imbalanced Datasets

In this section, we evaluate our novel BMPM model in comparison with three competitive classification methods, namely the Naive Bayesian classifier, the k-Nearest Neighbor methods and the decision tree C4.5, on two real world imbalanced datasets, the recidivism dataset and the rooftop dataset. Before we go into the experimental details, we first introduce these three techniques and adapt them to learn from imbalanced datasets according to previous research results [20, 26].

5.4.2.1 Modifying Three Learning Techniques

We investigate and modify three learning techniques, the Naive Bayesian classifier, the k-Nearest Neighbor method, and the decision tree C4.5 in the following.

The Naive Bayesian classifier [11, 18] is proposed based on a very simple assumption, i.e. each attribute is conditionally independent of each other when given the class variable. The decision in a two-category prediction task is made according to the calculation of the posterior probability $p(C|z)$, where C is the class variable and z represents the observation. When $p(C_1|z) \geq 0.5$ or another equivalent yet more convenient rule is satisfied, i.e. $p(C_1)p(z|C_1) \geq p(C_2)p(z|C_2)$, z is classified into C_1; otherwise, it is judged as C_2. Even with the strong conditional independency assumption, the Naive Bayesian classifier demonstrates a surprisingly good performance when compared with state-of-the-art classifiers [8, 19] such as Support Vector Machines [35] and C4.5 in many domains. By simply introducing a parameter τ into the decision rule $p(C_1)p(z|C_1) \geq \tau p(C_2)p(z|C_2)$, Naive Bayesian classifiers can be adapted to the imbalanced learning. For example, specifying $\tau < 1$ imposes a bias towards the C_1 class, whereas specifying $\tau > 1$ imposes a bias towards the C_2 class.

In the k-Nearest Neighbor classification [1], based on some distance measure, e.g. the Euclidean distance measure, k data points, which are the closest to the query point, are selected out. It then labels the query point as the most frequent class among the chosen k points. Although this method is very simple and may suffer from difficulties in high dimensions, it achieves satisfactory performance in many real domains. Following [26], we alter the distance measure δ_j for the class C_j to handle imbalanced learning tasks according to Eq.(5.8):

$$\delta_j = d_E(\boldsymbol{z}, \boldsymbol{z}_j) - \tau_j d_E(\boldsymbol{z}, \boldsymbol{z}_j) \,, \tag{5.8}$$

where $\boldsymbol{z}_j$ is the closest point from class C_j to the query point, and $d_E(\boldsymbol{z}, \boldsymbol{z}_j)$ represents the Euclidean distance measure. Similar to the Naive Bayesian classifier, by modifying τ_j the Nearest Neighbor method can build biased classifiers.

C4.5 is a kind of algorithm introduced by Quinlan for inducing classification models, also called decision trees, from data [31]. By selecting the attributes according to the gain ratios criterion, an information measure of homogeneity, C4.5 builds up a decision tree where each path from the root to a leaf represents a specific classification rule. We adapt C4.5 to learn from imbalanced dataset based on the similar method to [26], i.e. by changing the prior probability to bias the classification.

5.4.2.2 Evaluations on the Recidivism Dataset

The recidivism dataset was obtained from a cohort of releases of the North Carolina prison system during the time period from July 1, 1977 to June 30, 1978. There are totally $4,618$ individuals in this dataset, including a training set with $1,540$ individuals and a test set with $3,078$ individuals. In the training set, 570 (27.5%) individuals were recidivists and 970 (72.5%) were not. In the test set, $1,151$ individuals were recidivists and $1,927$ were not. Although this dataset is not skewed as severely as other reported datasets, for example, the fog dataset [28] and the rooftop dataset used in the next subsection, it is enough to use this dataset to evaluate the performance of the imbalanced learning [26].

We use the same processing method [32] to select and scale nine attributes that appear in Table 5.2, while six other attributes are dropped based on an insignificant test at the 5% level.

We compare the performance of our proposed Biased Minimax Probability Machine model, in both the linear (BMPML) and the Gaussian kernel setting (BMPMG), with the Naive Bayesian classifier, C4.5 and the k-Nearest Neighbor method. These methods are modified into the imbalanced learning according to the methods introduced in the previous section. We run k-NN methods for $k = 1, 3, 5, \ldots, 21$, but we only present the best three results for brevity. The width parameter for the Gaussian kernel is tuned via cross validation methods [13].

We first present the experimental results based on the MS criterion in Table 5.3. To be more comparable, we show the average of the accuracy for

Table 5.2. Attribute description in the recidivism dataset

Attribute	Description
TSERVED	Time served (in months)
AGE	Age (in months) at the time of release
PRIORS	Number of previous incarcerations
WHITE	Is the individual Caucasian?
FELON	Was the sentence for a felony?
LCHY	Does individual's record indicate a serious problem with alcohol?
JUNKY	Does individual's record indicate a serious problem with hard drugs?
PROPTY	Was individual's sentence for a crime against property?
MALE	Is the individual male?

each class when each classifier attains the point of the maximum sum. The
BMPML achieves an average accuracy of 0.6391 and the BMPMG achieves an
average accuracy of 0.6490, while the highest average accuracy among other
classifiers is given as 0.6272 by NB. Therefore, in this dataset, BMPML and
BMPMG outperform other methods in terms of the MS criterion.

Table 5.3. Performance on a recidivism prediction task based on the MS
criterion

Method	True negative rate	True positive rate	(True positive rate+true negative rate)/2
NB	0.6177	0.6377	0.6272
k-NN(9)	0.6255	0.5464	0.5860
k-NN(11)	0.6238	0.5542	0.5890
k-NN(13)	0.5569	0.6201	0.5885
C4.5	0.7405	0.4900	0.6153
BMPML	0.7037	0.5745	0.6391
BMPMG	0.7203	0.5778	0.6490

Let us next present the experimental results based on the ROC analysis. By setting the thresholds or costs by trials for NB, k-NN, and C4.5, the
ROC curves are generated with good shapes as evenly distributed along their
length as possible. As discussed in [26], although this generation method may
increase the running time for some methods, e.g. k-NN, it works well in C4.5
and NB and is sufficient to evaluate the performance of imbalanced learning.
For the BMPM model, since the lower bound β_0 serves as the accuracy indicators, we simply vary it from 0 to 1 to generate the corresponding ROC
curve. The ROC curves are shown in Fig. 5.3(a). As seen in this figure, the
performances of BMPML and BMPMG are once again superior to those of

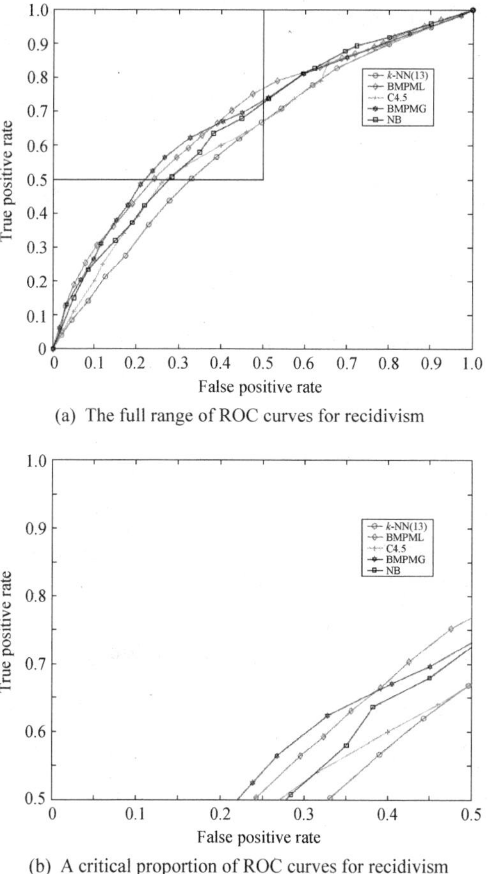

(a) The full range of ROC curves for recidivism

(b) A critical proportion of ROC curves for recidivism

Fig. 5.3. ROC curves for the recidivism dataset. Subfigure (a) shows a full range of the ROC curve, while (b) shows a critical proportion of the ROC curve, which is of more interest in real applications. Both figures demonstrate the superiority of the BMPM model, since the curves of BMPML and BMPMG cover those of other models in most parts and thus have a larger area

other methods, since their ROC curves cover those of other models in most parts. To quantitatively demonstrate the difference, in Table 5.4 we also show the areas beneath the ROC curves approximated by using the trapezoid rule. The BMPML and BMPMG show a consistent superiority to NB which is the best of the other three methods.

In addition, in real applications not all the portions of the ROC curve are of great interest [27]. Usually, those with a small false positive rate and a high true positive rate should be more of interest and importance [36]. We thus

Table 5.4. Performance on a recidivism prediction task based on the area of ROC curve

Method	Area under ROC curve
NB	0.6646
k-NN(11)	0.6155
k-NN(13)	0.6189
k-NN(17)	0.6148
C4.5	0.6383
BMPML	0.6842
BMPMG	0.6798

especially show the portion of the ROC curve in the range when the false positive rate $FP \in [0, 0.5]$ and the true positive rate $TP \in [0.5, 1]$. As shown in Fig. 5.3(b), in this range, the superiority of the BMPL and BMPMG is more obvious than the whole ROC curve analysis. This again demonstrates our model's advantages over other methods.

5.4.2.3 Evaluations on the Rooftop Dataset

The rooftop dataset consists of $17,829$ overhead images of Fort Hood, Texas, collected as part of the RADIUS project [7], which are of a military base. Depending on whether they are buildings (with a detected rooftop) or not, 781 images in this dataset are labeled as positive examples while $17,048$ images are labeled as negative examples. It is clearly observed that this is a severely skewed dataset. According to [7, 26], these images were taken from two different viewpoints, i.e. a nadir aspect and an oblique aspect and covered three different areas. Following [21, 26], we represent each of these images in nine continuous attributes which are extracted based on various image analysis. The detailed information about this dataset is summarized in Tables 5.5 and 5.6.

Table 5.5. Description of images in the rooftop dataset

Sub-dataset	Location	Image size	Aspect	#Positive	#Negative
1	A	2055 × 375	Nadir	71	2645
2	A	1803 × 429	Oblique	74	3349
3	B	670 × 645	Nadir	197	982
4	B	704 × 568	Oblique	238	1955
5	C	1322 × 642	Nadir	87	3722
6	C	1534 × 705	Oblique	114	4395

Table 5.6. Description of the attributes in the rooftop dataset

Attribute	Description
1	Evaluation of the edge support
2	Evaluation of the corner support
3	Evaluation of the parallel support
4	Evaluation of the OTV (Orthogonal Trihedral Vertex) support
5	Evaluation of the shadow corner support
6	Evaluation of gap overlap
7	Evaluation of displacement of edge support
8	Evaluation of crossing lines on any side of the hypothesis
9	Evaluation of existence of T-junction or L-junction on any side

We randomly split the rooftop data into a training set with 60% data and a test set with 40% data. We then construct classifiers from imbalanced data based on the training dataset and perform evaluations on the test dataset. We repeat this procedure ten times and use the average of the results as the performance metric. In such a setup, we compare our BMPM with other three approaches, i.e. NB, C4.5 and k-NN. Similar to the case in the recidivism dataset, NB, C4.5 and k-NN are modified to handle imbalanced data. The width parameter σ is chosen by cross validation methods again. Moreover, we still run k-NN with $k = 1, 3, 5, ..., 21$ and present the best three for brevity.

The results are summarized in Table 5.7 based on the MS criterion, and

Table 5.7. Performance on the rooftop dataset based on the MS criterion

Method	True negative rate	True positive rate	(True positive rate + True negative rate)/2
BMPML	0.8015 ± 0.0058	0.8231 ± 0.0063	0.8123 ± 0.0060
BMPMG	0.7997 ± 0.0087	0.8405 ± 0.0100	0.8201 ± 0.0091
k-NN(7)	0.7510 ± 0.0055	0.8069 ± 0.0062	0.7789 ± 0.0052
k-NN(13)	0.7409 ± 0.0051	0.8140 ± 0.0083	0.7774 ± 0.0061
k-NN(15)	0.7433 ± 0.0067	0.8211 ± 0.0072	0.7822 ± 0.0072
NB	0.7969 ± 0.0043	0.8177 ± 0.0080	0.8073 ± 0.0066
C4.5	0.8176 ± 0.0040	0.7942 ± 0.0063	0.8059 ± 0.0051

Fig. 5.4 and Table 5.8 based on the ROC analysis. As is clearly observed, for both criteria, the BMPM method demonstrates its superiority to the other methods, since it has higher sums of the accuracies and larger areas under the ROC curves. Similar to what we do in the recivisim dataset, we also plot the more critical portion of the ROC curve in Fig. 5.4(b). The predominance of BMPML and the BMPMG is even more obvious. To evaluate the performance more reliably, we perform a significance test based on both LabMRMC [5, 24]

and a t-test. The analysis shows that the accuracies of BMPML and BMPMG are significantly different from those of other methods at $P \leq 0.05$, both in terms of the MS criterion and the ROC curve criterion.

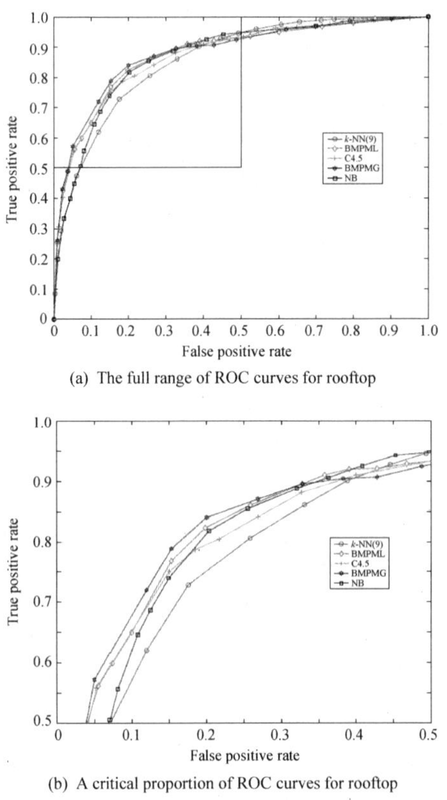

(a) The full range of ROC curves for rooftop

(b) A critical proportion of ROC curves for rooftop

Fig. 5.4. ROC curves for the rooftop dataset. We ran each method by randomly partitioning the dataset into a training dataset (60%) and a test dataset (40%). The evaluations were iterated 10 times. We then average the true positive rate and false positive rate to generate the ROC curves. Subfigure (a) shows a full range of the ROC curve, while (b) shows a critical proportion of the ROC curve, which is of more interest in real applications. Both figures demonstrate the superiority of the BMPML and BMPMG model to other models, since the curves of BMPML and BMPMG cover those of other models in most parts and thus have a larger area

Table 5.8. Performance on the rooftop dataset based on the area of ROC curve

Method	Area under ROC curve
BMPML	0.8791 ± 0.0061
BMPMG	0.8819 ± 0.0087
k-NN(9)	0.8601 ± 0.0091
k-NN(11)	0.8569 ± 0.0058
kNN(15)	0.8582 ± 0.0063
NB	0.8678 ± 0.0060
C4.5	0.8744 ± 0.0062

5.4.3 Evaluations on Disease Datasets

Diagnosing diseases contain a very similar characteristic to the imbalanced learning, since one class, usually the disease class needs to be given more bias than the other class. Therefore, the above discussed model modifications will be automatically applicable for this kind of tasks. In the following, we evaluate the performance of BMPM on two disease datasets, namely, the Breast-cancer dataset and the Heart-disease dataset, which are obtained from UCI machine learning repository. In the context of diagnosing diseases, the true positive rate is usually called sensitivity, while the true negative rate is called specificity. Therefore, we should maximize the sensitivity while maintaining the specificity acceptable. In the following, we present the experimental results still compared with the best three, namely the modified Naive Bayesian classifier, k-NN, and C4.5. We randomly split the data for each dataset into a training set with 80% data and a test set with 20% data. We then construct classifiers based on the training dataset and perform evaluations on the test dataset. We repeat this procedure ten times and use the average of the results as the performance metric.

We present the results based on the MS criterion in Table 5.9 for the breast-cancer dataset and Table 5.10 for the heart disease dataset. Obsereved from these two tables, the BMPM model also demonstrates a superiority to other three models. In addition, the t-test also shows that the accuracies of BMPML and BMPMG are significantly different from those of other three classifiers at $P \leq 0.05$.

We next present the experimental results based on the ROC analysis in Fig. 5.5(a) and Fig. 5.6(a). It is observed that BMPML and BMPMG perform better than other classifiers for both datasets, since in most parts the BMPM curves dominate those of other methods. More specifically, we calculate the areas under the ROC curves as illustrated in Table 5.11, based on the trapezoid rule. For the breast-cancer dataset, it produces a curve with an area of 0.9953 in the linear setting and a curve with an area of 0.9963 in

Table 5.9. Comparison of the model performance based on the MS criterion on the breast-cancer dataset

Method	Specificity	Sensitivity	(Specificity+Sensitivity)/2
BMPML	0.9684 ± 0.0029	0.9872 ± 0.0015	0.9778 ± 0.0021
BMPMG	0.9612 ± 0.0018	0.9915 ± 0.0011	0.9764 ± 0.0016
k-NN(11)	0.9900 ± 0.0047	0.9620 ± 0.0034	0.9760 ± 0.0029
k-NN(17)	0.9862 ± 0.0081	0.9664 ± 0.0058	0.9762 ± 0.0050
k-NN(7)	0.9721 ± 0.0071	0.9752 ± 0.0049	0.9737 ± 0.0058
NB	0.9366 ± 0.0059	0.9719 ± 0.0049	0.9543 ± 0.0051
C4.5	0.9378 ± 0.0074	0.9582 ± 0.0067	0.9480 ± 0.0072

Table 5.10. Comparison of the model performance based on the MS criterion on the heart disease dataset

Method	Specificity	Sensitivity	(Specificity+Sensitivity)/2
BMPML	0.8549 ± 0.0042	0.8158 ± 0.0013	0.8354 ± 0.0035
BMPMG	0.8403 ± 0.0053	0.8572 ± 0.0017	0.8488 ± 0.0026
k-NN(17)	0.7654 ± 0.0029	0.8837 ± 0.0018	0.8246 ± 0.0027
k-NN(7)	0.7754 ± 0.0038	0.8844 ± 0.0042	0.8299 ± 0.0037
k-NN(15)	0.7512 ± 0.0028	0.8653 ± 0.0037	0.8082 ± 0.0036
NB	0.7862 ± 0.0052	0.8024 ± 0.0031	0.7943 ± 0.0040
C4.5	0.8831 ± 0.0022	0.7065 ± 0.0018	0.7948 ± 0.0021

the Gaussian kernel, whereas the k-NN with $k = 11$ forms a curve with a smaller area equal to 0.9908, the best result of the k-NN, NB and C4.5. For the Heart disease dataset, the BMPM shows a curve with an area of 0.8814 in the linear setting and a curve with an area of 0.8932 in the Gaussian kernel setting. These two areas are both greater than those of the other methods, i.e. the k-NN classifier, NB and C4.5. In summary, the evaluations based on the area of the ROC curve quantitatively demonstrate the superiority of our BMPM model for both datasets.

In addition, as illustrated in Fig. 5.5(b) and Fig. 5.6(b), we show the critical portion of Fig. 5.5(a) and Fig. 5.6(a) respectively when the false positive rate is in the range of 0.0 to 0.5 and the true positive rate is in the range of 0.5 to 1.0. In this critical region, most parts of the ROC curves of BMPM cover the corresponding curves of other models in both datasets, which again demonstrates the superiority of the BMPM model.

Table 5.11. Comparison of the model performance based on the ROC analysis

Method	Area under ROC Curve	
	Breast-cancer	Heart
BMPML	0.9953 ± 0.0018	0.8814 ± 0.0056
BMPMG	0.9963 ± 0.0016	0.8932 ± 0.0043
k-NN(11)	0.9908 ± 0.0060	0.8701 ± 0.0038
k-NN(17)	0.9902 ± 0.0100	0.8689 ± 0.0050
k-NN(7)	0.9887 ± 0.0080	0.8596 ± 0.0038
NB	0.9841 ± 0.0060	0.8162 ± 0.0034
C4.5	0.9762 ± 0.0120	0.8301 ± 0.0038

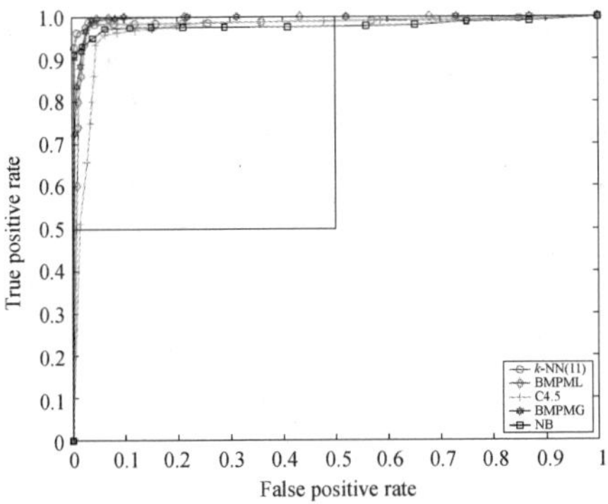

(a) The full range of ROC curves for breast-cancer

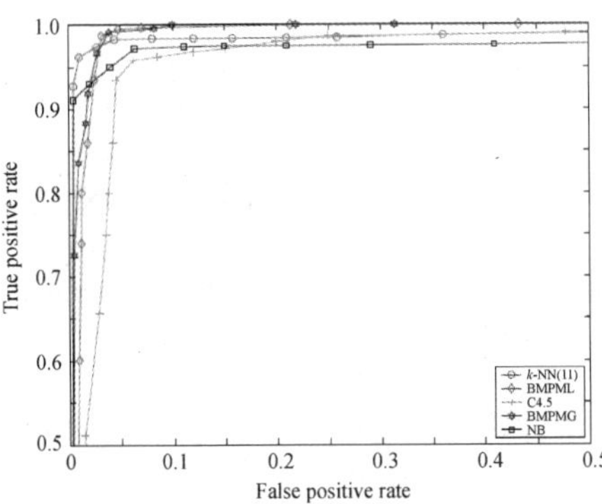

(b) A critical proportion of ROC curves for breast-cancer

Fig. 5.5. ROC curves for the breast-cancer dataset. The ROC curves of BMPML and BMPMG dominate those of other models and BMPMG yields the largest area under the ROC curve

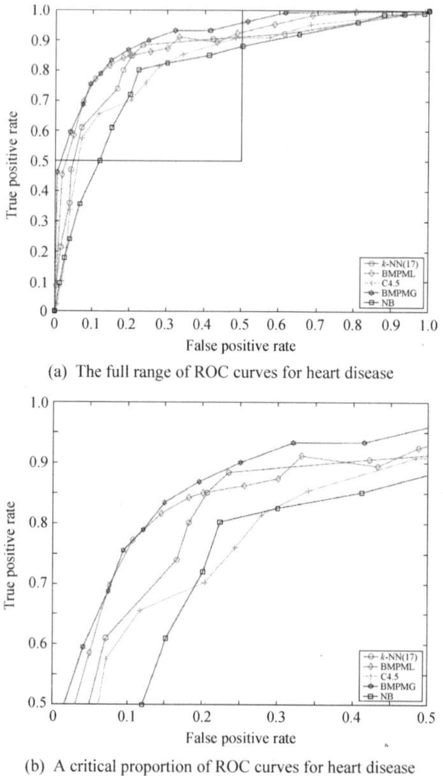

(a) The full range of ROC curves for heart disease

(b) A critical proportion of ROC curves for heart disease

Fig. 5.6. ROC curves for the heart disease dataset. The ROC curves of BMPML and BMPMG dominate those of other models and BMPMG yields the largest area under the ROC curve

5.5 When the Cost for Each Class Is Known

There exists cases in which the cost for each class can be given by experts. In the following, we show that the BMPM model can naturally be adapted to this type of tasks.

Assuming x and y are the minority class and the majority class respectively, it is easily verified that minimizing the optimization function given by Eq.(5.4) is equivalent to maximizing the following formulation:

$$\max \quad (r_x K_x + r_y K_y) ,$$

where r_x is the true positive rate or the accuracy of the class x, r_y is the true negative rate or the accuracy of the class y, K_x and K_y are two constants which are equal to $C_{F_p} N_y$ and $C_{F_n} N_x$ respectively (N_x, N_y are respectively the number of data points labeled as the classes x and y). Similar to the optimization procedure of MS, we can naturally modify the BMPM model in the following formulation:

$$\max_{\alpha,\beta,b,\boldsymbol{w}\neq\boldsymbol{0}} \quad (K_{\boldsymbol{x}}\alpha + K_{\boldsymbol{y}}\beta) \,,$$

$$\text{s.t.} \quad \inf_{\boldsymbol{x}\sim\{\overline{\boldsymbol{x}},\boldsymbol{\Sigma}_{\boldsymbol{x}}\}} Pr\{\boldsymbol{w}^{\mathrm{T}}\boldsymbol{x} \geq b\} \geq \alpha \,,$$

$$\inf_{\boldsymbol{y}\sim\{\overline{\boldsymbol{y}},\boldsymbol{\Sigma}_{\boldsymbol{y}}\}} Pr\{\boldsymbol{w}^{\mathrm{T}}\boldsymbol{y} \leq b\} \geq \beta \,.$$

The above optimization derives the classification boundary by maximizing the weighted lower bound of the real accuracies or the weighted worst-case real accuracies so as to minimize the overall classification risk. Moreover, similar to the MS case, it is easily validated that this optimization problem can be cast as a sequential BMPM problem. Hence, it can similarly be solved based on the method presented in Chapter 3.

5.6 Summary

In this chapter, we have applied a novel model named Biased Minimax Probability Machine to deal with the task of learning from imbalanced datasets. Given reliable estimation of the mean and covariance of data, this model constructs the classification boundary by directly controlling the lower bound of the real accuracy and thus provides a systematic and rigorous treatment on skewed data. We have evaluated the BMPM model on two real world imbalanced datasets and two disease datasets in terms of two criteria. In both criteria, the performances are shown to be the best when compared with other competitive methods such as the Naive Bayesian classifier, the k-Nearest Neighbor method, and the decision tree classifier, C4.5.

References

1. Aha D, Kibler D, Albert M (1991) Instance-based learning algorithms. Machine Learning 6:37–66
2. Bradley A (1997) The use of the area under the ROC curve in the evaluation of machine learning algorithm. Pattern Recognition 30(7):1145–1159
3. Cardie C, Howe N (1997) Improving minority class prediction using case specific feature weights. In Proceedings of the Fourteenth International Conference on Machine Learning (ICML-1997). San Francisco, CA: Morgan Kaufmann 57–65
4. Chawla N, Bowyer K, Hall L, Kegelmeyer W (2002) Smote: synthetic minority over-sampling technique. Journal of Artificial Intelligence Research 16:321–357
5. Dorfman K, Berbaum D, Metz C (1992) Receiver operating characteristic rating analysis: generalization to the population of readers and patients with the jackknife method. Investigative Radiology 27:723–731

6. Dori D, Liu W (1999) Sparse pixel vectorization: An algorithm and its performance evaluation. IEEE Trans. Pattern Analysis and Machine Intelligence 21:202–215

7. Firschein O, Strat T (1996) RADIUS: Image understanding for imagery intelligence. San Francisco, CA: Morgan Kaufmann

8. Friedman N, Geiger D, Goldszmidt M (1997) Bayesian network classifiers. Machine Learning 29:131–161

9. Grzymala-Busse JW, Goodwin LK, Zhang X (2003) Increasing sensitivity of preterm birth by changing rule strengths. Pattern Recognition Letters 24:903–910

10. Huang K, King I, Lyu MR (2003) Discriminative training of Bayesian chow-liu tree multinet classifiers. In Proceedings of International Joint Conference on Neural Network (IJCNN-2003), Oregon, Portland, U.S.A. 1:484–488

11. Huang K, King I, Lyu MR (2003) Finite mixture model of bound semi-naive Bayesian network classifier. In Proceedings of the International Conference on Artificial Neural Networks (ICANN-2003), Lecture Notes in Artificial Intelligence, Long paper. Heidelberg: Springer-Verlag 2714:115–122

12. Jaakkola TS, Haussler D (1998) Exploiting generative models in discriminative classifiers. In Advances in Neural Information Processing Systems (NIPS)

13. Kohavi R (1995) A study of cross validation and bootstrap for accuracy estimation and model selection. In Proceedings of the Fourteenth International Joint Conference on Artificial Intelligence (IJCAI-1995). San Francisco, CA: Morgan Kaufmann 338–345

14. Kubat M, Holte R, Matwin S (1998) Machine learning for the detection of oil spills in satellite radar images. Machine Learning 30(2-3):195–215

15. Kubat M, Matwin S (1997) Addressing the curse of imbalanced training sets: One-sided selection. In Proceedings of the Fourteenth International Conference on Machine Learning (ICML-1997). San Francisco, CA: Morgan Kaufmann 179–186

16. Lanckriet GRG, Ghaoui LE, Bhattacharyya C, Jordan MI (2001) Minimax probability machine. In Advances in Neural Information Processing Systems (NIPS)

17. Lanckriet GRG, Ghaoui LE, Bhattacharyya C, Jordan MI (2002) A robust minimax approach to classification. Journal of Machine Learning Research 3:555–582

18. Langley P, Iba W, Thompson K (1992) An analysis of Bayesian classifiers. In Proceedings of National Conference on Artificial Intelligence 223–228

19. Lerner B, Lawrence ND (2001) A comparison of state-of-the-art classification techniques with application to cytogenetics. Neural Computing and Applications 10(1):39–47

20. Lewis D, Catlett J (1994) Heterogeneous uncertainty sampling for supervised learning. In Proceedings of the Eleventh International Conference on Machine Learning (ICML-1994). San Francisco, CA: Morgan Kaufmann 148–156

21. Lin C, Nevatia R (1998) Building detection and description from a single intensity image. Computer Vision and Image Understanding 72:101–121

22. Ling C, Li C (1998) Data mining for direct marketing:problems and solutions. In Proceedings of the Fourth International Conference on Knowledge Discovery and Data Mining (KDD-1998). Menlo Park, CA: AAAI Press 73–79

23. Liu W, Dori D (1997) A protocol for performance evaluation of line detection algorithms. Machine Vision and Application 9:240–250

24. Maloof MA (2002) On machine learning, ROC analysis, statistical tests of significance. In Proceedings of the Sixteenth International Conference on Pattern Recognition. Los Alamitos, CA: IEEE Press 204–207
25. Maloof MA (2003) Learning when data sets are imbanlanced and when costs are unequal and unknown. In Proceedings of International Conference on Machine Learning (ICML-2003)
26. Maloof MA, Langley P, Binford TO, Nevatia R, Sage S (2003) Improved rooftop detection in aerial images with machine learning. Machine Learning 53:157–191
27. Mcclish D (1989) Analyzing a portion of the ROC curve. Medical Decision Making 9(3):190–195
28. Nugroho AS, Kuroyanagi S, Iwata A (2002) A solution for imbalanced training sets problem by combnet and its application on fog forecasting. IEICE TRANS. INF. & SYST, E85-D(7)
29. Provost F (2000) Learning from imbanlanced data sets. In Proceedings of the Seventeenth National Conference on Artificial Intelligence (AAAI 2000)
30. Provost F, Fawcett T (1997) Analysis and visulization of classifier performance: comparison under imprecise class and cost distributions. In Proceedings of the Third International Conference on Knowledge Discovery and Data Mining. Menlo Park, CA: AAAI Press 43–48
31. Quinlan JR (1993) C4.5: Programs for Machine Learning. San Mateo, CA: Morgan Kaufmann Publishers
32. Schmidt P, Witte A (1988) Predicting Recidivism Using Survival Models. New York, NY: Spring-Verlag
33. Swets J (1988) Measureing the accuracy of diagnostic systems. Science 240:1285–1293
34. Swets J, Pickett R (1982) Evaluation of Diagnoistic Systems: Methods from Signal Detection Theory. New York, NY: Springer-Verlag
35. Vapnik VN (1999) The Nature of Statistical Learning Theory. New York, NY: Springer-Verlag, 2nd edition
36. Woods K, Kegelmeyer Jr WP, Bowyer K (1997) Combination of multiple classifiers using local accuracy estimates. IEEE Tansactions on Pattern Analysis and Machine Intelligence 19(4):405–410

6

Extension II: A Regression Model from M^4

In this chapter, we present a novel regression model which is directly motivated from the Maxi-Min Margin Machine(M^4) model described in Chapter 4. Regression is one of the problems in supervised learning. The objective is to learn a model from a given dataset, $\{(\boldsymbol{x}_1, y_1), \ldots, (\boldsymbol{x}_N, y_N)\}$, and then based on the learned model, to make accurate predictions of y for future values of $\boldsymbol{x}$. Support Vector Regression (SVR), a successful method in dealing with this problem contains the good generalization ability [20, 17, 8, 6]. The standard SVR adopts the ℓ_2-norm to control the functional complexity and chooses an ϵ-insensitive loss function with a fixed tube (margin) to measure the empirical risk. By introducing the ℓ_2-norm, the optimization problem in SVR can be transformed to a quadratic programming problem. On the other hand, the ϵ-tube has the ability to tolerate noise in data and fixing the tube enjoys the advantages of simplicity. These settings are in a global fashion and are effective in common applications, but they lack the ability and the flexibility to capture the local trend in some applications. For example, in stock markets, the data are highly volatile and the associated variance of noise varies over time. In such cases, fixing the tube cannot capture the local trend of data and cannot tolerate the noise adaptively.

One typical illustration can be seen in Fig. 6.1. In this figure, the data contain larger noise as the $\boldsymbol{x}$ value of the data becomes larger. However, the SVR cannot flexibly and suitably handle it. As shown in Fig. 6.1(a), with a fixed ϵ-margin (set to 0.04) SVR considers the data globally and equally: The derived approximating function in SVR deviates from the actual data trend. On the other hand, as illustrated in Fig. 6.1(b), if we adequately consider the local volatility of data by adaptively and automatically setting a small margin in low volatile regions and a larger margin in high volatile areas, the resulting approximating function (the solid line in Fig. 6.1(b)) would be more suitable and reasonable.

Targeting to solve these problems, we propose the Local Support Vector Regression (LSVR) model. We will show that with consideration of the local

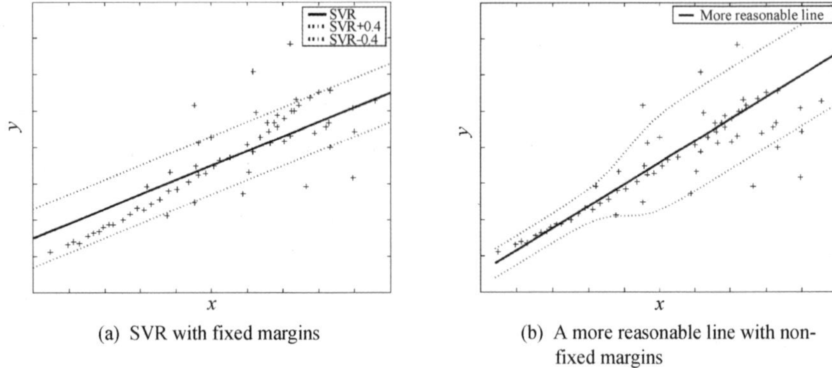

(a) SVR with fixed margins

(b) A more reasonable line with non-fixed margins

Fig. 6.1. Illustration of the ϵ-insensitive loss function with fixed and non-fixed margins in the feature space. In (b), a non-fixed margin setting is more reasonable. It can moderate the effect of the noise by enlarging (shrinking) the margin width in the local area with large (small) variance of noise

data trend, our model provides a systematic and automatic scheme to locally and flexibly adapt the margin. Moreover, we will also demonstrate that this novel LSVR model can derive special cases, containing a very similar physical meaning to the standard SVR. Another critical feature of our model is that the associated optimization of LSVR can be cast as a Second Order Cone Programming (SOCP) problem which can be efficiently solved in polynomial time [11]. The margin setting in the novel LSVR model is different from that in our previous work [21]. Concretely, the tube here is adapted directly based on the functional complexity and the local trend of data. This hence provides a more systematic and more rigorous way to moderate the margin automatically. This model can be seen as an extension to the regression model of M^4. In M^4, the main purpose is to build a classification boundary for different classes, while in LSVR the goal is to model a function approximating the data. Therefore, M^4 considers different data trends for different classes, while LSVR focuses on employing different data trends in different data regions. This is more valuable with the framework of regression tasks.

The rest of this chapter is organized as follows: the linear LSVR model with its theoretical background is presented in Section 6.1. In Section 6.2, we demonstrate how the standard SVR can be considered as the special case of our proposed model. In Section 6.3, we show the link between our proposed LSVR model and the general large margin classifier M^4. The kernelized LSVR is tackled by utilizing the Mercer's kernel in Section 6.5. Section 6.6 provides an additional interpretation on the issue of controlling the complexity of the LSVR model. Section 6.7 presents the experiments on both synthetic and real data. The chapter is concluded in Section 6.8.

6.1 A Local Support Vector Regression Model

In this section, we first present the problem and model definition of the LSVR model. We then detail its interpretation and its appealing characteristics. After that we state its corresponding optimization method.

6.1.1 Problem and Model Definition

A basic idea to avoid overfitting in function approximation is to restrict the class of admissible solutions by a regularization term. A common method is to find a function, $f : \mathbb{R}^d \mapsto \mathbb{R}$, based on an N-instance dataset $D = \{(\boldsymbol{x}_i, y_i) \mid \boldsymbol{x}_i \in \mathbb{R}^d,\ y_i \in \mathbb{R},\ i = 1, \ldots, N\}$ by minimizing the following regularized functional risk:

$$R_{\mathrm{reg}}[f] = \Omega[f] + C \cdot R_{\mathrm{emp}}[f],$$

where $C > 0$ is a regularization parameter used as the tradeoff between the minimal empirical risk $R_{\mathrm{emp}}[f]$ and the smoothness or functional complexity controlled by $\Omega[f]$.

Support Vector Regression is a successful regression model following this idea. It attempts to find an approximating function in the linear form:

$$f(\boldsymbol{x}) = \boldsymbol{w}^{\mathrm{T}}\boldsymbol{x} + b, \quad \boldsymbol{w}, \boldsymbol{x} \in \mathbb{R}^d, b \in \mathbb{R}. \tag{6.1}$$

For the complexity term $\Omega[f]$, SVR selects ℓ_2-norm or other ℓ_p-norm of $\boldsymbol{w}$. To measure the empirical risk $R_{\mathrm{emp}}[f]$, the standard SVR uses an ϵ-insensitive loss function [20].

In order to improve the flexibility of the standard SVR, we propose a new regression model, namely Local Support Vector Regression (LSVR). The objective is to learn the function in Eq.(6.1) approximating the data in D by making the function locally as less volatile as possible while keeping the error as small as possible. We formulate this objective as follows:

$$\min_{\boldsymbol{w}, b, \xi_i, \xi_i^*} \ \frac{1}{N} \sum_{i=1}^{N} \sqrt{\boldsymbol{w}^{\mathrm{T}} \boldsymbol{\Sigma}_i \boldsymbol{w}} + C \sum_{i=1}^{N} (\xi_i + \xi_i^*), \tag{6.2}$$

$$\mathrm{s.t.} \ \ y_i - (\boldsymbol{w}^{\mathrm{T}}\boldsymbol{x}_i + b) \leq \epsilon \sqrt{\boldsymbol{w}^{\mathrm{T}} \boldsymbol{\Sigma}_i \boldsymbol{w}} + \xi_i,$$

$$(\boldsymbol{w}^{\mathrm{T}}\boldsymbol{x}_i + b) - y_i \leq \epsilon \sqrt{\boldsymbol{w}^{\mathrm{T}} \boldsymbol{\Sigma}_i \boldsymbol{w}} + \xi_i^*, \tag{6.3}$$

$$\xi_i \geq 0, \ \ \xi_i^* \geq 0, \ \ i = 1, \ldots, N,$$

where ξ_i and ξ_i^* are the corresponding up-side and down-side errors at the i-th point, respectively, ϵ is a positive constant, $\boldsymbol{\Sigma}_i$ is the covariance matrix formed by the i-th data point and those data points close to it.

6.1.2 Interpretations and Appealing Properties

In this section, beginning with stating the physical meaning of the term, $\boldsymbol{w}^{\mathrm{T}}\boldsymbol{\Sigma}_i\boldsymbol{w}$, we interpret our novel LSVR model.

Suppose $y_i = \boldsymbol{w}^{\mathrm{T}}\boldsymbol{x}_i + b$ and $\bar{y}_i = \boldsymbol{w}^{\mathrm{T}}\bar{\boldsymbol{x}}_i + b$. We have the variance around the i-th data point as

$$\Delta_i = \frac{1}{2k+1}\sum_{j=-k}^{k}(y_{i+j} - \bar{y}_i)^2 = \frac{1}{2k+1}\sum_{j=-k}^{k}[\boldsymbol{w}^{\mathrm{T}}(\boldsymbol{x}_{i+j} - \bar{\boldsymbol{x}}_i)]^2 = \boldsymbol{w}^{\mathrm{T}}\boldsymbol{\Sigma}_i\boldsymbol{w},$$

where $2k$ is the number of data points closest to the i-th data point. Therefore, $\Delta_i = \boldsymbol{w}^{\mathrm{T}}\boldsymbol{\Sigma}_i\boldsymbol{w}$ actually captures the volatility in the local region around the i-th data point. In addition, Δ_i can also measure the local functional complexity around the i-th data, since it reflects the smoothness of the corresponding local region. This will be in details addressed later in Section 6.6.

By using the first meaning of $\Delta_i = \boldsymbol{w}^{\mathrm{T}}\boldsymbol{\Sigma}_i\boldsymbol{w}$ (representing the local volatility), LSVR can systematically and automatically vary the tube: If the i-th data point lies in the area with a larger variance of noise, it will contribute to a larger $\epsilon\sqrt{\boldsymbol{w}^{\mathrm{T}}\boldsymbol{\Sigma}_i\boldsymbol{w}}$ or a larger local margin. This will result in reducing the impact of the noise around the point; on the other hand, in the case that the i-th data point is in the region with a smaller variance of noise, the local margin (tube), $\epsilon\sqrt{\boldsymbol{w}^{\mathrm{T}}\boldsymbol{\Sigma}_i\boldsymbol{w}}$, will be smaller. Therefore, the corresponding point would contribute more in the fitting process. In comparison, the standard SVR adopts a fixed margin, which treats each point equally and therefore lacks the ability to tolerate the change in noise.

By engaging the second compelling property of $\Delta_i = \boldsymbol{w}^{\mathrm{T}}\boldsymbol{\Sigma}_i\boldsymbol{w}$, namely, a measure in describing the local functional complexity, LSVR controls the overall smoothness of the approximating function by minimizing the average of Δ_i as seen in Eq.(6.2). Intuitively, the margin around each point can be neither too large nor too small: If the margin is too large, the local data trend may not be captured for "over-tolerating" data; if the margin is too small, the local data trend may be "over-emphasized" resulting in a highly zig-zag approximating curve. Therefore by adding the regularization term, a trade-off can be achieved via adapting the parameter C.

6.2 Connection with Support Vector Regression

We now analyze the connection of the LSVR model with the standard Support Vector Regression model. By considering the data trend globally and equally, i.e. setting $\boldsymbol{\Sigma}_i = \boldsymbol{\Sigma}$, for $i = 1,\ldots,N$, we can transform the optimization of Eq.(6.2) as follows:

$$\min_{\boldsymbol{w},b,\xi_i,\xi_i^*} \quad \sqrt{\boldsymbol{w}^{\mathrm{T}}\boldsymbol{\Sigma}\boldsymbol{w}} + C\sum_{i=1}^{N}(\xi_i + \xi_i^*) \,,$$

$$\text{s.t.} \quad y_i - (\boldsymbol{w}^{\mathrm{T}}\boldsymbol{x}_i + b) \leq \epsilon\sqrt{\boldsymbol{w}^{\mathrm{T}}\boldsymbol{\Sigma}\boldsymbol{w}} + \xi_i \,,$$

$$(\boldsymbol{w}^{\mathrm{T}}\boldsymbol{x}_i + b) - y_i \leq \epsilon\sqrt{\boldsymbol{w}^{\mathrm{T}}\boldsymbol{\Sigma}\boldsymbol{w}} + \xi_i^* \,, \tag{6.4}$$

$$\xi_i \geq 0, \quad \xi_i^* \geq 0, \quad i = 1,\ldots,N \,.$$

Further, if $\boldsymbol{\Sigma} = \boldsymbol{I}$, we obtain:

$$\min_{\boldsymbol{w},b,\xi_i,\xi_i^*} \quad \left(\|\boldsymbol{w}\| + C\sum_{i=1}^{N}(\xi_i + \xi_i^*) \right) \,, \tag{6.5}$$

$$\text{s.t.} \quad y_i - (\boldsymbol{w}\boldsymbol{x}_i + b) \leq \|\boldsymbol{w}\|\epsilon + \xi_i \,,$$

$$(\boldsymbol{w}\boldsymbol{x}_i + b) - y_i \leq \|\boldsymbol{w}\|\epsilon + \xi_i^* \,, \tag{6.6}$$

$$\xi_i \geq 0, \quad \xi_i^* \geq 0, \quad i = 1,\ldots,N \,.$$

The above optimization problem is very similar to the ℓ_1-norm SVR, except that it has a margin related to the complexity term. In the following, we will prove that the above optimization is actually equivalent to the ℓ_1-norm SVR in a meaningful sense.

Lemma 6.1. *The LSVR model with setting $\boldsymbol{\Sigma}_i = \boldsymbol{I}$ is equivalent to the ℓ_1-norm SVR in the sense that: (1) Assuming a unique ϵ_1^* exists for making ℓ_1-norm SVR optimal (i.e. setting ϵ to ϵ_1^* will make the objective function minimal), if for ϵ_1^* the ℓ_1-norm SVR achieves a solution $\{\boldsymbol{w}^*,b^*\} = SVR(\epsilon_1^*)$, then the LSVR can produce the same solution by setting the parameter $\epsilon = \frac{\epsilon_1^*}{\|\boldsymbol{w}_1^*\|}$, i.e. $LSVR(\frac{\epsilon_1^*}{\|\boldsymbol{w}_1^*\|}) = SVR(\epsilon_1^*)$; (2) Assuming a unique ϵ_2^* exists for making the special case of LSVR optimal (i.e. setting ϵ to ϵ_2^* will make the objective function minimal), if for ϵ_2^* the special case of LSVR achieves a solution $\{\boldsymbol{w}_2^*,b_2^*\} = LSVR(\epsilon_2^*)$, then the ℓ_1-norm SVR can produce the same solution by setting the parameter $\epsilon = \epsilon_2^*\|\boldsymbol{w}_2^*\|$, i.e. $SVR(\epsilon_2^*\|\boldsymbol{w}_2^*\|) = LSVR(\epsilon_1^*)$.*

Proof. Since (1) and (2) are very similar statements, we only prove (1). When ϵ of the special case of LSVR is setting to $\frac{\epsilon_1^*}{\|\boldsymbol{w}_1^*\|}$, the value of the objective function of LSVR will be at least smaller than the one by simply setting $\{\boldsymbol{w},b\} = \{\boldsymbol{w}_1^*,b_1^*\}$, since $\{\boldsymbol{w}_1^*,b_1^*\}$ is easily verified to satisfy the constraints of LSVR. Namely,

$$\text{LSVR}\left(\frac{\epsilon_1^*}{\|\boldsymbol{w}_1^*\|}\right) \succeq \text{SVR}(\epsilon_1^*) \,, \tag{6.7}$$

where we use $\succeq$ to represent "superior to". We assume the solution for $\epsilon = \frac{\epsilon_1^*}{\|\boldsymbol{w}_1^*\|}$ in LSVR as $\{\boldsymbol{w}_2,b_2\}$. Similarly, by setting $\epsilon = \epsilon_1^*\frac{\|\boldsymbol{w}_2\|}{\|\boldsymbol{w}_1^*\|}$ in SVR, we have:

$$\text{SVR}\left(\epsilon_1^*\frac{\|\boldsymbol{w}_2\|}{\|\boldsymbol{w}_1^*\|}\right) \succeq \text{LSVR}\left(\frac{\epsilon_1^*}{\|\boldsymbol{w}_1^*\|}\right) \,. \tag{6.8}$$

Combining Eqs.(6.7) and (6.8), we have:

$$\text{SVR}\left(\epsilon_1^* \frac{\|\boldsymbol{w}_2\|}{\|\boldsymbol{w}_1^*\|}\right) \succeq \text{LSVR}\left(\frac{\epsilon_1^*}{\|\boldsymbol{w}_1^*\|}\right) \succeq \text{SVR}\left(\epsilon_1^*\right). \tag{6.9}$$

Since ϵ_1^* is the unique ϵ making the objective of SVR minimal, Eq.(6.9) implies that $\boldsymbol{w}_2 = \boldsymbol{w}_1^*$.

In addition, if in LSVR we use the item of $\boldsymbol{w}^{\mathrm{T}}\boldsymbol{\Sigma}\boldsymbol{w}$ instead of its square root form as the structure risk or complexity risk, a similar proof will also be applicable that the ℓ_2-norm SVR is equivalent to the special case of LSVR with $\boldsymbol{\Sigma}_i = \boldsymbol{\Sigma}$. In summary, we can see that the LSVR model actually contains the standard SVR model as special cases.

6.3 Link with Maxi-Min Margin Machine

The LSVR model can also be considered as an extension of the general large margin classifier, Maxi-Min Margin Machine (M^4) presented previously in this book or [10]. Within the framework of binary classifications for class $\boldsymbol{x}$ and $\boldsymbol{y}$, the M^4 is formulated as follows:

$$\max_{\rho,\boldsymbol{w}\neq\boldsymbol{0},b} \quad \rho, \tag{6.10}$$

$$\text{s.t.} \quad \frac{(\boldsymbol{w}^{\mathrm{T}}\boldsymbol{x}_i + b)}{\sqrt{\boldsymbol{w}^{\mathrm{T}}\boldsymbol{\Sigma}_x\boldsymbol{w}}} \geq \rho, \quad i = 1, 2, \ldots, N_{\boldsymbol{x}}, \tag{6.11}$$

$$\frac{-(\boldsymbol{w}^{\mathrm{T}}\boldsymbol{y}_j + b)}{\sqrt{\boldsymbol{w}^{\mathrm{T}}\boldsymbol{\Sigma}_y\boldsymbol{w}}} \geq \rho, \quad j = 1, 2, \ldots, N_{\boldsymbol{y}}, \tag{6.12}$$

where $\boldsymbol{\Sigma}_x$ and $\boldsymbol{\Sigma}_y$ refer to the covariance matrices of the $\boldsymbol{x}$ and the $\boldsymbol{y}$ data, respectively.

Within the framework of classifications, M^4 considers different data trends for different classes. Analogously, in the novel LSVR model we allow different data trends for different regions, which is more suitable for the regression purpose.

6.4 Optimization Method

In order to solve the optimization problem of Eq.(6.2), we introduce auxiliary variables, $t_1, \ldots, t_N$, and transform the problem as follows:

$$\min_{\boldsymbol{w},b,t_i,\xi_i,\xi_i^*} \left(\frac{1}{N}\sum_{i=1}^{N} t_i + C\sum_{i=1}^{N}(\xi_i + \xi_i^*) \right), \tag{6.13}$$

$$\text{s.t. } y_i - (\boldsymbol{w}^{\mathrm{T}}\boldsymbol{x}_i + b) \leq \epsilon\sqrt{\boldsymbol{w}^{\mathrm{T}}\boldsymbol{\Sigma}_i\boldsymbol{w}} + \xi_i,$$

$$(\boldsymbol{w}^{\mathrm{T}}\boldsymbol{x}_i + b) - y_i \leq \epsilon\sqrt{\boldsymbol{w}^{\mathrm{T}}\boldsymbol{\Sigma}_i\boldsymbol{w}} + \xi_i^*, \tag{6.14}$$

$$\sqrt{\boldsymbol{w}^{\mathrm{T}}\boldsymbol{\Sigma}_i\boldsymbol{w}} \leq t_i, \tag{6.15}$$

$$t_i \geq 0, \quad \xi_i \geq 0, \quad \xi_i^* \geq 0, \quad i = 1,\ldots,N.$$

It is clear that Eqs.(6.14) and (6.15) are non-convex constraints. This may present difficulties in optimizing the LSVR problems. In the following, we relax the optimization to a Second Order Cone Programming (SOCP) problem [11] by replacing $\sqrt{\boldsymbol{w}^{\mathrm{T}}\boldsymbol{\Sigma}_i\boldsymbol{w}}$ with its upper bound t_i:

$$\min_{\boldsymbol{w},b,t_i,\xi_i,\xi_i^*} \left(\frac{1}{N}\sum_{i=1}^{N} t_i + C\sum_{i=1}^{N}(\xi_i + \xi_i^*) \right),$$

$$\text{s.t. } y_i - (\boldsymbol{w}^{\mathrm{T}}\boldsymbol{x}_i + b) \leq \epsilon t_i + \xi_i,$$

$$(\boldsymbol{w}^{\mathrm{T}}\boldsymbol{x}_i + b) - y_i \leq \epsilon t_i + \xi_i^*,$$

$$\sqrt{\boldsymbol{w}^{\mathrm{T}}\boldsymbol{\Sigma}_i\boldsymbol{w}} \leq t_i,$$

$$t_i \geq 0, \quad \xi_i \geq 0, \quad \xi_i^* \geq 0, \quad i = 1,\ldots,N.$$

Since t_i is closely related to $\sqrt{\boldsymbol{w}^{\mathrm{T}}\boldsymbol{\Sigma}_i\boldsymbol{w}}$, weighting the margin width with t_i will contain a meaning similar to the original motivation, i.e. adapting the margin flexibly. More importantly, the relaxed form is a linear programming problem under quadratic cone constraints, or more specifically it is a Second Order Cone Programming. Therefore, this problem can be solved in polynomial time by many general optimization packages, e.g. Sedumi [18, 19].

6.5 Kernelization

In this section we extend the above linear regression model to the non-linear one by using the Mercer's kernel. Suppose the training data are mapped into a kernel space or a feature space by the mapping function, $\varphi : \mathbb{R}^d \mapsto \mathbb{R}^f$. Then, the objective in the feature space is transformed as follows:

$$\min_{\boldsymbol{w},b,t_i,\xi_i,\xi_i^*} \left(\frac{1}{N}\sum_{i=1}^{N} t_i + C\sum_{i=1}^{N}(\xi_i + \xi_i^*) \right), \tag{6.16}$$

$$\text{s.t. } y_i - (\boldsymbol{w}^{\mathrm{T}}\varphi(\boldsymbol{x}_i) + b) \leq \epsilon t_i + \xi_i,$$

$$(\boldsymbol{w}^{\mathrm{T}}\varphi(\boldsymbol{x}_i) + b) - y_i \leq \epsilon t_i + \xi_i^*,$$

$$\sqrt{\boldsymbol{w}^{\mathrm{T}}\boldsymbol{\Sigma}_i^{\varphi}\boldsymbol{w}} \leq t_i,$$

$$t_i \geq 0, \quad \xi_i \geq 0, \quad \xi_i^* \geq 0, \quad i = 1,\ldots,N.$$

In order to utilize the Mercer's kernel, we first present the following theorem.

Theorem 6.2. *If the corresponding local covariance Σ_i^φ can be estimated by the mapped training data, i.e. $\hat{\varphi}_i$, Σ_i^φ can be written as*

$$\hat{\varphi}_i = \frac{1}{2k+1} \sum_{j=-k}^{k} \varphi(\boldsymbol{x}_{i+j}) \,, \tag{6.17}$$

$$\Sigma_i^\varphi = \frac{1}{2k+1} \sum_{j=-k}^{k} (\varphi(\boldsymbol{x}_{i+j}) - \hat{\varphi}_i)(\varphi(\boldsymbol{x}_{i+j}) - \hat{\varphi}_i)^{\mathrm{T}}, \tag{6.18}$$

where we just consider $2k$ data points which are the closest to the i-th data, then the optimal $\boldsymbol{w}$ lies in the span of the mapped training data.

Proof. Suppose $\boldsymbol{w} = \boldsymbol{w}_{\mathrm{p}} + \boldsymbol{w}_{\mathrm{o}}$, where $\boldsymbol{w}_{\mathrm{p}}$ is the projection of $\boldsymbol{w}$ in the span of the mapped training data, $\boldsymbol{w}_{\mathrm{o}}$ is the orthogonal component to the span. Since $\boldsymbol{w}_{\mathrm{rmo}}^{\mathrm{T}}\varphi(\boldsymbol{x}_i) = 0$, $i = 1, \ldots, N$, we can easily know that:

$$\boldsymbol{w}^{\mathrm{T}}\varphi(\boldsymbol{x}_i) = \boldsymbol{w}_{\mathrm{p}}^{\mathrm{T}}\varphi(\boldsymbol{x}_i) \,,$$

$$\boldsymbol{w}^{\mathrm{T}}\Sigma_i^\varphi \boldsymbol{w} = \boldsymbol{w}_{\mathrm{p}}^{\mathrm{T}}\Sigma_i^\varphi \boldsymbol{w}_{\mathrm{p}} \,.$$

Therefore, we can omit $\boldsymbol{w}_{\mathrm{o}}$ since it disappears in the optimization. We then set it to 0 and obtain $\boldsymbol{w} = \boldsymbol{w}_{\mathrm{p}}$, i.e. the optimal $\boldsymbol{w}$ lies in the span of the mapped training data.

By using Theorem 6.2, we write $\boldsymbol{w}$ as $\sum_{j=1}^{N} \mu_j \varphi(\boldsymbol{x}_j)$ and substitute it into Eq.(6.17). By rewriting Eq.(6.17) in the kernel form by a kernel function $K(\boldsymbol{z}_1, \boldsymbol{z}_2) = \varphi(\boldsymbol{z}_1)^{\mathrm{T}}\varphi(\boldsymbol{z}_2)$, we then obtain:

$$\boldsymbol{w}^{\mathrm{T}}\varphi(\boldsymbol{x}_i) = \sum_{j=1}^{N} \mu_j K(\boldsymbol{x}_i, \boldsymbol{x}_j) = \boldsymbol{\mu}^{\mathrm{T}}\boldsymbol{K}_i \,,$$

$$\boldsymbol{w}^{\mathrm{T}}\Sigma_i^\varphi \boldsymbol{w} = \boldsymbol{\mu}^{\mathrm{T}}\boldsymbol{L}_i^{\mathrm{T}}\boldsymbol{L}_i\boldsymbol{\mu} \,,$$

where $\boldsymbol{\mu} = [\mu_1, \ldots, \mu_N]^{\mathrm{T}}$, $\boldsymbol{K}_i = [K(\boldsymbol{x}_1, \boldsymbol{x}_i) \ldots K(\boldsymbol{x}_N, \boldsymbol{x}_i)]^{\mathrm{T}}$, $K_{ij} = K(\boldsymbol{x}_i, \boldsymbol{x}_j)$,

$$\boldsymbol{L}_i = \frac{1}{\sqrt{2k+1}}(\boldsymbol{K}_{[i-k:i+k,N]} - \mathbf{1}_{2k+1}\boldsymbol{l}_i^{\mathrm{T}}), \quad \boldsymbol{K}_{[i-k:i+k,N]} = \begin{pmatrix} \boldsymbol{K}_{i-k,1} & \cdots & \boldsymbol{K}_{i-k,N} \\ \vdots & \ddots & \vdots \\ \boldsymbol{K}_{i+k,1} & \cdots & \boldsymbol{K}_{i+k,N} \end{pmatrix},$$

$(\boldsymbol{l}_i^{\mathrm{T}})_t = \frac{1}{2k+1} \sum_{j=-k}^{k} K(\boldsymbol{x}_{i+j}, \boldsymbol{x}_t)$, and $\mathbf{1}_{2k+1}$ is a column vector with ones of dimension $2k+1$.

Consequently, the corresponding objective in Eq.(6.16) becomes:

$$\min_{\boldsymbol{\mu},b,t_i,\xi_i,\xi_i^*} \left(\frac{1}{N}\sum_{i=1}^{N}t_i + C\sum_{i=1}^{N}(\xi_i + \xi_i^*)\right),$$

$$\text{s.t. } y_i - (\boldsymbol{\mu}^{\mathrm{T}}\boldsymbol{K}_i + b) \le \epsilon t_i + \xi_i ,$$

$$(\boldsymbol{\mu}^{\mathrm{T}}\boldsymbol{K}_i + b) - y_i \le \epsilon t_i + \xi_i^* ,$$

$$\sqrt{\boldsymbol{\mu}^{\mathrm{T}}\boldsymbol{L}_i^{\mathrm{T}}\boldsymbol{L}_i\boldsymbol{\mu}} \le t_i ,$$

$$t_i \ge 0, \quad \xi_i \ge 0, \quad \xi_i^* \ge 0, \quad i = 1,\dots,N .$$

Hence we only need a kernel function in the optimization without knowing a specific mapping function and it can be easily solved by the SOCP methods.

6.6 Additional Interpretation on $\boldsymbol{w}^{\mathrm{T}}\boldsymbol{\Sigma}_i\boldsymbol{w}$

We now interpret in terms of sparse approximation [2, 3, 7, 5, 4, 9, 14] why $\boldsymbol{w}^{\mathrm{T}}\boldsymbol{\Sigma}_i\boldsymbol{w}$ can be considered as the local complexity around the data point $\boldsymbol{x}_i$.

In [7], Girosi has demonstrated an equivalence between sparse approximation and Support Vector Machines. In the view of sparse approximation, the regression can be regarded as the task of approximating data using linear superpositions of basis functions selected from a large, redundant set of basis functions, called dictionary [12]. A common sense in choosing a good approximating function is that one should not only approximate the given data as accurately as possible, more importantly, one should use as few as possible basis functions. Therefore, a sparsity concept is invoked, i.e. the approximating function should be sparse in using the basis functions. When it is connected with Support Vector Regressions, the readers can regard that a basis function is associated with each data point (note that the regression function can be represented as the linear combination form in the kernel space). The fact that SVR contains the property of sparsity, i.e. only a small fraction of data points (support vectors) makes contributions to the final approximating function, may therefore explain why it has achieved a great success. The measure of sparsity of the approximating function f, which is also regarded as the measure of complexity is formulated as follows:

$$\Omega[f] = \left(\sum_{i=1}^{N}\delta_i\right)^p , \tag{6.19}$$

$$\text{where, } \delta_i = \begin{cases} 1, & \text{if } \boldsymbol{x}_i \text{ appears ;} \\ 0, & \text{otherwise .} \end{cases} \tag{6.20}$$

It is well known that the ℓ_0-norm of a vector counts the number of elements different from zero. The complexity term can also be described as:

$$\Omega[f] = \|\boldsymbol{w}\|_{\ell_0}^p . \tag{6.21}$$

However, due to involving in minimizing a combinatorial term as the above, it is extremely difficult to perform the optimization in practice. Therefore, instead, one often uses ℓ_1-norm as its approximated version, i.e.

$$\Omega[f] = \|\boldsymbol{w}\|_{\ell_1}^p \ . \tag{6.22}$$

When p is set to 1, it therefore leads to the standard ℓ_1-norm SVR. When one looks back on the LSVR model, minimizing $(1/N) \sum_{i=1}^{N} \sqrt{\boldsymbol{w}^{\mathrm{T}} \boldsymbol{\Sigma}_i \boldsymbol{w}}$ presents another approximated version to the sparsity, since it also tries to make $\boldsymbol{w}$ as sparse as possible.[1] Another advantage of using $(1/N) \sum_{i=1}^{N} \sqrt{\boldsymbol{w}^{\mathrm{T}} \boldsymbol{\Sigma}_i \boldsymbol{w}}$ is that it leads to an easy solving method as illustrated in Section 6.4.

6.7 Experiments

In this section, we report the experiments on both synthetic sinc datasets and real world datasets. The SOCP problem associated with our LSVR model is solved by a general software, Sedumi [18, 19]. The SVR algorithm is performed by LIBSVM [1].

6.7.1 Evaluations on Synthetic Sinc Data

Fifty examples (x_i, y_i) are generated from a sinc function [16], where x_i are drawn uniformly from $[-3, \ 3]$, and $y_i = \sin(\pi x_i)/(\pi x_i) + \tau_i$, with τ_i drawn from a Gaussian with zero mean and variance σ^2. Two cases are evaluated. One is with $\sigma = 0$. The standard deviation of the data in the other case increases linearly from 0.5 at $x = -3$ to 1.5 at $x = 3$. It is clearly observed that in the second case, the variance of noise is different in different regions. We use the default parameters $C = 100$, the RBF kernel $K(u, v) = \exp(-\|u - v\|^2)$.

Table 6.1 reports the average results over 100 random trails with different ϵ values. Fig. 6.2 illustrates the difference between the LSVR model and the SVR algorithm when $\epsilon = 0.2$. For the case I, $\sigma = 0.0$, the LSVR model can adjust the tube automatically to fit the data with a smaller Mean Square Error (MSE), which can be seen in Fig. 6.2(c). However, containing a fixed tube, the SVR algorithm lacks the flexibility (see Fig. 6.2(a)). This also yields that the MSE increases as ϵ increases. As reported in Table 6.1, when $\epsilon \geq 0.8$, there are no support vectors in SVR and MSE is the largest. In case II, the LSVR model has smaller MSE's and smaller STD's for all ϵ's. Fig. 6.2(d) also shows that the obtained approximating function in LSVR is smoother than that in SVR.

---

[1]Intuitively, when $\boldsymbol{w}$ is sparser, $(1/N) \sum_{i=1}^{N} \sqrt{\boldsymbol{w}^{\mathrm{T}} \boldsymbol{\Sigma}_i \boldsymbol{w}}$ would be smaller.

Table 6.1. Experimental results (MSE±STD) of the LSVR model and the SVR algorithm on the sinc data with different ϵ values

ϵ	Case I: $\sigma = 0.0$		Case II: Varying σ	
	LSVR	SVR	LSVR	SVR
0.0	0	0	0.1825±0.1011	0.3101±0.1165
0.2	0.0004	0.0160	0.2338±0.0888	0.2761±0.1111
0.4	0.0016	0.0722	0.1917±0.0726	0.2217±0.0840
0.6	0.0044	0.1695	0.1540±0.0687	0.2384±0.0867
0.8	0.0082	0.1748	0.1333±0.0674	0.2333±0.1096
1.0	0.0125	0.1748	0.1115±0.0597	0.2552±0.1218
2.0	0.0452	0.1748	0.0959±0.0421	0.2616±0.1517

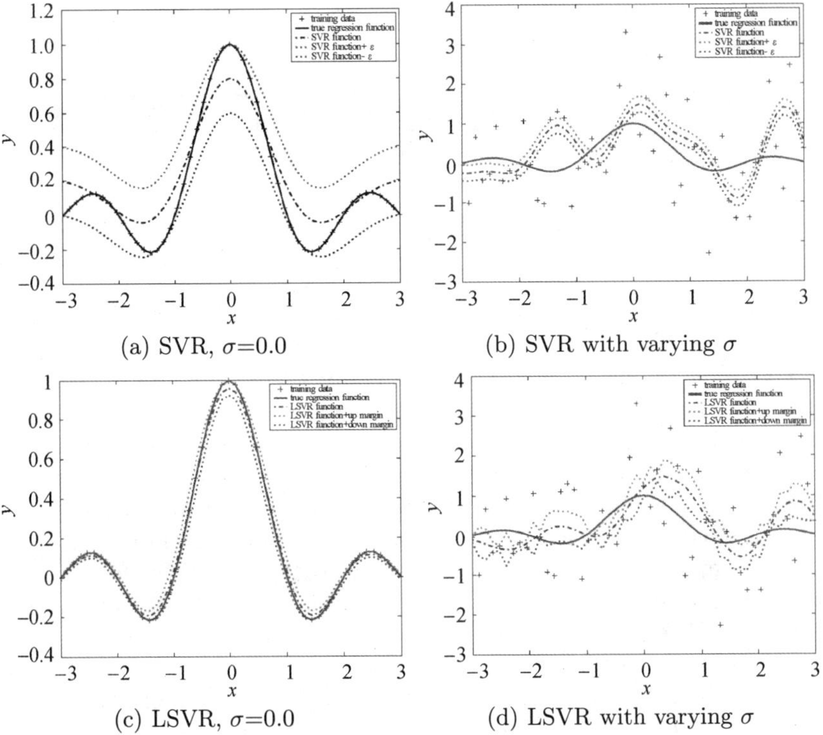

(a) SVR, σ=0.0

(b) SVR with varying σ

(c) LSVR, σ=0.0

(d) LSVR with varying σ

Fig. 6.2. Experimental results on synthetic sinc data with ϵ=0.2

6.7.2 Evaluations on Real Financial Data

We evaluate our model on the financial time series data which are highly volatile and non-stationary. The experimental data are three major indices: (1) the Dow Jones Industrial Average (DJIA), (2) the NASDAQ, and (3) the Standard & Poor 500 index (S&P500) in the period from January 2, 2004 to April 30, 2004. We choose this period of data because three indices data contain different statistical properties as reported in Table 6.2. Especially, one may note that the data in this period for three indices contain largely different skewness. In this way, the diversity in the data may not bias the comparison of the models.

Table 6.2. Summary statistics of normalized returns of DJIA, NASDAQ and S&P500 in the experiments. These indices show different statistical properties.

Moments	DJIA		NASDAQ		S&P500	
	Train	Test	Train	Test	Train	Test
Mean	0.0000	−0.2850	−0.0000	−0.4819	0.0000	−0.3858
S.D.	1.0000	0.9957	1.0000	1.1312	1.0000	1.1298
Skew	−0.0678	0.1684	0.0928	0.3256	−0.1298	−0.0102
Kurt	2.5437	2.7706	2.6600	1.8631	2.5308	2.4124

Following the procedure in [15], we convert the daily closing prices (d_t) of these indices to continuously compounded returns $(r_t = \log(d_{t+1}/d_t))$ and set the ratio of the number of the training return series to the number of test return series to $5 : 1$. We perform normalization on these return series by $R_t = (r_t - Mean(r_t))/SD(r_t)$, where the means and standard deviations are computed for each individual index in the training period.

We compare the performance of the LSVR model against the SVR. The predicted system is modelled as $\hat{R}_t = f(\boldsymbol{x}_t)$, where $\boldsymbol{x}_t$ takes the previous four days' normalized returns as indicators, i.e. $\boldsymbol{x}_t = (R_{t-4}, R_{t-3}, R_{t-2}, R_{t-1})$. Here this simple setting we employ is based on the suggestions in [15]: A suitable selection for the sequent values is four. We then apply the modelled function f to test the performance by one-step ahead prediction. The trade-off parameter C and the parameter of the RBF kernel $(\boldsymbol{K}(\boldsymbol{u},\boldsymbol{v}) = \exp(-\beta\|\boldsymbol{u} - \boldsymbol{v}\|^2))$, (C, β), are obtained by a five-fold cross-validation conducting the SVR on the following paired points: $[2^{-5}, 2^{-4}, \ldots, 2^{10}] \times [2^{-5}, 2^{-4}, \ldots, 2^{10}]$. We obtain the corresponding parameters as $(2^4, 2^{-3})$ for DJIA, $(2^{-3}, 2^1)$ for NASDAQ, and $(2^0, 2^2)$ for S&P500.

As suggested in [15], there is a relationship in the sequential five days' values. We select $k = 2$, i.e. five days' values, to model the local volatility. Since when $\epsilon \geq 2.0$, there are no support vectors in SVR, we just set the ϵ

values from $0.0, 0.2, \ldots, 1.0$, to 2.0. The corresponding results are reported in Table 6.3. As observed, the LSVR model demonstrates a consistent superiority to the SVR algorithm, even though the paired parameters (C, β) are not tuned for our LSVR model. Furthermore, a paired t-test [13] performed on the best results of both models in Table 6.3, shows that the LSVR model outperforms SVR with $\alpha = 10\%$ significance level for a one-tailed test.

Table 6.3. Experimental results of the LSVR model and the SVR algorithm on the financial data with different ϵ values

ϵ	DJIA		NASDAQ		S&P500	
	LSVR	SVR	LSVR	SVR	LSVR	SVR
0.0	0.9204	1.3241	1.2897	1.3050	1.2372	1.2833
0.2	0.9835	1.1274	1.2896	1.3246	1.2399	1.2831
0.4	0.9341	0.9156	1.2898	1.3314	1.2442	1.2952
0.6	0.9096	0.9387	1.2901	1.3404	1.2540	1.2887
0.8	0.9273	0.9450	1.2904	1.3891	1.2788	1.2798
1.0	0.9434	0.9713	1.2908	1.4105	1.3044	1.2664
2.0	0.9666	1.0337	1.2928	1.3619	1.2643	1.3220

6.8 Summary

In this chapter, we propose a Local Support Vector Regression model. Different from the standard Support Vector Regression model, our novel model offers a systematic and automatic scheme to locally and flexibly adapt the margin. Therefore, it can tolerate the noise adaptively. We demonstrate that the promising model can not only capture the local information of the data in approximating functions, but also can branch out similar models to the standard SVR. The experiments conducted on sinc datasets and three indices data from stock markets show that our model outperforms the standard SVR. One future work of this model is to investigate efficient methods to directly solve the original optimization of LSVR instead of solving a relaxed form. In addition, both theoretical and empirical comparisons between the true solution and the approximated relaxed solution quantitatively are also valuable research topics in the future.

References

1. Chang CC, Lin CJ (2001) LIBSVM: A Library for Support Vector Machines
2. Chen S (1995) Basis Pursuit. PhD thesis, Department of Statistics, Standford University

3. Chen S, Donoho D, Saunders M (1995) Atomic decomposition by basis pursuit. Technique Report 479, Department of Statistics, Standford University

4. Coifman RR, Wickerhauser MV (1992) Entropy-based algorithms for best-basis selection. IEEE Transactions on Information Theory 38(2):713–718

5. Daubechies I (1992) Ten lectures on wavelets. In CBMS-NSF Regional Conferences Series in Applied Mathematics. Philadelphia, PA: SIAM

6. Drucker H, Burges C, Kaufman L, Smola A, Vapnik VN (1997) Support Vector Regression Machines. In Mozer Michael C, Jordan Michael I, Petsche Thomas, editors, Advances in Neural Information Processing Systems. Cambridge, MA: The MIT Press 9:155–161

7. Girosi F (1998) An equivalence between sparse approximation and support vector machines. Neural Computation 10(6):1455–1480

8. Gunn S (1998) Support vector machines for classification and regression. Technical Report NC2-TR-1998-030, Faculty of Engineering and Applied Science, Department of Electronics and Computer Science, University of Southampton

9. Harpur GF, Prager RW (1996) Development of low entropy coding in a recurrent network. Networks 7:277–284

10. Huang K, Yang H, King I, Lyu MR (2004) Learning large margin classifiers locally and globally. In the 21st International Conference on Machine Learning (ICML-2004)

11. Lobo M, Vandenberghe L, Boyd S, Lebret H (1998) Applications of second order cone programming. Linear Algebra and Its Applications 284:193–228

12. Mallat S, Zhang Z (1993) Matching pursuit in a time-frequency dictionary. IEEE Transactions on Signal Processing 41(12):3397–3415

13. Montgomery Douglas C, Runger George C (1999) Applied statistics and probability for engineers. New York, NY: John & Wileys, 2nd edition

14. Olshausen BA, Field DJ (1996) Emergence of simple-cell receptive field properties by learning a sparse code for natural images. Nature 381:607–609

15. Pompe Bernd (2002) Mutual information and relevant variables for predictions. In Soofi Abdols, Cao Liangyue, editors, Modelling and forecasting financial data: techniques of nonlinear dynamics. Boston, MA: Kluwer Academic Publishers 61–92

16. Schölkopf B, Bartlett P, Smola A, Williamson R (1999) Shrinking the Tube: A New Support Vector Regression Algorithm. In Kearns MS, Solla SA, Cohn DA, editors, Advances in Neural Information Processing Systems. Cambridge, MA: The MIT Press 11:330–336

17. Smola A, Schölkopf B (1998) A tutorial on support vector regression. Technical Report NC2-TR-1998-030, NeuroCOLT2

18. Sturm JF (1999) Using sedumi 1.02, a matlab toolbox for optimization over symmetric cones. Optimization Methods and Software 11:625–653

19. Sturm JF (2000) Central region method. In Frenk JBG, Roos C, Terlaky T, Zhang S, editors, High Performance Optimization. Kluwer Academic Publishers 157–194

20. Vapnik VN (1999) The Nature of Statistical Learning Theory. New York, NY: Springer-Verlag 2nd edition

21. Yang H, King I, Chan L, Huang K (2004) Financial Time Series Prediction Using Non-fixed and Asymmetrical Margin Setting with Momentum in Support Vector Regression. In Rajapakse JC, Wang L, editors, Neural Information Processing: Research and Development, Studies in Fuzziness and Soft Computing. New York, NY: Springer-Verlag 152:334–350

7

Extension III: Variational Margin Settings within Local Data in Support Vector Regression

In Chapter 6, we propose a Local Support Vector Regression Model to include the local information of data. In this chapter, we consider another extension of the Support Vector Regression (SVR) which also includes the local information of data for a specific application, i. e. financial engineering. Both these models are motivated from the local viewpoint of data.

SVR is derived from the Support Vector Machine which is based on the principle of Structural Risk Minimization (SRM). Due to its solid theoretical ground, SVR has been applied successfully in time series prediction [9, 10]. Usually, when SVR is applied in time series forecasting, it uses the ϵ-insensitive loss function to measure the empirical risk. This loss function contains an ϵ margin. It not only measures the training error (empirical risk), but also controls the sparsity of the solution (the number of support vectors). When the width of ϵ-margin increases, it may tend to reduce the number of support vectors. Extremely, a too wide margin may result in a constant regression function. When the width of ϵ-margin decreases, it may increase the number of support vectors. Ultimately, all the data points are used for support vectors [19]. In this case, it may include the data noise in seeking the regression function. Hence, setting the width of ϵ-margin is very important. It affects the complexity and the generalization of the regression function indirectly.

Normally, the setting of ϵ is fixed, which is a kind of global setting. However, in some applications, e. g. financial engineering, the global setting will not be an optimal choice. Since financial data are usually volatile and noisy, we extend the previous global margin setting to a variation one which includes the local information of data.

In the following, we will first describe the SVR model briefly in Section 7.1. We then indicate the problem of margin settings in Section 7.2. To solve the problem of margin settings, we propose a general ϵ-insensitive loss function for SVR in Section 7.3. We further aim at a specific application, i. e. financial engineering by introducing momentum and including GARCH model for the variational margin settings in Section 7.4. After the detailed experimental setup and experimental results in Section 7.5, we conclude the chapter with discussions in Section 7.6.

7.1 Support Vector Regression

The aim of SVR is to find a function f with parameters $\boldsymbol{w}$ and b by minimizing the regression error as follows:

$$R_{\mathrm{reg}}(f) = \frac{1}{2}\langle \boldsymbol{w}, \boldsymbol{w}\rangle + C\sum_{i=1}^{N} l(f(\boldsymbol{x}_i), y_i) , \tag{7.1}$$

where $\langle,\rangle$ denotes the inner product. This Euclidean norm $\langle \boldsymbol{w}, \boldsymbol{w}\rangle$ measures the flatness of the function f. Minimizing $\langle \boldsymbol{w}, \boldsymbol{w}\rangle$ will make the regression function as flat as possible [16].

The function f is then defined as

$$f(\boldsymbol{x}, \boldsymbol{w}, b) = \langle \boldsymbol{w}, \phi(\boldsymbol{x})\rangle + b , \tag{7.2}$$

where $\phi(\boldsymbol{x}) : \boldsymbol{x} \to \Omega$, maps $\boldsymbol{x} \in \boldsymbol{X}(\mathbb{R}^d)$ into a high (possible infinite) dimensional space Ω, and $b \in \mathbb{R}$.

There are several loss functions which could be used to measure the regression error, e.g. squared loss function, Huber's loss function, ϵ-insensitive loss function, etc. In SVR, the ϵ-insensitive loss function is used to measure the loss [19] (illustrated in Fig. 7.1):

$$l_\epsilon(y, f(\boldsymbol{x})) = \begin{cases} 0, & \text{if} \quad |y - f(\boldsymbol{x})| < \epsilon ; \\ |y - f(\boldsymbol{x})| - \epsilon, & \text{otherwise} . \end{cases} \tag{7.3}$$

The advantage of this loss function is that it could affect the seeking of regression function implicitly.

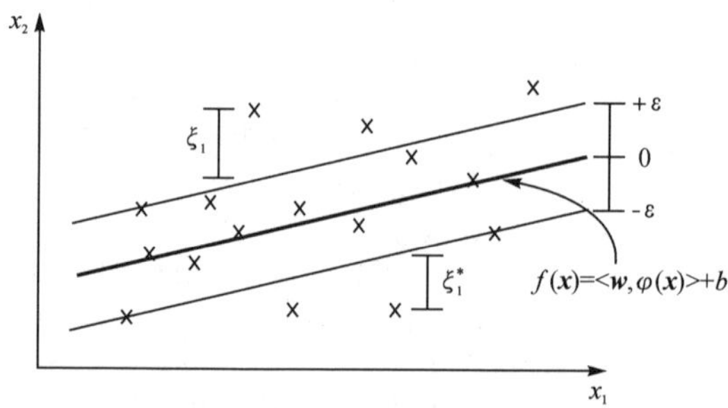

Fig. 7.1. Linear regression in the feature space by ϵ loss function

To solve the minimization of Eq.(7.1) with loss function of Eq.(7.3) is equivalent to solving the following constrained minimization problem:

$$\min \quad \Upsilon(\boldsymbol{w}, b, \boldsymbol{\xi}^{(*)}) = \frac{1}{2}\langle \boldsymbol{w}, \boldsymbol{w}\rangle + C\sum_{i=1}^{N}(\xi_i + \xi_i^*) , \tag{7.4}$$

subject to

$$
\begin{aligned}
y_i - (\langle \boldsymbol{w}, \boldsymbol{\phi}(\boldsymbol{x}_i)\rangle + b) &\leq \epsilon + \xi_i , \\
(\langle \boldsymbol{w}, \boldsymbol{\phi}(\boldsymbol{x}_i)\rangle + b) - y_i &\leq \epsilon + \xi_i^* , \\
\xi_i^{(*)} &\geq 0 .
\end{aligned}
\tag{7.5}
$$

Here and below, for every i, it ranges from 1 to N and $(*)$ is a shorthand implying both the variables with and without asterisks. ξ_i and ξ_i^* measure the up error and down error for the sample point $(\boldsymbol{x}_i, y_i)$, respectively, see Fig. 7.1.

A standard method to find the optimal solution of the above minimization problem in Eq.(7.4), further finding the function f in Eq.(7.2), is to construct the dual problem of this optimization problem (primal problem) by the Lagrange Method and to translate the (primal) minimization problem to maximize its dual function. Therefore, the optimization becomes a Quadratic Programming (QP) problem as follows [19]:

$$
\begin{aligned}
\min \quad Q(\boldsymbol{\alpha}^{(*)}) = &\frac{1}{2}\sum_{i=1}^{N}\sum_{j=1}^{N}(\alpha_i - \alpha_i^*)(\alpha_j - \alpha_j^*)\langle \phi(\boldsymbol{x}_i), \phi(\boldsymbol{x}_j)\rangle \\
&+ \sum_{i=1}^{N}(\epsilon - y_i)\alpha_i + \sum_{i=1}^{N}(\epsilon + y_i)\alpha_i^* ,
\end{aligned}
\tag{7.6}
$$

subject to

$$\sum_{i=1}^{N}(\alpha_i - \alpha_i^*) = 0, \quad \alpha_i^{(*)} \in [0, C] . \tag{7.7}$$

After solving this QP problem, we obtain the objective function as:

$$f(\boldsymbol{x}) = \sum_{i=1}^{N}(\alpha_i - \alpha_i^*)\langle \phi(\boldsymbol{x}_i), \phi(\boldsymbol{x})\rangle + b ,$$

where α, α^* are the Lagrange multipliers used to pull and push f towards to the observation y. Those sample points $(\boldsymbol{x}_i, y_i)$ with nonzero α_i or α_i^* are called support vectors.

By using the trick of kernel function, one could define the kernel function as the inner product of mapping function, i. e. $K(\boldsymbol{x}, \boldsymbol{z}) = \langle \phi(\boldsymbol{x}), \phi(\boldsymbol{z})\rangle$. Therefore, one only needs to specify a kernel function without considering the mapping function or the feature space explicitly. The property of the kernel function is that it should satisfy the Mercer's Theorem [6, 14].

Four kernel functions are common used:

Linear function: $K(\boldsymbol{x}_k, \boldsymbol{x}_l) = \langle \boldsymbol{x}_k, \boldsymbol{x}_l \rangle$;
Polynomial function with parameter d, $K(\boldsymbol{x}_k, \boldsymbol{x}_l) = (\langle \boldsymbol{x}_k, \boldsymbol{x}_l \rangle + 1)^d$;
Radial Basis Function (RBF) with parameter β:

$$K(\boldsymbol{x}_k, \boldsymbol{x}_l) = \exp(-\beta \|\boldsymbol{x}_k - \boldsymbol{x}_l\|^2) , \tag{7.8}$$

Hyperbolic tangent: $K(\boldsymbol{x}_k, \boldsymbol{x}_l) = \tanh(2\langle \boldsymbol{x}_k, \boldsymbol{x}_l \rangle + 1)$.

7.2 Problem in Margin Settings

Since the width of ϵ-margin holds the ability to affect the complexity and the generalization of the regression function indirectly, it is very important to seek an optimal value for different applications. Commonly, the ϵ is difficult to control [10], as one does not know beforehand which one is able to fit the curve better.

Usually, there are several methods to deal with it. Firstly, most practitioners set the value of ϵ as a non-negative constant value just for convenience. For example, in [18], they simply set the margin width to 0. This amounts to the least modulus loss function. In other instances, the margin width has been set to a very small value [5, 9, 20]. The second method is the cross-validation technique, e. g. [4, 10]. It is usually too expensive in terms of computation. A more efficient approach is to use another variant called ν-SVR [12, 13, 14, 15], which determines ϵ by using another parameter ν. It is stated that ν may be easier to specify than ϵ. Another approach by Smola, et al. [17] is to find the "optimal" choice of ϵ based on maximizing the statistical efficiency of a location parameter estimator. They showed that the asymptotically optimal ϵ should be scaled linearly with the input noise of training the data, and this was verified experimentally. Recently, a regularization path was proposed for SVR to seek optimal parameters in [7, 21].

In financial time series, however, the data are noisy and high volatile. The fixed margin setting is not suitable for this special application. We therefore extend the fixed ϵ margin setting to variational ones.

7.3 General ϵ-insensitive Loss Function

First, we note that the margin in ϵ-insensitive loss function contains two characteristics: fixed and symmetrical. Based on these two characteristics, we have proposed a general ϵ-insensitive loss function and classified the margin into four cases in [22]: Fixed and Symmetrical Margin (FASM), Fixed and

Asymmetrical Margin (FAAM), Non-fixed and Symmetrical Margin (NASM) and Non-fixed and Asymmetrical Margin (NAAM). Table 7.1 gives a simple description of these four categories. FASM is equivalent to the margin in ϵ-insensitive loss function, see Fig. 7.2(a). FAAM is divided into up margin and down margin, each margin is fixed but they are not equal (Fig. 7.2(b)). While NASM is with equal up margin and down margin, but they are varied with data (Fig. 7.2(c)). NAAM combines two characteristics of the margin (Fig. 7.2(d)).

Table 7.1. Margin categories

	Symmetrical	Asymmetrical
Fixed	FASM	FAAM
Non-fixed	NASM	NAAM

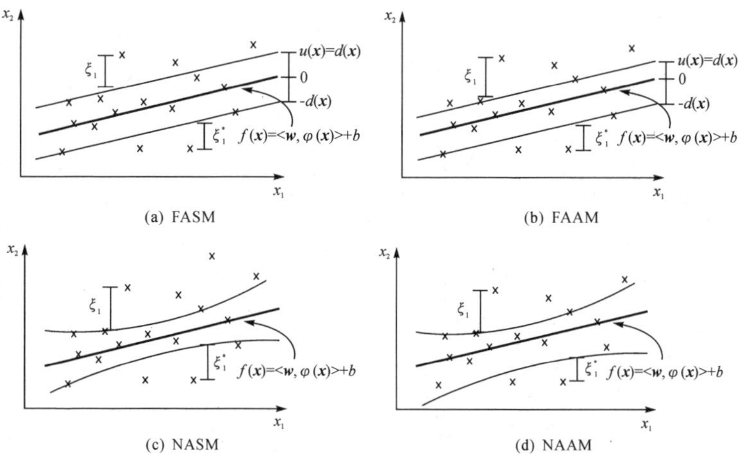

Fig. 7.2. Four categories in general ϵ-insensitive loss function of SVR

In the following, we will derive the SV formula based on the general ϵ-insensitive loss function. The general ϵ-insensitive loss function splits the margin in the original ϵ-insensitive loss function into two parts: up margin and down margin,

$$l'_\epsilon(f(\boldsymbol{x}_i)-y_i) = \begin{cases} 0, & \text{if } -d(\boldsymbol{x}_i) < y_i - f(\boldsymbol{x}_i) < u(\boldsymbol{x}_i); \\ y_i - f(\boldsymbol{x}_i) - u(\boldsymbol{x}_i), & \text{if } y_i - f(\boldsymbol{x}_i) \geq u(\boldsymbol{x}_i); \\ f(\boldsymbol{x}_i) - y_i - d(\boldsymbol{x}_i), & \text{if } f(\boldsymbol{x}_i) - y_i \geq d(\boldsymbol{x}_i), \end{cases} \tag{7.9}$$

where $d(\boldsymbol{x}_i), u(\boldsymbol{x}_i) \geq 0$, are two functions determining the down-margin and up margin at point $\boldsymbol{x}_i$ respectively. When $d(\boldsymbol{x})$ and $u(\boldsymbol{x})$ are both constant functions and $d(\boldsymbol{x}) = u(\boldsymbol{x})$, Eq.(7.9) amounts to the ϵ-insensitive loss function in Eq.(7.3) and we label it as FASM (Fixed and Symmetrical Margin). When $d(\boldsymbol{x})$ and $u(\boldsymbol{x})$ are both constant functions but $d(\boldsymbol{x}) \neq u(\boldsymbol{x})$, this case is labeled as FAAM (Fixed and Asymmetrical Margin). In the case of NASM (Non-fixed and Symmetrical Margin), $d(\boldsymbol{x}) = u(\boldsymbol{x})$ but are varied with the data. The last case is with a non-fixed and asymmetrical margin (NAAM) where $d(\boldsymbol{x})$ and $u(\boldsymbol{x})$ are varied with the data and $d(\boldsymbol{x}) \neq u(\boldsymbol{x})$.

In the same way, we use the standard method to find the solution of Eq.(7.1) with the cost function of Eq.(7.9) as [19] and obtain:

$$\min_{\boldsymbol{w},b,\boldsymbol{\xi}^{(*)}} \left\{ \frac{1}{2}\langle \boldsymbol{w}, \boldsymbol{w}\rangle + C \sum_{i=1}^{N}(\xi_i + \xi_i^*) \right\}, \tag{7.10}$$

subject to

$$y_i - \langle \boldsymbol{w}, \phi(\boldsymbol{x}_i)\rangle - b \leq u(\boldsymbol{x}_i) + \xi_i \ ,$$
$$\langle \boldsymbol{w}, \phi(\boldsymbol{x}_i)\rangle + b - y_i \leq d(\boldsymbol{x}_i) + \xi_i^* \ ,$$
$$\xi_i^{(*)} \geq 0 \ .$$

Using the standard primal-dual method as above, we also obtain a QP problem as follows:

$$\min \quad \Phi(\boldsymbol{\alpha}^{(*)}) = \frac{1}{2}\sum_{i=1}^{N}\sum_{j=1}^{N}(\alpha_i - \alpha_i^*)(\alpha_j - \alpha_j^*)\langle \phi(\boldsymbol{x}_i), \phi(\boldsymbol{x}_j)\rangle$$
$$+ \sum_{i=1}^{N}(u(\boldsymbol{x}_i) - y_i)\alpha_i + \sum_{i=1}^{N}(d(\boldsymbol{x}_i) + y_i)\alpha_i^* \ , \tag{7.11}$$

subject to

$$\sum_{i=1}^{N}(\alpha_i - \alpha_i^*) = 0, \quad \alpha_i, \alpha_i^* \in [0, C] \ .$$

This QP problem is very similar to the original QP problem in Eq.(7.6), therefore, we just need to modify the SMO algorithm a little bit to implement this QP problem. Practically, we add a new data structure to store both margins: up margin, $u(\boldsymbol{x})$, and down-margin, $d(\boldsymbol{x})$. This will not impact the time complexity of the SVR algorithm; we just need more space linear to the size of data points to store the corresponding margins. We modify the LIBSVM from [5] to implement the SVR algorithm.

After solving this QP problem, we then obtain the regression function:

$$f(\boldsymbol{x}) = \sum_{i=1}^{N}(\alpha_i - \alpha_i^*)\langle \phi(\boldsymbol{x}_i), \phi(\boldsymbol{x})\rangle + b \ , \tag{7.12}$$

where $\boldsymbol{\alpha}$, $\boldsymbol{\alpha}^*$ are corresponding Lagrange multipliers also used to pull and push f towards to the observation y.

The computation of b is exploited by the Karush-Kuhn-Tucker (KKT) conditions. Here, they are:

$$\alpha_i(u(\boldsymbol{x}_i) + \xi_i - y_i + \langle \boldsymbol{w}, \phi(\boldsymbol{x}_i) \rangle + b) = 0 \ ,$$
$$\alpha_i^*(d(\boldsymbol{x}_i) + \xi_i^* + y_i + \langle \boldsymbol{w}, \phi(\boldsymbol{x}_i) \rangle - b) = 0 \ ,$$

and

$$(C - \alpha_i)\xi_i = 0 \ ,$$
$$(C - \alpha_i^*)\xi_i^* = 0 \ .$$

Therefore, b can be computed as follows:

$$b = \begin{cases} y_i - \langle \boldsymbol{w}, \phi(\boldsymbol{x}_i) \rangle - u(\boldsymbol{x}_i), \text{ for } \alpha_i \in (0, C) \ ; \\ y_i - \langle \boldsymbol{w}, \phi(\boldsymbol{x}_i) \rangle + d(\boldsymbol{x}_i), \text{ for } \alpha_i^* \in (0, C) \ . \end{cases}$$

When no $\alpha_i^{(*)} \in (0, C)$, methods e.g. [5] are used.

7.4 Non-fixed Margin Cases

7.4.1 Momentum

In [23], we have focused on the case of NAAM. More specially, we have added a momentum term in the margin setting. The margin is a linear combination of the standard deviation and the momentum. The up margin and down-margin are set in the following forms:

$$\begin{aligned} u(\boldsymbol{x}_i) &= \lambda_1 \cdot \sigma(\boldsymbol{x}_i) + \mu \cdot \Delta(\boldsymbol{x}_i), \quad i = 1, \ldots, N, \\ d(\boldsymbol{x}_i) &= \lambda_2 \cdot \sigma(\boldsymbol{x}_i) - \mu \cdot \Delta(\boldsymbol{x}_i), \quad i = 1, \ldots, N, \end{aligned} \tag{7.13}$$

where $\sigma(\boldsymbol{x}_i)$ is the standard deviation of input $\boldsymbol{x}_i$, $\Delta(\boldsymbol{x}_i)$ is the momentum at point $\boldsymbol{x}_i$, λ_1, λ_2 are both positive constants and μ is a non-negative constant. Therefore, the width of margin at point $\boldsymbol{x}_i$ is:

$$W(\boldsymbol{x}_i) = (\lambda_1 + \lambda_2) \cdot \sigma(\boldsymbol{x}_i) \ .$$

It is determined by $\sigma(\boldsymbol{x}_i)$ and the sum of λ_1 and λ_2. Here we called λ_1, λ_2 as the coefficients of the margin width. We also called μ as the coefficient of momentum and we know that the margin setting of Eq.(7.13) includes the case of NASM (when $\mu = 0$).

From [22], when $\mu \neq 0$ and $\Delta(x) > 0$, the up margin is larger than the down-margin and we can under-predict the stock price. While $\mu \neq 0$ and

$\Delta(x) < 0$, the up margin is smaller than the down-margin and we can over-predict the stock price. A simple illustration is shown in Fig. 7.3. Based on these observations, in our prediction we assume that we are risk aversion, or downside risk aversion. When the stock price reveals an uptrend, we know that it will not be always up, so we tend to under-predict the stock prices in this case. On the contrary, when the stock price goes down, we tend to over-predict it. We add this information in the margin setting by controlling the momentum term.

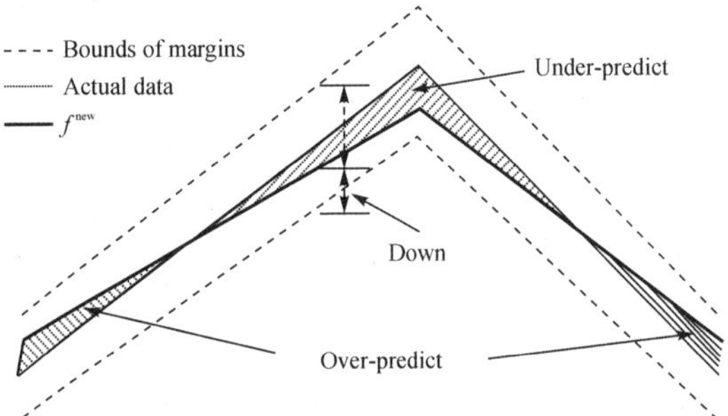

Fig. 7.3. Margin settings: dashed lines are the bounds of margins; dashed-dotted lines are actual data series; solid-bold lines are the new objective function, f^{new}, by new margin settings. The upper shadow area is the case of new objective function under-predicted to the actual function; the lower shadow parts are the case of "over-predicted"

Actually, there are many ways to calculate the momentum. For example, the simplest way is to set it as a constant. In this chapter, we will concentrate on using the Exponential Moving Average (EMA). The reason of using EMA is that it is time-varying and can reflect the uptrend and down-tendency of the financial data. A little deficiency is that there exists the lag problem. An n-day's EMA sequence begins from the first day, i.e. $EMA_1 = y_1$ and the following is calculated by:

$$EMA_i = EMA_{i-1} \times (1 - r) + y_i \times r \, ,$$

where $r = 2/(1 + n)$, and y_i is the information about day i, e.g. the closing price in day i, the volume in day i, etc. Here, the current day's momentum is set as the difference between the current day's EMA and the EMA in the previous k day, i.e.

$$\Delta(x_i) = EMA_i - EMA_{i-k} \, .$$

7.4.2 GARCH

In the above methods, the datasets we used in the experiments are the price of the share [22, 23]. We use the standard deviation of input x_t, which can reflect the volatility of the financial time series over time, to determine the width of margin at time t in our prediction. Actually, the Generalized AutoRegressive Conditionally Heteroscedastic (GARCH) model [3] is a more common used model to reflect the volatility of the financial time series.

The standard $GARCH$(p, q) model with Gaussian shocks takes the following form:

$$y_t = c_0 + \boldsymbol{x}_t^{\mathrm{T}}\boldsymbol{b} + \epsilon_t, \quad \epsilon_t|\Psi_{t-1} = N(0, \sigma_t^2) \,,$$

where

$$\sigma_t^2 = \kappa_0 + \sum_{i=1}^{p} \lambda_i \sigma_{t-i}^2 + \sum_{j=1}^{q} \mu_j \epsilon_{t-j}^2 \,.$$

This GARCH toolbox is applied to the return series. So we use the continuous compounded return as the data series and use the σ_t calculated by $GARCH$(1,1) as the width of margin at time t.

7.5 Experiments

In this section, we will perform the experiments by using the momentum and GARCH models to set the margins. Before illustrating the experiments, we define the accuracy and risk measurement first.

7.5.1 Accuracy Metrics and Risk Measurement

In order to measure the prediction performance of our model, we define the Mean Absolute Error (MAE).

Let a_t and p_t be the actual values respectively and predicted values at day t, let m be the number of testing data.

Definition 7.1. Mean Absolute Error (MAE) *measures the discrepancy between the actual and predicted values; the smaller the value of MAE, the closer are the predicted values to the actual values. MAE is calculated by:*

$$MAE = \frac{1}{m} \sum_{t=1}^{m} |a_t - p_t| \,. \tag{7.14}$$

We also consider the risk of using this model in the prediction. Actually, risk is a term frequently encountered in strategic management and financial literature. However, risk has a variety of different meanings and rarely is the meaning used in a particular project clarified in [2]. In financial literature, Markowitz first formulated the portfolio selection into a mathematical model [8]. In his model, the "return" of a portfolio is measured by the expected value of the random portfolio return and the associated "risk" is quantified by the variance of the portfolio return. However, the use of variance to measure risk makes no distinction between gains and losses. Markowitz also proposed to use semi-variance to measure the risk of loss. That is the sum of the squares of negative deviations from the mean divided by the total number of observations:

$$\frac{1}{m}\sum_{t=1}^{m}[\min(r_t - \mu, 0)]^2 .$$

The great advantage of the use of semi-variance over variance is that it does not include positive gains, so what is considered as risk takes into account only negative deviations. However, minimizing downside does not mean minimizing only negative deviations. For example, if the distribution, like the normal curve, is symmetric, minimizing variance and semi-variance will lead to the same problem. The only case that justifies the use of semi-variance is when the presence of skewness is observed [1]. A generalization of semi-variance is given in [1]:

$$\text{downside risk} \Rightarrow \frac{1}{m}\sum_{t=1}^{m}[\min(r_t - \mu, 0)]^k , \tag{7.15}$$

where k is any power that one chooses; when $k=1$, it should be considered the absolute value of the term in the brackets and μ is a chosen benchmark (not necessarily the mean).

Based on Eq.(7.15), we choose $k=1$ and define the following risk measurements.

Definition 7.2. Upside Mean Absolute Error (UMAE) *measures upside risk; the smaller the value of UMAE, the smaller the upside risk. UMAE is defined as:*

$$UMAE = \frac{1}{m}\sum_{\substack{t=1 \\ a_t \geq p_t}}^{m} (a_t - p_t) . \tag{7.16}$$

Definition 7.3. Downside Mean Absolute Error (DMAE) *measures the downside risk; the smaller the value of DMAE, the smaller the downside risk. DMAE is defined as:*

$$DMAE = \frac{1}{m}\sum_{\substack{t=1 \\ a_t < p_t}}^{m} (p_t - a_t) . \tag{7.17}$$

7.5.2 Momentum

We compare the modified SVR algorithm by adapting margins using momentum with the AutoRegression (AR) model and the Radial Basis Function (RBF) method. The results are presented as follows one by one for three algorithms.

7.5.2.1 SVR Algorithm

Two datasets are used in this experiment:

HSI: daily closing prices of Hong Kong's Hang Seng Index (HSI) from January 2nd, 1998 to December 29, 2000.

DJIA: daily closing prices of Dow Jones Industrial Average (DJIA) from January 2nd, 1998 to December 29, 2000.

The ratio of the number of training data and the number of testing data is set to 5:1. Therefore, the corresponding initial training time periods are obtained and listed as in Table 7.2.

Table 7.2. Indices, time periods and parameters for momentum experiments

Indices	Initial training time periods	C	β
HSI	$02/01/1998 - 04/07/2000$	16000	2^{-27}
DJIA	$02/01/1998 - 29/06/2000$	8000	2^{-22}

Furthermore, we model the system as $p_t = f(\boldsymbol{x}_t)$, where f is learned by the SVR algorithm from the training data, $\boldsymbol{x}_t = (a_{t-4}, a_{t-3}, a_{t-2}, a_{t-1})$, a_t is the daily closing index in day t.

Before generating the model, we do a cross-validation on the initial training data to determine the parameters that are needed in SVR. They are C, the cost of error and β, the parameter of kernel function. The corresponding parameters are also listed in Table 7.2. With these parameters we begin to build the model by SVR from the initial training data. After obtaining the predictive value, we shift the input window to the next time-step and train the model again to obtain the next day's price. This one-step ahead prediction is done as the window shifted for the remaining data.

Non-fixed Cases: The margins setting is followed as Eq.(7.13). In the case of NASM, we set $\lambda_1 = \lambda_2 = 1/2$ and $\mu = 0$, thus the overall margin width at day t is equal to the standard deviation of input $\boldsymbol{x}_t$, $\sigma(\boldsymbol{x}_t)$.

In the case of NAAM, we also fix $\lambda_1 = \lambda_2 = 1/2$, hence we have a fair comparison of NASM case. In addition, we have to determine three parameters, i.e. n, the length of EMA; k, the lag of EMA; μ, the coefficient of momentum. We have performed the following experiments to test their effects:

(a) At first, we set $k = 1$, $\mu = 1$ and use 10, 30, 50, 100 as the length of EMA respectively. From the result of Table 7.3 we can see that the DMAE values in all cases of NAAM are smaller than that in NASM case, thus we have a smaller downside risk in NAAM case; this exactly meets our assumption. We also see that the MAE gradually decreases with the increase of the length of EMA, and that when the length equals 100, the MAE and the DMAE are the smallest in all cases of NAAM for dataset HSI. For dataset DJIA, when the length equals 30, the MAE and the DMAE are also the smallest in all cases of NAAM.

Table 7.3. Effect of the length of EMA on HSI with parameters $(k, \mu)=(1,1)$

Type	n	HSI			DJIA		
		MAE	UMAE	DMAE	MAE	UMAE	DMAE
NASM		216.78	104.58	112.20	85.33	40.29	45.04
NAAM	10	222.43	115.64	106.79	85.68	43.13	42.55
	30	218.18	114.04	104.14	84.12	41.82	42.30
	50	217.93	113.38	104.55	84.57	42.12	42.45
	100	216.50	113.04	103.46	84.80	42.41	42.39

In the following, we will use the best length of EMA from the above experiments for the corresponding datasets, i.e. $n = 100$ for data set HSI and $n = 30$ for dataset DJIA.

(b) When testing the effect of lag k, we let $\mu = 1$ and set k to 1, 2, 4, 8 respectively for both datasets. The results are listed in Table 7.4. They show that the MAE increases with increasing of the lag of EMA. These indicate that the results when the lag of EMA equals 1 are superior to the other cases.

Table 7.4. Effect of the distance of EMA on HSI and DJIA

k	HSI with $(n, k) = (100, 1)$			DJIA with $(n, k) = (30, 1)$		
	MAE	UMAE	DMAE	MAE	UMAE	DMAE
1	216.50	113.04	103.46	84.12	41.82	42.30
2	219.02	125.30	93.72	85.42	43.91	41.51
4	228.25	149.36	78.88	90.99	49.16	41.83
8	260.73	200.74	59.99	103.77	58.03	45.74

(c) Here, we set $k = 1$ and $\mu = 1, 1/2, 1/4, 1/8$ respectively for both datasets to see the effect of the μ. From Table 7.5, we see that the DMAE increases gradually with decreasing of the coefficient of EMA and that the MAE is smaller than the value in the NASM case. The change of the MAE for dataset HSI in (2–4 columns of) Table 7.5 is fluctuating and the MAE in (5–7 columns of) Table 7.5 increases gradually with the decrease of the coefficient of EMA.

Table 7.5. Effect of the coefficient of momentum on HSI and DJIA

μ	HSI with $(n, k) = (100, 1)$			DJIA with $(n, k) = (30, 1)$		
	MAE	UMAE	DMAE	MAE	UMAE	DMAE
1	216.50	113.04	103.46	84.12	41.82	42.30
1/2	216.55	108.97	107.58	84.88	41.32	43.56
1/4	216.19	106.36	109.83	85.02	41.14	43.88
1/8	216.41	105.32	111.08	85.22	40.86	44.36

We also plot the daily closing prices of HSI with 100 days' EMA and the prices of DJIA with 30 days' EMA in Fig. 7.4 and Fig. 7.5 respectively, and list the Average Standard Deviations (ASD) of input x of the training datasets HSI and DJIA, respectively in Table 7.6, the Average of Absolute Momentums (AAM) of input x for the best length of both training datasets respectively in Table 7.6. We can observe that the ASD of HSI is higher than that of DJIA and that the ratio of AAM to ASD is smaller for HSI than that for DJIA.

Table 7.6. ASD and AAM

Dataset	ASD	AAM		Ratio
		n	Δ	
HSI	182.28	100	20.80	0.114
DJIA	79.95	30	15.64	0.196

Now, we will make a summary for the above experiments. At first, we can know the effects of n, k and μ from the above experiments results. Following these results, we can say that a suitable setting for k and μ will both be 1, which can be applied when a new dataset comes. The only parameter needed to determine is the length of EMA, n, this may refer to the ASD of the training dataset. When the ASD is larger, we may use a longer length of EMA. On the contrary, when the ASD is smaller, we may use a shorter length of EMA.

Fixed Cases: After considering the non-fixed margin cases, we also test the predictive results of fixed margins. Actually, for dataset HSI, we let

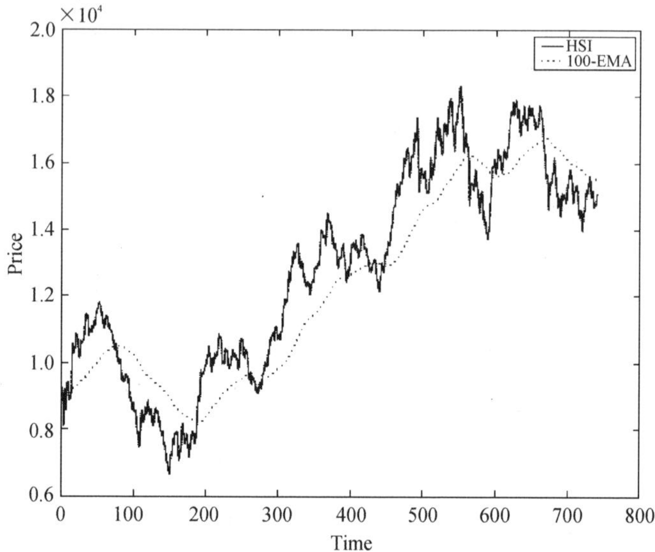

Fig. 7.4. HSI with 100 days' EMA

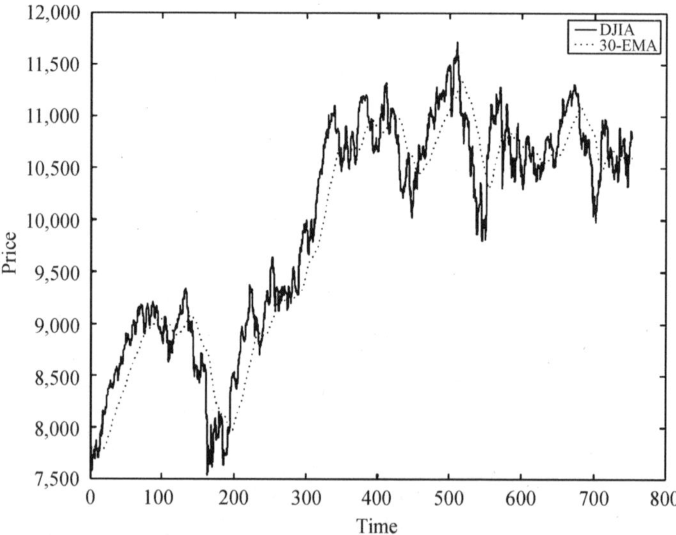

Fig. 7.5. DJIA with 30 days' EMA

the width of margin equal to 200 (approximate to the ASD of HSI), i.e. $u(\boldsymbol{x}) + d(\boldsymbol{x}) = 200$. The up-margin $u(\boldsymbol{x})$ ranges from 0 to 200, each increment is one-tenth of 200, i.e. 20. The results are listed in (1−5 columns of) Table 7.7. Similarly, for dataset DJIA, we let the width of margin equal to 90 (approximate to ASD of DJIA), i.e. $u(\boldsymbol{x}) + d(\boldsymbol{x}) = 90$. The up-margin

$u(x)$ ranges from 0 to 90, each increment is also one-tenth of 90, i.e. 9. The results are listed in (6−10 columns of) Table 7.7. We can see that for both datasets, as the up-margin increases, the DMAE tends to decrease.

Table 7.7. Results of FASM and FAAM for HSI and DJIA

HSI $[u(x)+d(x)]$					DJIA $[u(x)+d(x)]$				
$u(x)$	$d(x)$	MAE	UMAE	DMAE	$u(x)$	$d(x)$	MAE	UMAE	DMAE
0	200	236.04	62.24	173.80	0	90	91.63	20.45	71.18
20	180	230.85	69.65	161.20	9	81	89.14	23.70	65.44
40	160	226.29	77.37	148.92	18	72	87.35	27.31	60.04
60	140	222.24	85.34	136.90	27	63	86.09	31.18	54.91
80	120	219.35	93.90	125.45	36	54	85.30	35.28	50.02
100	100	217.83	103.14	114.69	45	45	85.45	39.86	45.59
120	80	217.35	112.90	104.45	54	36	86.33	44.80	41.53
140	60	217.88	123.16	94.72	63	27	87.40	49.83	37.57
160	40	219.49	133.97	85.52	72	18	88.64	54.95	33.69
180	20	221.66	145.05	76.61	81	9	90.80	60.53	30.27
200	0	224.83	156.64	68.19	90	0	93.75	66.51	27.24

Comparing the results in Table 7.3 with the results in Table 7.7 (the experimental results are plotted in Fig. 7.6(b) and Fig. 7.7(b) respectively), we can see that NASM and NAAM are both superior to FASM and FAAM in both datasets.

In the following, we will perform other models, such as AR models and RBF network, on the above two datasets. The best results of all the models are illustrated in Fig. 7.6(a) for HSI and Fig. 7.7(a) respectively.

7.5.2.2 AR Models

For AR models, we use the AR model with order 4 to predict the prices of HSI and DJIA, hence we can compare the AR model with NASM, NAAM in SVR with the same order. The results are listed in the Table 7.8. From these results, we can see that NASM and NAAM are superior to AR model with the same order.

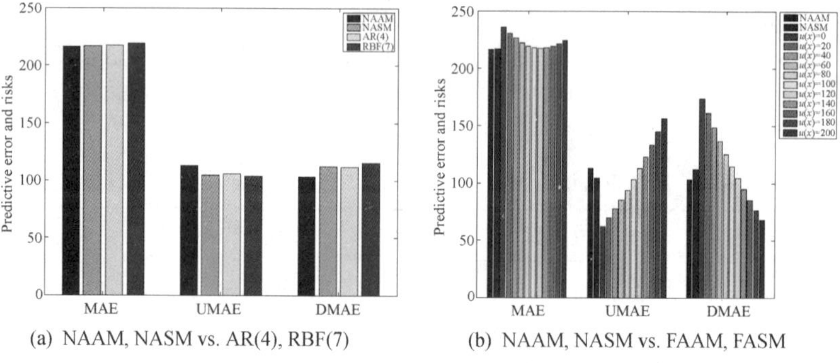

(a) NAAM, NASM vs. AR(4), RBF(7)   (b) NAAM, NASM vs. FAAM, FASM

Fig. 7.6. Experimental results of HSI

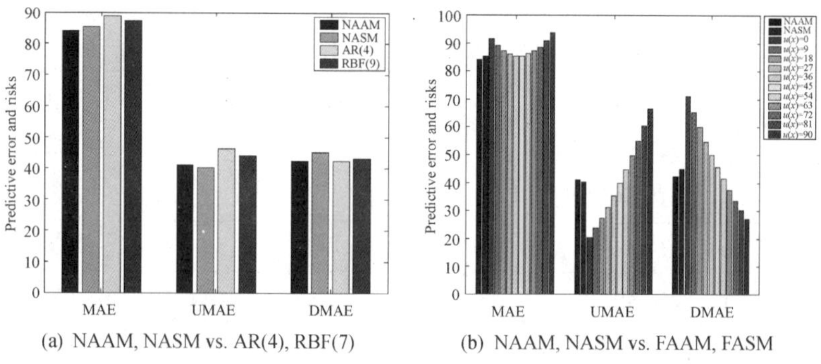

(a) NAAM, NASM vs. AR(4), RBF(7)   (b) NAAM, NASM vs. FAAM, FASM

Fig. 7.7. Experimental results of DJIA

Table 7.8. Results on AR(4)

Dataset	MAE	UMAE	DMAE
HSI	217.75	105.96	111.79
DJIA	88.74	46.36	42.38

7.5.2.3 RBF Network

For the RBF network, we use the RBF network which was implemented in
NETLAB [11] and perform the one-step-ahead prediction to predict the prices
of HSI and DJIA. Concretely, we let other parameters as default and set the
number of hidden units to 3, 5, 7, 9 to learn f by training the RBF network
on the training samples, and obtain the results in Table 7.9 for both datasets.
Comparing the results in Table 7.3 with the results in Table 7.9, we can see
that NASM and NAAM are also better than RBF network.

Table 7.9. Effect of number of hidden units on HSI and DJIA

Hidden No.	HSI			DJIA		
	MAE	UMAE	DMAE	MAE	UMAE	DMAE
3	386.65	165.08	221.57	88.31	44.60	43.71
5	277.83	128.92	148.91	98.44	48.46	49.98
7	219.32	104.15	115.17	90.53	46.22	44.31
9	221.81	109.46	112.35	87.23	44.09	43.14

7.5.3 GARCH

In this experiment, the experimental data are 3 years' daily closing indices (2000–2002) from stock markets in different countries:

Nikkei225: Nikkei225 Stock Average from Japan, the daily closing prices are plotted in Fig. 7.11(a);

DJIA00-02: Dow Jones Industrial Average (DJIA) from USA, the daily closing prices are plotted in Fig. 7.13(a);

FTSE100: FTSE100 index from UK, the daily closing prices are plotted in Fig. 7.15(a).

In the data processing step, the daily closing prices of these indices are converted to continuously compounded returns and the ratio of the number of training data to the number of testing data is set to 5:1. Therefore, we obtain and list the corresponding training and testing periods in Table 7.10.

Table 7.10. GARCH experimental data description

Indices	Training period	Testing period
Nikkei225	4 Jan., 2000 − 2 Jul., 2002	4 Jul., 2002 − 30 Dec., 2002
DJIA00-02	3 Jan., 2000 − 3 Jul., 2002	5 Jul., 2002 − 31 Dec., 2002
FTSE100	4 Jan., -2000 − 3 Jul., 2002	4 Jul., 2002 − 31 Dec., 2002

7.5.3.1 $GARCH(1,1)$

We apply the Matlab toolbox to calculate the GARCH model. In the Matlab toolbox, Before running the SVR algorithm, we run the $GARCH(1,1)$ model to determine the width of margin in SVR. For Nikkei225, we obtain the parameter estimates and their standard errors in Table 7.11, i. e. the best fits for Nikkei225 by (1,1) is:

$$y_t = 0.49468 + \epsilon_t,$$
$$\sigma_t^2 = 0.00073917 + 0.8682\sigma_{t-1}^2 + 0.077218\epsilon_{t-1}^2 .$$

Table 7.11. GARCH parameter for Nikkei225

Parameter	Value	Standard error	T statistic
c_0	0.49468	0.0045008	109.9083
κ_0	0.00073917	0.00034866	2.1200
$GARCH(1)$	0.8682	0.048144	18.0334
$ARCH(1)$	0.077218	0.027279	2.8306

We also show that the log-likelihood contours of $GARCH(1,1)$ model fit to the returns of dataset, Nikkei225 Fig. 7.8(a) The log-likelihood contours are plotted in a GARCH coefficient-ARCH coefficient $(G_1 - A_1)$ plane, holding the parameters c_0 and κ_0 fixed at their maximum likelihood estimates 0.49468 and 0.00073917, respectively. The contours confirm the results in Table 7.11. The maximum log-likelihood value occurs at the coordinates $G_1 = GARCH(1) = 0.8682$ and $A_1 = ARCH(1) = 0.077218$. This figure also reveals a highly negative correlation between the estimates of the G_1 and A_1 parameters of the $GARCH(1,1)$ model. It implies that a small change in the estimate of the G_1 parameter is nearly compensated for a corresponding change of opposite sign in the A_1 parameter. The innovations, standard deviations (σ_t) and returns of Nikkei225 are shown in Fig. 7.8(b).

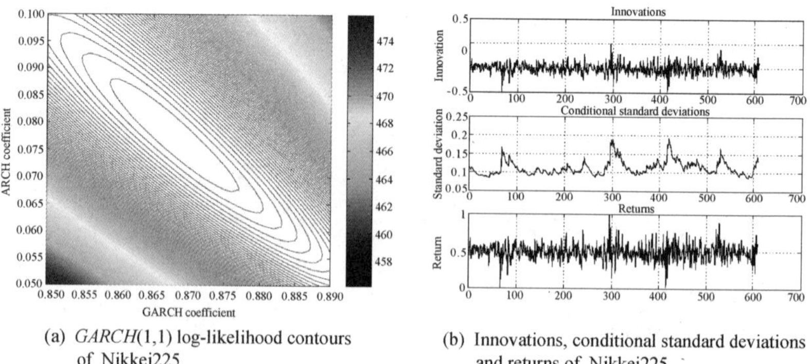

(a) $GARCH(1,1)$ log-likelihood contours of Nikkei225

(b) Innovations, conditional standard deviations and returns of Nikkei225

Fig. 7.8. $GARCH(1,1)$ of Nikkei225. The color-coded bar at the right of (a) indicates the height of the log-likelihood surface of the $GARCH(1,1)$ plane

For dataset DJIA00-02, $GARCH(1,1)$ parameter estimates are listed in Table 7.12, therefore, the best fits for DJIA00-02 by $GARCH(1,1)$ is

$$y_t = 0.60363 + \epsilon_t ,$$
$$\sigma_t^2 = 0.00056832 + 0.85971\sigma_{t-1}^2 + 0.092295\epsilon_{t-1}^2 .$$

Table 7.12. GARCH parameter for DJIA00-02

Parameter	Value	Standard error	T statistic
c_0	0.60363	0.0041185	146.5631
κ_0	0.00056832	0.00023491	2.4193
$GARCH(1)$	0.85971	0.031773	27.0580
$ARCH(1)$	0.092295	0.020352	4.5350

The corresponding log-likelihood contours of DJIA00-02 are plotted in Fig. 7.9(a), the maximum log-likelihood value occurs at the coordinates $G_1 = GARCH(1) = 0.85971$ and $A_1 = ARCH(1) = 0.09229$. The corresponding innovations, standard deviation and returns of DJIA00-02 are shown in Fig. 7.9(b).

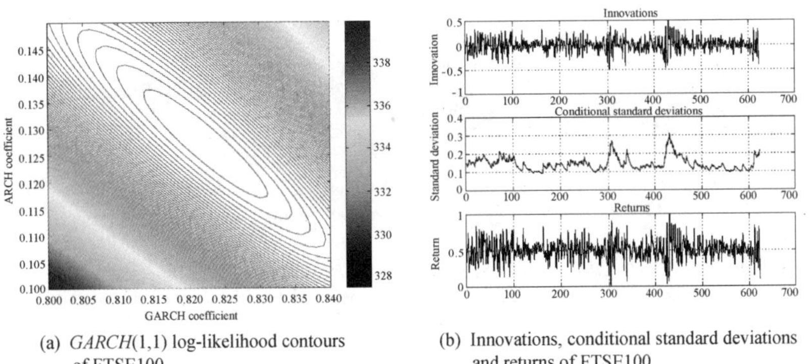

(a) $GARCH(1,1)$ log-likelihood contours of FTSE100

(b) Innovations, conditional standard deviations and returns of FTSE100

Fig. 7.9. $GARCH(1,1)$ of FTSE100. The color-coded bar at the right of (a) indicates the height of the log-likelihood surface of the $GARCH(1,1)$ plane

For dataset FTSE100, $GARCH(1,1)$ parameter estimates are listed in Table 7.13 therefore, the best fits for FTSE100 by $GARCH(1,1)$ is

$$y_t = 0.50444 + \epsilon_t \ ,$$
$$\sigma_t^2 = 0.0011599 + 0.82253\sigma_{t-1}^2 + 0.12693\epsilon_{t-1}^2 \ .$$

Table 7.13. GARCH parameter for FTSE100

Parameter	Value	Standard error	T statistic
c_0	0.50444	0.0053313	94.6180
κ_0	0.0011599	0.00049206	2.3573
$GARCH(1)$	0.82253	0.04906	16.7658
$ARCH(1)$	0.12693	0.034698	3.6582

The corresponding log-likelihood contours of FTSE100 are plotted in Fig. 7.10(a). The maximum log-likelihood value occurs at the coordinates $G_1 = GARCH(1) = 0.82253$ and $A_1 = ARCH(1) = 0.12693$. The corresponding innovations, standard deviation and returns of FTSE100 are shown in Fig. 7.10(b).

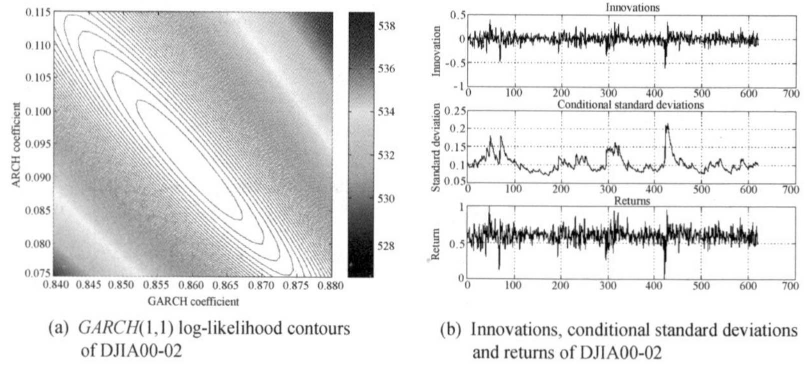

(a) $GARCH(1,1)$ log-likelihood contours of DJIA00-02

(b) Innovations, conditional standard deviations and returns of DJIA00-02

Fig. 7.10. $GARCH(1,1)$ of DJIA00-02. The color-coded bar at the right of (a) indicates the height of the log-likelihood surface of the $GARCH(1,1)$ plane

7.5.3.2 SVR Algorithm

For SVR algorithm, the experimental procedure consists of three steps: at first, we normalize the return value by $t_i = (r_i - r_{\text{low}})/(r_{\text{high}} - r_{\text{low}})$, where r_i is the actual return of the stock at day i, r_{low} and r_{high} are the correspondingly minimum and maximum return in the training data, respectively. Then, we train the normalized training data once and then obtain the normalized predicted return value $p_{n_i} = f(x_i)$, where $x_i = (t_{i-4}, t_{i-3}, t_{i-2}, t_{i-1})$. Finally, we unnormalize p_{n_i}, convert the result to price and obtain the corresponding predicted price p_i.

Before running the SVR algorithm, we have to choose two parameters: C, the cost of error; β, the parameter of kernel function. Here the parameters we choose are the same respectively for different indices. They are listed in Table 7.14.

Table 7.14. Parameters in GARCH experiments for NASM

Indices	C	β
Nikkei225	2	2^{-4}
DJIA	2	2^{-4}
FTSE100	2	2^{-4}

Here, we just consider the case of NASM. The margin setting is as Eq.(7.13). Concretely, we set the margin width to σ calculated by $GARCH(1,1)$ from return series y, therefore $\lambda_1 = \lambda_2 = 1/2$ and $\mu = 0$. For fixed margin cases, we set the margin width as 0.1, i.e. $u(x) + d(x) = 0.1$, and each increment is 0.02. The corresponding results are shown in the Tables 7.15−7.17. We also plot the training and testing data results of NAAM in Figs. 7.12(a) and 7.12(b) for index Nikkei225, in Figs. 7.14(a) and 7.14(b) for index DJIA00-02, in Figs. 7.16(a) and 7.16(b) for index FTSE100, respectively. From these results, we can see that for FTSE100 index, NASM outperforms in the prediction than in fixed margin cases. For Nikkei225, when $u(x) = 0.06, d(x) = 0.04$ and $u(x) = 0.08, d(x) = 0.02$, the predicted results are better than NASM. For DJIA00-02, when $u(x) = 0.06, d(x) = 0.04$, the predicted result is slightly better than NASM.

7.5.3.3 AR Models

We also use AR model with different orders (1−6) to predict the prices of the above three indices. The experimental procedure is to apply the AR model on training return series and to obtain the predicted return value from testing data. Then we convert the predicted return values to price values. We obtain the experimental results and show them in Table 7.18. After comparing the results in Tables 7.15 and 7.17 with the results in 2−4 and 8−10 columns of Table 7.18, we can see that for Nikkei225 and FTSE100 index, the NASM method is better than AR model. For DJIA, we can see that NASM method is slight worse than $AR(1)$, but better than other order of AR model.

For index Nikkei225, the predictive error and risks comparison results graphs are shown in Fig. 7.11(b), the corresponding bar values are from

Table 7.15. SVR results for Nikkei225

Type	$u(\boldsymbol{x})$	$d(\boldsymbol{x})$	MAE	UMAE	DMAE
NASM	σ	σ	124.37	55.97	68.40
FAAM	0	0.10	141.60	30.70	110.90
	0.02	0.08	131.25	39.02	92.23
	0.04	0.06	125.63	49.66	75.97
	0.06	0.04	123.11	61.81	61.30
	0.08	0.02	124.00	75.63	48.37
	0.10	0	129.19	91.56	37.63

Table 7.16. SVR results for DJIA00-02

Type	$u(\boldsymbol{x})$	$d(\boldsymbol{x})$	MAE	UMAE	DMAE
NASM	σ	σ	129.56	62.74	66.83
FAAM	0	0.10	139.82	41.56	98.26
	0.02	0.08	134.33	49.16	85.17
	0.04	0.06	130.49	57.56	72.93
	0.06	0.04	128.51	66.87	61.64
	0.08	0.02	129.65	77.72	51.94
	0.10	0	133.76	90.02	43.74

Table 7.17. SVR results for FTSE100

Type	$u(\boldsymbol{x})$	$d(\boldsymbol{x})$	MAE	UMAE	DMAE
NASM	σ	σ	69.61	33.42	36.19
FAAM	0	0.10	73.46	25.93	47.53
	0.02	0.08	71.98	28.52	43.46
	0.04	0.06	70.83	31.27	39.56
	0.06	0.04	70.10	34.22	35.88
	0.08	0.02	69.86	37.42	32.45
	0.10	0	70.26	40.92	29.34

Table 7.18. AR results

Order	Nikkei225			DJIA00-02			FTSE100		
	MAE	UMAE	DMAE	MAE	UMAE	DMAE	MAE	UMAE	DMAE
1	125.31	53.40	71.91	128.58	61.67	66.91	71.44	33.9	37.53
2	125.68	53.31	72.36	130.00	62.08	67.92	71.40	33.46	37.94
3	125.67	53.37	72.30	130.56	62.50	68.06	70.41	32.76	37.65
4	125.22	52.91	72.31	131.20	62.93	68.27	69.96	32.76	37.20
5	125.32	53.08	72.24	131.27	62.90	68.38	70.12	32.89	37.23
6	125.40	52.72	72.68	131.32	62.89	68.43	69.99	32.78	37.21

Table 7.15 and (2−4 columns of) Table 7.18. The predictive error and risks of DJIA00-02 are shown in Fig. 7.13(b), where the corresponding bar values are from Table 7.16 and (5−7 columns of) Table 7.18. The predictive error and risks of FTSE100 are shown in Fig. 7.15(b), where the corresponding bar values are from Table 7.17 and (8−10 columns of) Table 7.18.

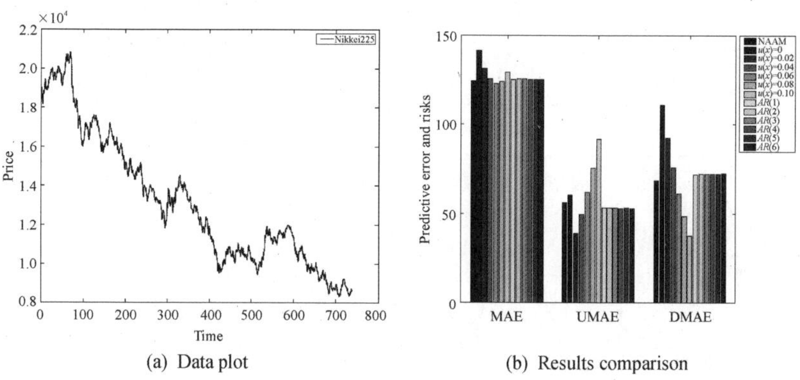

(a) Data plot   (b) Results comparison

Fig. 7.11. Nikkei225 data plot and experimental results graphs

7.6 Discussions

Having described the experiments and their results, we know that NASM is superior to FASM and FAAM generally. One reason is that NASM catches the stock market information and adds the information into the setting of the

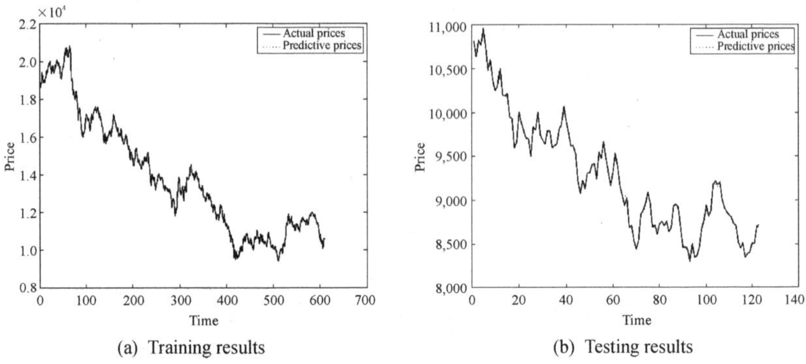

(a) Training results   (b) Testing results

Fig. 7.12. Experimental results graphs using GARCH method for Nikkei225

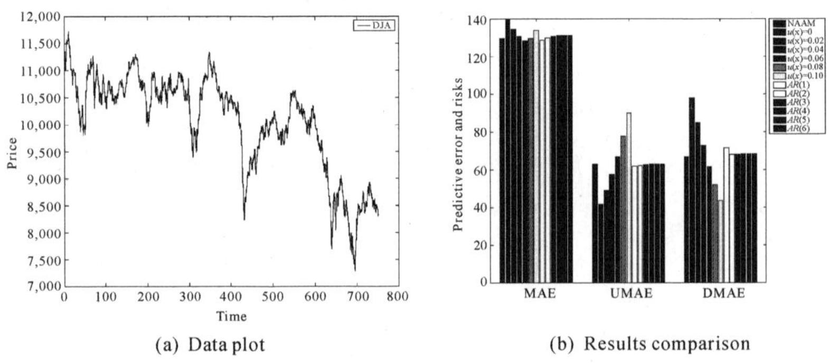

(a) Data plot   (b) Results comparison

Fig. 7.13. DJIA00-02 data plot and experimental results graphs

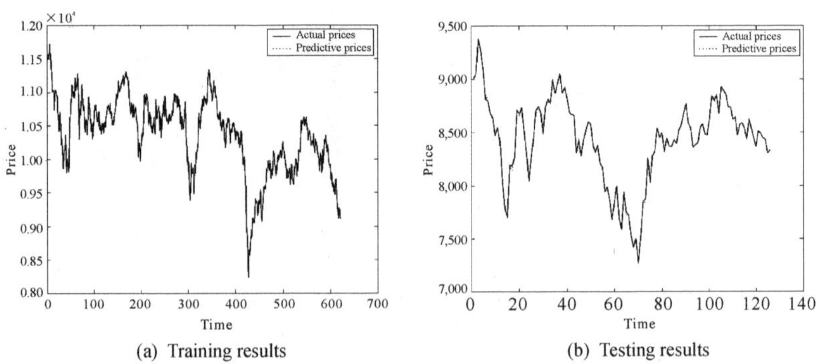

(a) Training results   (b) Testing results

Fig. 7.14. Experimental results graphs using GARCH method for DJIA00-02

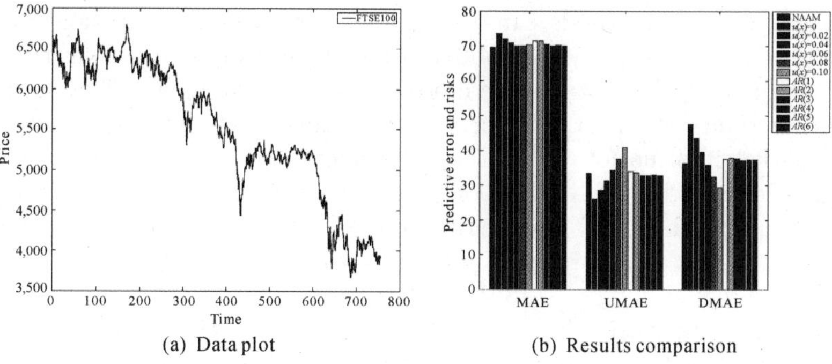

(a) Data plot

(b) Results comparison

Fig. 7.15. FTSE100 data plot and experimental results graphs

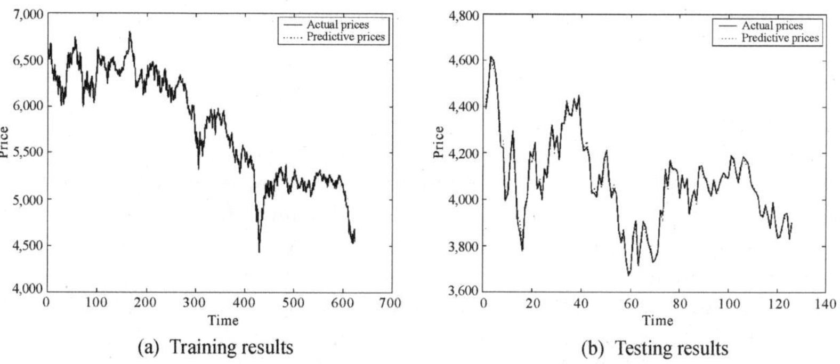

(a) Training results

(b) Testing results

Fig. 7.16. Experimental results graphs using GARCH method for FTSE100

margin. This provides helpful information for the prediction. Another reason is that by using NASM, the margin width is determined by a meaningful value. This value changes with the stock market. Obviously, this method is more flexible than fixed margin cases and avoids risk of getting bad predictive results partially when the margin values are determined by random selection in the fixed margin cases.

Furthermore, we know that NAAM may be better than NASM. For example, by adding a momentum, we may not only improve the accuracy of prediction, but also reduce the predictive downside risk.

Another notice is that by cautiously selecting parameters, SVR algorithm has similar predictive performance to other models, from Figs. 7.6(a) and 7.7(a). However, for a novice, the SVR libraries are easy to run. Since every local optimum is the global optimum, it guarantees the user to find an optimal solution easily and stably. This advantage is very useful for a novice to learn a new model, or library, and strengthen his confidence of learning new things comparing with learning other non-linear model, e. g. RBF networks.

In general, our methods can be considered as a model selection, determining the parameter, ϵ. We do not consider the setting of other parameters, such as C and β. We just use the cross-validation technique to find suitable values for them. However, this procedure is time-consuming. We may add some market information to set these parameters, e. g. [4]. In addition, the margin width set by GARCH model is too wide; we may need to add more useful terms to shrink it. This can be one of our future works. A valuable experience is that the normalized procedure will be helpful for selecting suitable parameters easily and stably.

Finally, we turn to a key weakness of our model: the predictive model does not lead to direct profit making in real life and we do not provide the confidence of these predictive models. However, we may find some useful information through using our model to predict the stock market prices; the predictive results may provide some helpful suggestions.

References

1. Gustavo M, de Athayde (2001) Building a Mean-downside Risk Portfolio Frontier. In: Sortino F.A, Satchell S.E, editors, Managing Downside Risk in Financial Markets: Theory, Practice and Implementation. Oxford, Boston:Butterworth-Heinemann 194–211
2. Baird IS, Howard T (1990) What Is Risk Anyway? Using and Measuring Risk in Strategic Management. In Bettis Richard A and Thomas Howard, editors, Risk, Strategy and Management. Greenwich, Conn: JAI Press 21–51
3. Bollerslev T (1986) Generalized Autoregressive Conditional Heteroskedasticity. Econometrics 31:307–327
4. Cao LJ, Chua KS, Guan LK (2003) c-Ascending Support Vector Machines for Financial Time Series Forecasting. In International Conference on Computational Intelligence for Financial Engineering (CIFEr2003) 329–335
5. Chang CC, Lin CJ (2001) LIBSVM: A Library for Support Vector Machines
6. Cristianini N, Shawe-Taylor J (2000) An Introduction to Support Vector Machines(and Other Kernel-based Learning Methods). Cambridge, U.K.; New York: Cambridge University Press
7. Hastie T, Rosset S, Tibshirani R, Zhu J (2004) The entire regularization path for the support vector machine. Journal of Machine Learning Research 5:1391–1415
8. Markowitz H (1952) Portfolio Selection. Journal of Finance 7:77–91
9. Mukherjee S, Osuna E, Girosi F (1997) Nonlinear Prediction of Chaotic Time Series Using Support Vector Machines. In Principe J, Giles L, Morgan N, Wilson E, editors, IEEE Workshop on Neural Networks for Signal Processing VII. IEEE Press 511–519
10. Müller KR, Smola A, Rätsch G, Schölkopf B, Kohlmorgen J, Vapnik V (1997) Predicting Time Series with Support Vector Machines. In Gerstner W, Germond A, Hasler M, and Nicoud JD, editors, ICANN. New York, NY: Springer 999–1004
11. Nabney IT (2002) Netlab: Algorithms for Pattern Recognition. New York, NY: Springer

12. Schölkopf B, Chen PH, Lin CJ (2003) A Tutorial on ν-Support Vector Machines. Technical Report, National Taiwan University

13. Schölkopf B, Bartlett P, Smola A, Williamson R (1998) Support Vector Regression with Automatic Accuracy Control. In Niklasson L, Bodén M, and Ziemke T, editors, Proceedings of ICANN'98 Perspectives in Neural Computing. Berlin 111–116

14. Schölkopf B, Bartlett P, Smola A, Williamson R (1999) Shrinking the Tube: A New Support Vector Regression Algorithm. In Kearns MS, Solla SA, Cohn DA, editors, Advances in Neural Information Processing Systems. Cambridge, MA: The MIT Press 11: 330–336

15. Schölkopf B, Smola AJ, Williamson R, Bartlett P (1998) New Support Vector Algorithms. Technical Report NC2-TR-1998-031, GMD and Australian National University

16. Smola A, Schölkopf B (1998) A tutorial on support vector regression. Technical Report NC2-TR-1998-030, NeuroCOLT2

17. Smola AJ, Murata N, Schölkopf B, Müller KR (1998) Asymptotically Optimal Choice of ε-Loss for Support Vector Machines. In Proc. of Seventeenth Intl. Conf. on Artificial Neural Networks

18. Trafalis TB, Ince H (2000) Support Vector Machine for Regression and Applications to Financial Forecasting. In Proceedings of the IEEE-INNS-ENNS International Joint Conference on Neural Networks (IJCNN2000). IEEE 6: 348–353

19. Vapnik VN (1999) The Nature of Statistical Learning Theory. New York, NY: Springer, 2nd edition

20. Vapnik VN, Golowich S, Smola AJ (1997) Support Vector Method for Function Approximation, Regression Estimation and Signal Processing. In Mozer M, Jordan M, Petshe T, editors, Advances in Neural Information Processing Systems. Cambridge, MA: The MIT Press 9: 281–287

21. Wang G, Yeung DY, Lochovsky FH (2006) Two-dimensional solution path for support vector regression. In The 23rd International Conference on Machine Learning. Pittsburge, PA: 1993–1000

22. Yang H, Chan L, King I (2002) Support Vector Machine Regression for Volatile Stock Market Prediction. In Yin Hujun, Allinson Nigel, Freeman Richard, Keane John, and Hubbard Simon , editors, Intelligent Data Engineering and Automated Learning — IDEAL 2002. NewYork, NY: Springer 2412 of LNCS: 391–396

23. Yang H, King I, Chan L (2002) Non-fixed and Asymmetrical Margin Approach to Stock Market Prediction Using Support Vector Regression. In International Conference on Neural Information Processing — ICONIP 2002, 1968

8

Conclusion and Future Work

In this chapter, a summary of this book is provided. We will review the whole journey of this book, which starts from two schools of learning thoughts in the literature of machine learning, and then motivate the resulting combined learning thought including Maxi-Min Margin Machine, Minimum Error Minimax Probability Machine and their extensions. Following that, we then present both future perspectives within the proposed models and beyond the developed approaches.

8.1 Review of the Journey

Two paradigms exist in the literature of machine learning. One is the school of global learning approaches; the other is the school of local learning approaches. Global learning enjoys a long and distinguished history, which usually focuses on describing phenomena by estimating a distribution from data. Based on the estimated distribution, the global learning methods can then perform inferences, conduct marginalizations, and make predictions. Although containing many good features, e.g. a relatively simple optimization and the flexibility in incorporating global information such as structure information and invariance, etc., these learning approaches have to assume a specific type of distribution a prior. However, in general, the assumption itself may be invalid. On the other hand, local learning methods do not estimate a distribution from data. Instead, they focus on extracting only the local information which is directly related to the learning task, i.e. the classification in this book. Recent progress following this trend has demonstrated that local learning approaches, e.g. Support Vector Machine (SVM), outperform the global learning methods in many aspects. Despite of the success, local learning actually discards plenty of important global information on data, e.g. the structure information. Therefore, this restricts the performance of this types of learning schemes. Motivated from the investigations of these two types of learning approaches, we therefore suggest to propose a hybrid learning framework. Namely, we should learn from data globally and locally.

Following the hybrid learning thought, we thus develop a hybrid model named Maxi-Min Margin Machine (M^4), which successfully combines two largely different but complementary paradigms. This new model is demonstrated to contain both appealing features in global learning and local learning. It can capture the global structure information from data, while it can also provide a task-oriented scheme for the learning purpose and inherit the superior performance from local learning. This model is theoretically important in the sense that M^4 contains many important learning models as special cases including Support Vector Machines, Minimax Probability Machine (MPM), and Fisher Discriminant Analysis; the proposed model is also empirically promising in that it can be cast as a Sequential Second Order Cone Programming problem yielding a polynomial time complexity.

The idea of learning from data locally and globally is also applicable in regression tasks. Directly motivated from the Maxi-Min Margin Machine, a new regression model named Local Support Vector Regression (LSVR) is proposed in this book. LSVR is demonstrated to provide a systematic and automatic scheme to locally and flexibly adapt the margin which is globally fixed in the standard Support Vector Regression (SVR), a state-of-the-art regression model. Therefore, it can tolerate the noise adaptively. The proposed LSVR is promising in the sense that it not only captures the local information of the data in approximating functions, but more importantly, includes special cases, which enjoy a physical meaning very much similar to the standard SVR. Both theoretical and empirical investigations demonstrate the advantages of this new model.

Besides the above two important models, another important contribution of this book is that we also develop a novel global learning model called Minimum Error Minimax Probability Machine (MEMPM). Although still within the framework of global learning, this model does not need to assume any specific distribution beforehand and represents a distribution-free Bayes optimal classifier in a worst-case scenario. This thus makes the model distinguished from the traditional global learning models, especially the traditional Bayes optimal classifier. One promising feature of MEMPM is that it can derive an explicit accuracy bound under a mild condition, leading to a good generalization performance for future data.

The fourth contribution of this book is that we develop the Biased Minimax Probability Machine (BMPM) model. Even though it is a special case of MEMPM, we highlight this model because BMPM provides the first systematic and rigorous approach for a kind of important learning tasks, namely, the biased learning or imbalanced learning. Different from traditional imbalanced (biased) learning methods, BMPM can quantitatively and explicitly incorporate a bias for one class and consequently emphasize the more important class. A series of experiments demonstrate that BMPM is very promising in imbalanced learning and medical diagnosis.

8.2 Future Work

The models developed in this book bridge the gap between local learning and global learning. This brings a new viewpoint for both existing local models and global models. Following the viewpoint of learning from data both globally and locally, there seems to be a lot of immediate directions both inside and beyond the proposed models in this book.

8.2.1 Inside the Proposed Models

There are certainly a lot of work for improving the proposed models in this book.

First, all the models proposed in this book including Minimum Error Minimax Probability Machine, Maxi-Min Margin Machine and Local Support Vector Machine, involve in solving either a single Second Order Cone Programming or a Sequential Second Order Cone Programming problem. Although many optimization programs have demonstrated their good performance and mathematic tractability in solving this kind of problems, they are designed for general purposes and may not adequately exploit the specific properties in our models. Therefore, it is highly possible and valuable to develop some special optimization algorithms for speeding up their training. In particular, Maxi-Min Margin Machine enjoys the feature of sparsity. By taking advantages of this property, researchers have developed fast optimization algorithms for Support Vector Machine. It is therefore very interesting to investigate whether similar procedures can be applied here. This interesting topic deserves much attention and remains to be an open problem.

Second, an immediate problem for Minimum Error Minimax Probability Machine is the possible presence of local optimum in the practical optimization procedures. While empirical evidence shows that the global optimum can be attained in most of cases, the local optimum may occur when two types of data are not well-separated. Conventional simulated annealing [6, 14] or deterministic annealing methods [11, 12] are certainly possible ways to attack this problem, however a formal approach that is either a regularization augment or an algorithmic approximation may be proved more appropriate.

Third, as shown in this book, all the proposed models apply the kernelization trick to extend their applications to nonlinear tasks. However, it is well known that some global information, e.g. the structure information, may not be well kept when the data are mapped from the original space to the feature space. This may restrict the power of learning from data both globally and locally. Motivated from this view, it is thus highly valuable to develop techniques to retain the global information of data when performing the projection from the original space to the feature space. This can also be considered as a task on how to choose a suitable kernel, which currently attracts much interest in the machine learning community [4, 15].

Another important future direction for the proposed classification models, i.e. Minimum Error Minimax Probability Machine and Maxi-Min Margin Machine, is how to extend the current binary classifications into multi-way classifications. Although one vs. all and one vs. one [1, 16] approaches present the main tools for conducting the upgrading, one always prefers to a more systematic and more rigorous approach.

8.2.2 Beyond the Proposed Models

Although several important models have been motivated and developed from the viewpoint of learning from data both globally and locally, beyond these models there are plenty of work deserving future investigations.

One natural question is whether other famous local models or global models can be extended by engaging the viewpoint of learning from data globally and locally. For example, Neural Networks, a large family of popular learning models, might be also considered as modelling data in a local fashion. It is therefore very interesting to investigate whether global information can also be incorporated into these kinds of learning processes.

It is noted that the learning discussed in this book is restricted within the framework of either classification or regression tasks. Both tasks belong to the so-called supervised learning [5, 9, 18]. However, the other largely different learning paradigm, unsupervised learning [10, 13, 17], and the recently emerging semi-supervised learning [2, 3, 8, 7] are not considered. Therefore, exploring possible applications of hybrid learning in this field presents a straightforward and immediate ongoing topic.

References

1. Allwein EL, Schapire RE, Singer Y (2000) Reducing multiclass to binary: A unifying approach for margin classifiers. Journal of Machine Learning Research 1:113–141
2. Altun Y, McAllester D, Belkin M (2005) Maximum margin semi-supervised learning for structured variables. In Advances in Neural Information Processing Systerm (NIPS 18)
3. Ando R, Zhang T (2005) A framework for learning predictive structures from multiple tasks and unlabeled data. Journal of Machine Learning Research 6:1817C1853
4. Bach FR, Lanckriet GRG, Jordan MI (2004) Multiple kernel learning, conic duality, and the SMO algorithm. In Proceedings of International Conference on Machine Learning (ICML-2004)
5. Bartlett PL (1998) Learning theory and generalization for neural networks and other supervised learning techniques. In Neural Information Processing Systems Tutorial

6. Cerny V (1985) Thermodynamical approach to the traveling salesman problem: An efficient simulation algorithm. J. Opt. Theory Appl. 45(1):41–51

7. Chapelle O, Zien A, Scholkopf B (2006) Semi-supervised learning. Cambridge, MA: The MIT Press

8. Chawla NV, Karakoulas G (2005) Learning from labeled and unlabeled data: An empirical study across techniques and domains. Journal of Artificial Intelligence Research 23:331C366

9. Dietterich TG (1997) Machine learning research: Four current directions. AI Magazine 18(4):97–136

10. Dougherty James, Kohavi Ron, Sahami Mehran (1995) Supervised and unsupervised discretization of continuous features. In International Conference on Machine Learning 194–202

11. Dueck G (1993) New optimization heuristics :the great deluge algorithm and the record-to-record travel. Journal of Computational Physics 104:86–92

12. Dueck G, Scheurer T (1990) Threshold accepting: A general purpose optimization algorithm. Journal of Computational Physics 90:161–175

13. Figueiredo M, Jain AK (2002) Unsupervised learning of finite mixture models. Transaction on Pattern Analysis and Machine Intelligence 24(3):381–396

14. Kirkpatrick S, Gelatt Jr CD, Vecchi MP (1983) Optimization by simulated annealing. Science 220:671–680

15. Lanckriet GRG, Cristianini N, Ghaoui LEl, Bartlett PL, Jordan MI (2004) Learning the kernel matrix with semidefinite programming. Journal of Machine Learning Research

16. Rifkin R, Klautau A (2004) In defense of one vs. all classification. Journal of Machine Learning Research 5:101–141

17. Steck H, Jaakkola T (2002) Unsupervised active learning in large domains. In Proceedings of the Eighteenth Annual Conference on Uncertainty in Artificial Intelligence

18. Wettig Hannes, Grunwald Peter, Roos Teemu (2002) Supervised naive Bayes parameters. In Alasiuru P, Kasko S, editors, The Art of Natural and Artificial: Proceedings of the 10th Finnish Artificial Intelligence Conference 72–83

Index